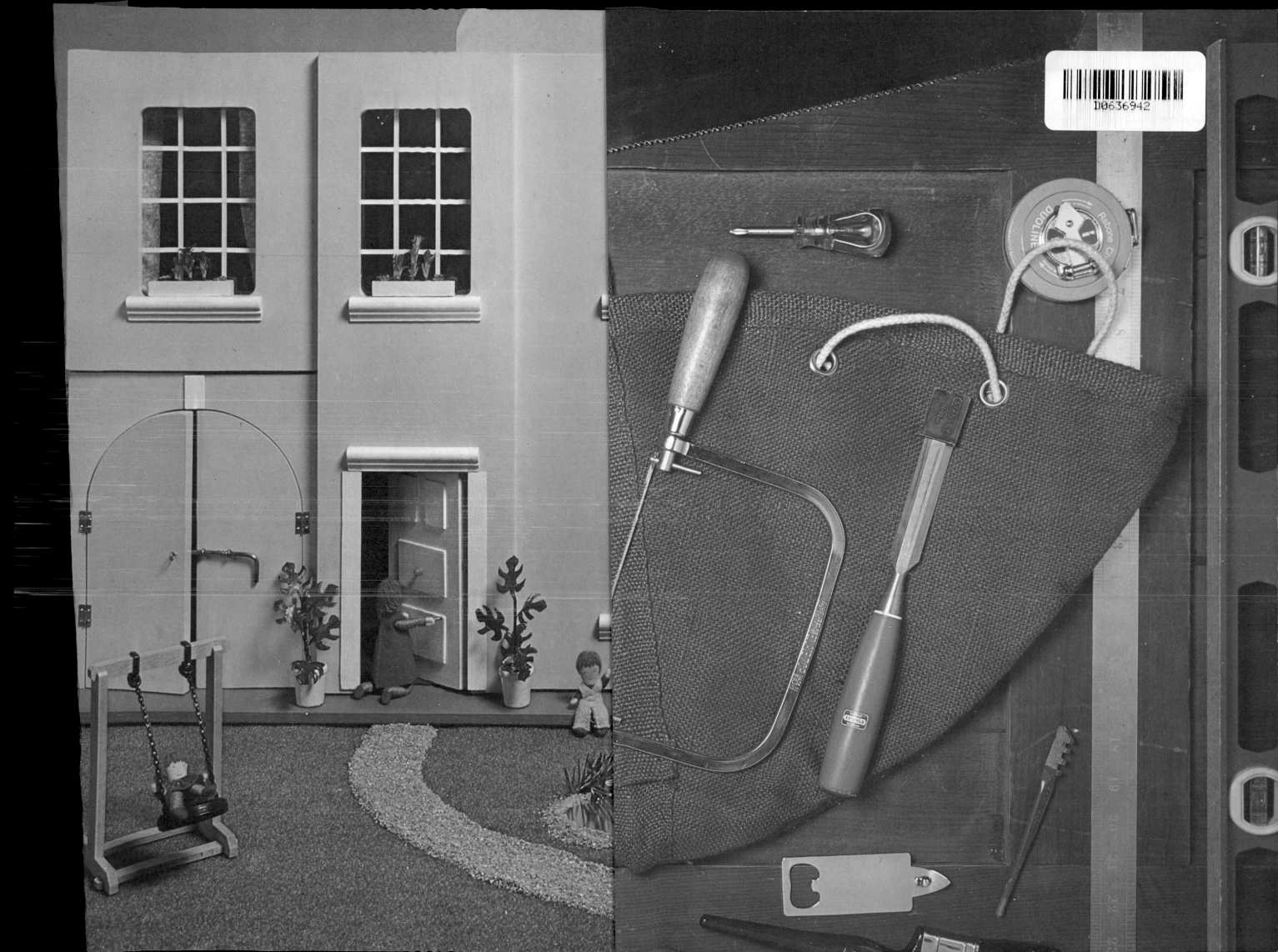

The all colour guide to
DIY

Barry Thompson

Galley Press

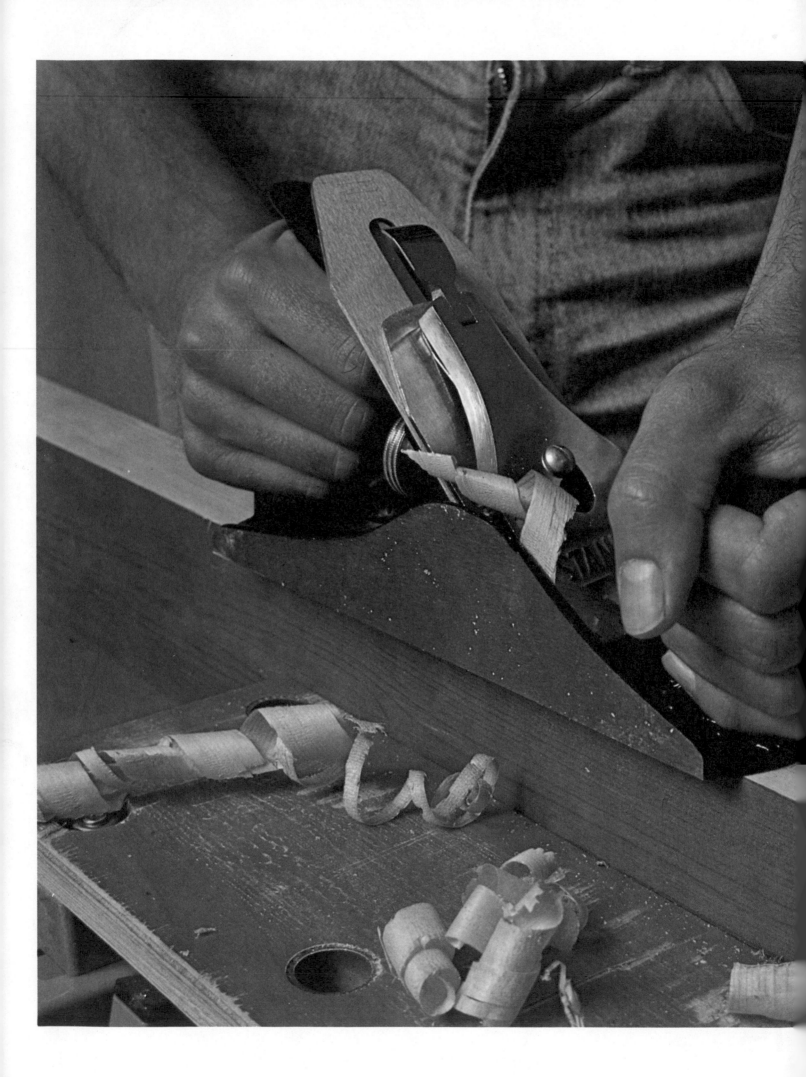

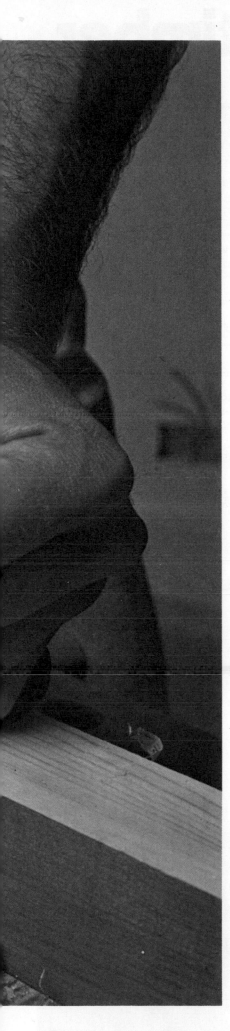

Contents

First published 1978 by Galley Press
in association with Cathay Books
59 Grosvenor Street London W1

ISBN 0 904644 61 8

© 1978 Hennerwood Publications Limited
Produced by Mandarin Publishers Limited
22A Westlands Road, Quarry Bay, Hong Kong

Printed in Singapore

Woodwork: talking timber

Timber remains the most widely used product in do-it-yourself activities; it is, perhaps, the most versatile of materials and can afford immense satisfaction in use.

It is important to choose the right wood for the right job. Basically, there are two types of timber–natural and man-made boards. Natural timbers are, basically, hardwoods and softwoods, consisting of very many types. There are many types of man-made timbers, the most common being chipboard, blockboard, hardboard and plywood.

In choosing timber you must take into account whether the wood is to be used in the house or out of doors. For outdoor use, timber must withstand all kinds of weather and should be durable and rot-resistant. These include teak, oak, sweet chestnut and western red cedar.

Teak and oak, while expensive, are the best choice for uses such as garden furniture. Sweet chestnut, cheaper and lighter in weight, may not always be so easily obtainable. Western red cedar, however, is durable, lightweight, soft and fairly cheap.

Softwood, if partially protected and used for such purposes as, for example, the framework of a shed, can be used out of doors. Softwood is widely used for making kitchen furniture, such as sink and kitchen units. Deal (redwood) is widely used and should be free from knots; it is not easy to obtain free of knots in larger sizes.

Other major softwoods are western red cedar, douglas fir, hemlock and parana pine. These are normally knot-free in most sizes but more expensive than deal.

Hardwood, such as beech or ramin, are used where two surfaces are in moving contact, such as a drawer or a folding chair. Where timber is in contact with food, such as a breadboard, it needs to be hard and close-grained, so that particles of food cannot lodge. Sycamore and beech are suitable.

Types of timber
Some of the best-known timbers, uses, properties and characteristics are as follows:

Mahogany
This is easy to work and nails, screws and glues well. Care is needed in staining, but it will varnish and polish.
Uses: high-class joinery, general utility work and furniture.

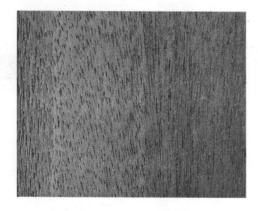

Birch
This is a whitish to light board, easy to work, turns well and stains, polishes and glues.
Uses: general joinery, moulding and furniture.

Douglas fir
Light, reddish-brown in colour and reasonably easy to work. It requires care in nailing and screwing and produces good results in finishing, though the grain tends to lift; glues well.
Uses: all types of joinery and constructional work.

Elm
Yellowish-brown in colour, variable to work but takes a good finish. Nails, screws, stains and polishes well. It needs careful selection and seasoning.
Uses: general joinery and furniture.

European whitewood
A non-resinous wood which is white to pale-straw in colour. Nails, screws and glues well and finishes satisfactorily.
Uses: general joinery and carpentry.

Oak
Moderately easy to work but requires care in nailing and screwing. Stains, polishes, varnishes and glues well. There is a liability to corrosion when in contact with metal in damp conditions.
Uses: high-class carpentry, joinery and furniture.

Parana pine
Creamy-brown in colour and easy to use. Care in selection is needed, since this has a liability to twist. This often has highly attractive graining. Finishes excellently; needs care in seasoning to avoid twisting.
Uses: interior purposes, work tops and general carpentry.

Teak
This has a greasy feel but works moderately well. Nails and screws satisfactorily with care and varnishes and polishes well.
Uses: high-class work, including draining boards and garden furniture.

Western red cedar
This is easy to use and finishes satisfactorily, though grain tends to lift. Liable to corrode metals under damp conditions; a very light wood.
Uses: exterior joinery, weatherboards, shingles, and related work.

Red Meranti-Red Seraya
Pink to reddish-brown and generally easy to work. Nails, screws, glues, stains and polishes well.
Uses: joinery and construction work.

Western Hemlock
A non-resinous, pale brown softwood. Moderately easy to saw, with fair nailing, screwing and finishing properties.
Uses: all types of general joinery.

Timber terminology
Timber may be bought sawn, planed all round *(PAR)*, or planed both sides *(PBS)*. Planing of timber entails a loss of about 3·5mm, so a 25mm piece of planed wood ends up at only 22mm. Similarly, a board measuring 152mm ends up at only 146mm. Unedged boards *(UE)* retain the shape of the tree at the edges; sawn-edged boards *(SE)* have unplaned edges.

When buying timber use, where possible, standard sizes; these are cheaper. Allow a little extra on lengths, in particular, for cutting and for dirty or gritty ends. A good rule is to add an extra 13mm for every 610mm. Always reject material with large knots as this would be weak. Where there is a knot, there is often a bend or twist in the wood.

Timber with traces of bark at the edges, reducing the effective width, is called waney-edged. End splits or 'shakes' are another common fault and sometimes extend a long way up the board. The other main fault is that of cupped boards—a warped curve across the width.

Timber terms and faults

Planed all round (PAR) sides and edges

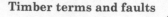

Planed both sides (PBS) edges stay sawn

Unedged (UE) sides are sawn or planed. Edges show the shape of the tree

Machine planed board showing: **1** Loss of thickness at end **2** Saw marks **3** Gash in the edge caused by log carriage.

A large knot in the edge may cause weakness and a change in shape

This shows a wane or waney-edged board

End shakes—first few centimetres are useless

Cupping—heart side has become rounded

Bowing—bending along the entire grain

Board can become badly twisted

Springing—a board may bend edgeways

Sapwood on edge is lighter in colour and attracts woodworm It should therefore be inspected for bore holes

Board cut across the pith. This is liable to warp, and pith is often surrounded by very small knots

Compression shake— a common defect

Man-made timbers

Chipboard

The most widely used of man-made boards, it is made from resin-bonded chips. Available unsurfaced, veneered and pre-finished, it does not lend itself to being worked in the same way as natural timbers but can be cut and planed at the ends. Another name for chipboard is particle board.

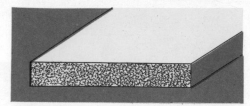

It is made in various grades for use as flooring and other decking surfaces. It has the advantage over natural timber of being far less subject to expansion and contraction from the effects of changes in humidity.

The four main grades of chipboard are *standard*, which is the cheapest and can be used in places where it will not be readily seen; *painting grade*, suitable for decorating; *flooring grade*, the strongest; and *exterior grade*, treated for resistance to water.

Pre-finished boards are either timber laminated or laminated in plastic. Edging strips are made to match the surface finishes.

Plywood

Widely used for woodworking jobs such as panelling and making drawer bottoms. Plywoods are veneers—thin sheets of timber glued together under pressure, with the grain at right angles to the adjacent sheets.

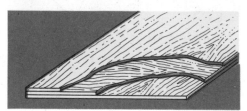

Ply always has an odd number of sheets, since an even number would be liable to warp. It ranges from two-ply, 0·8mm thick, up to 25mm for 11-ply and is made in both hardwood and softwood, such as birch and beech and West African and Gaboon mahogany.

Ordinary ply deteriorates in damp conditions, though mahogany ply will stand up to the weather if joined with a waterproof glue. A weather-proof grade is called WBP, an abbreviation for water and boil-proof.

Ply is also made with a decorative hardwood veneer on one face and is also available plastic-laminated.

Fibre building boards

These are made in several standard sizes and thicknesses and can be decorated or obtained predecorated. There are two main types—insulating board and hardboard.

Hardboard is made from softwood which has been pulped and drawn back into sheet form under heat and pressure. Standard hardboard has one smooth surface and one

rippled surface. Double-faced hardboard is made for use in situations where both sides will show. Other hardboards include oil-tempered, which has to stand up to external conditions, and enamelled and plastic-surfaced boards, for panelling and decorative uses.

Medium hardboard is made for heavier uses, such as partitioning. Hardboards range from 3mm to 6mm in thickness; medium boards are from 6mm to 13mm thick.

There is a wide variety of fibre building boards, ranging from perforated board,

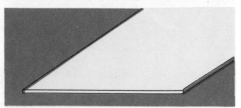

known as pegboard, which has good acoustical qualities and can be used to fix light objects through the perforations, to laminated fibre wallboard, made up of thin layers of board bonded together. Insulating boards are lightly compressed in manufacture and have a textured surface. These are used to provide thermal insulation and for the reduction of sound.

Blockboard

This is made up of thin timber outer veneers with a core of solid wood and is sometimes called coreboard. Thicknesses are between 19mm and 25mm and the surface is smooth. It is stronger than chipboard and is used for heavy-duty work, such as shelving. Blockboard is very stable and unlikely to warp.

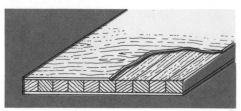

The edges of the board are not attractive, and these are filled and painted or covered with an edging strip, where the edges are likely to be seen.

Boards can be veneered, but it is usually best to have this done professionally, using specialized equipment. An alternative is laminboard—used for high-grade cabinet making—which has no edge gaps or flaws.

Cutting and finishing man-made boards

These can be cut with a panel or tenon saw. When cutting hardboard, avoid excess pressure, or you may tear the board, and always cut from the face side. Edges can be finished with a smoothing plane.

Chipboard has a tendency to 'break out' on the underside. To prevent this, mark the line of the cut right round the timber and score this with a marking knife; this will avoid splintering. Adhesive tape is an alternative. This can be applied along the line of the cut to avoid splintering or breaking out.

When cutting boards, always cut through the surface which will be seen, as this will present a clearer line.

Character walls in timber

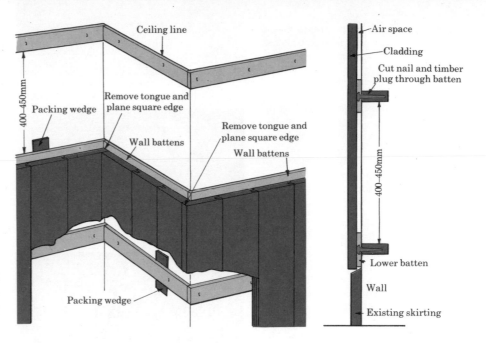

Natural timber, either in plank form or sheeting, provides a durable and attractive wall surface. This can be fixed in a variety of ways–usually on battens or with adhesive on to a wall surface. The quality of the finished effect depends on the care taken in preparing the wall surfaces and during fixing.

One of the easiest to use and most attractive modern wall finishes is natural wood cladding. All the richness, variation and colour of natural timber can be used to decorate wall areas in any room in the home. Easy to fix, and virtually maintenance-free, wood cladding offers many interesting decorative possibilities.

Types of cladding
Timber cladding is available in two main forms:

● Standard-sized natural or pre-finished panels;

● Solid timber planking or boarding, either square-edged or tongued and grooved.

Both types of cladding are easy to fix, but cladding in panel form is usually quicker.

Surfaces
Wood panel cladding or timber planking can be fixed to any even, dry surface. If the wall surface is very irregular it is best to fix battens to allow for this unevenness.

The space behind also allows less pleasing visual features, such as pipes, to be concealed, yet remain accessible behind the cladding. This space can also be easily insulated.

Fixing methods vary according to the surface. Usually surfaces of concrete, brick or insulating blocks are battened. In some cases, cladding may be fixed direct to surfaces using adhesive, provided these are even. Impact or slower-setting adhesives can be used on hardboard, chipboard or plaster surfaces.

New plaster surfaces should not be directly clad for at least eight weeks, to allow the plaster time to dry out.

Damp treatment
Damp walls must be treated before fixing cladding. If there is any suspicion of this, treat the surface with a damp-resistant

coating, such as a rubber or asphalt solution, brushed over the area.

Alternative damp-prevention methods include lining the wall with 500-gauge polythene sheeting, to provide a vertical damp-proof membrane, with metallic foil, or with a heavy-duty, bitumen-impregnated paper.

The battens and the back of the cladding should be treated with a clear timber preservative to prevent attack by moisture or fungi. Avoid a coloured preservative as this might bleed through the surface.

Insulation
Insulation material, such as expanded polystyrene sheeting, mineral rock wool or glass-fibre quilt, can be inserted between the wall surface and the panelling. This will provide thermal and some sound insulation, and help to prevent condensation by raising the touch temperature of the wall surface. In warmer conditions, a layer of insulation material gives a measure of heat insulation.

Panelling
Wood panelling is available in a wide range of timber veneers and provides a quick way to cover large areas. Panels are made in thicknesses from 4mm–6mm and in sheet sizes of between 2·44m × 1·22m to 3·05m × 1·22m.

Surfaces may be pre-finished, usually with a clear coat of alkyd resin, and v-grooved to represent random planking, or simply left in a natural condition.

Wood panelling may also be treated to make it fire resistant. The grooves in panels are usually located to correspond with batten centres at 400mm.

The long edge of each board is bevelled to match the adjoining panel and form a v-groove at the joint; veneers may not be matched for grain and colour.

Natural wood, with veneers of regular width, may be matched for grain and colour.

Preparation of panels
Before fixing, panels must be conditioned to room temperatures. This is done by bringing them into the room where they are to be fixed and leaving them to stand, loosely stacked, against the wall for two days, to acclimatize them both to room temperature and humidity.

Planed 19mm × 50mm timber is best used for battening, as unplaned timber may vary in size. Space the vertical battens at 400mm centres. Horizontal battens provide additional fixing points. Add five to ten per cent of the run of battening for cutting wastage.

Close-fitting 400mm horizontal battens are used where conditions are absolutely dry. If there is any likelihood of moisture, batten widths should be reduced to 305mm to allow a free flow of air at the back of the panels.

The uprights must be truly vertical. Hollows and irregularities in the wall surface must be corrected to prevent panel surface distortion. Concave irregularities can be corrected by blocking out the recesses with small slivers of hardboard or plywood between the wall and the battening. Convex irregularities can be overcome by shaping the rear of the batten or flattening the wall.

Where gaps are not being left between horizontal battens, fix a top and bottom batten, 25mm to 50mm down from the ceiling and upwards from the floor or skirting, checking these with a spirit level. At each end of walls, fit vertical battens; those at door openings may need trimming to fit architraves.

Battens may be fixed with screws or masonry nails. Walls may have to be plugged to accommodate screws, which should be of a non-rusting type. Battens should be fixed at intervals of 380mm.

Work from one end, partly fixing each vertical batten at 400mm centres, and check that each is upright before fixing finally. Place intermediate horizontal battens at intervals of 320mm above each other.

With light fittings or power points,

first fix a square of battening around them, so that the panel can be fixed once a hole is cut out for the switch or point.

Selecting panels

Before fixing, arrange the panels along the wall to get the most pleasing effects. Where the veneer is a natural wood surface, colour may vary from sheet to sheet. At this stage, the most economical way of using the panelling can be worked out and the most attractive graduation of graining and colour chosen.

Cutting edges and bevelling

Panels should be cut with a 8–10 point hand saw with the face side upwards. First, score the panel surface with a sharp marking knife. This will prevent splitting.

Use a metal straight edge and take care not to allow the knife to slip or you will mark and mar the panel face. Hold the saw at as flat an angle as possible as this will ensure a smooth cut.

A power saw can also be used; set this so that it projects not more than 50mm below the thickness of the panel. With a hand-held power saw, cut the panel face side downwards; with a bench saw, the panel is cut face side upwards.

When cutting with either a hand or power saw, it is a good precaution to cover the cutting line with masking tape, to ensure a split-free edge.

Where a panel has to be cut and butted against another, use a sharp plane with a fine set to impart a bevelled edge. Plane away from the panel edge to prevent splintering. Colour match this edge to the next v-groove with a dye or colourizer.

Get cladding

Start cladding from one corner and fix systematically along the surface area. Allow a 3mm gap at the ceiling and floor or skirting for ventilation. Offer up the first section, position it carefully and check its accuracy with a spirit level along the edge. The remaining panels should then be true when fixed. Fix the panels using 19mm–25mm panel or lost-head pins.

Each panel edge should meet in the centre of a vertical batten. Dovetail pin at about 75mm intervals through the v-grooves and at intervals through the grooves into the battens along each panel.

Drive the pins just below the face of the panel with a nail punch. The small surface holes left can be filled with bees-wax or a proprietary stopper.

A smear of woodworking adhesive can be applied to the edges of each board and the tops of battens to prevent panels from bowing between the panel-pin fixings.

Before working round switches or points, switch off the current. Unscrew and lift out the point. Locate the panel temporarily in position and drill a hole to align with the switch patrice. Pull the wires through the hole, measure the size of the switch backing, then enlarge the hole.

Use a handyman's knife or pad saw to cut out the hole. First score the surface and then carefully cut deeply until you

Cut, fit and nail battens to the wall; allow ventilation gaps at cross battens

Mark out panels accurately before you cut. Wrong cutting lines can prove costly

Fix lost-head pins through grooves into battens and punch down just below surface

Holes for fittings can be easily cut out, using a sharp handyman's knife

Establish centres are correct, so that fixings of panels can be made accurately

Cut pre-finished panels on the face side, using a fine-toothed panel saw

A sharp cutting knife and a straight edge can also be used to cut panelling

A proprietary adhesive, such as Gun-O-Prene, can be used to fix the panels

are through. Use a metal straight edge to guide the handyman's knife so that this does not slip and mark the surface. Re-connect the wires and reposition the switch.

Pin through the panel around the square batten support. Mark the fixing positions of the screws of the switch or point with a bradawl, drill holes and screw the plate of the unit back on.

Scribing

Where the ceiling line is uneven, the top of the panel should be scribed to match the contour. Cut the panel slightly over-size and hold it tightly against the ceiling. Place a piece of scrap plywood or hard-board hard to the ceiling and at right angles to the cladding.

Run this along the ceiling with a mark-ing knife held beneath and transfer or scribe this contour on to the face of the panel. It may help to keep the panel accurately in position if it is temporarily pinned. Check the position carefully before cutting.

Ceiling cladding

A ceiling can be clad in a similar way to a wall surface. First, fix a batten framework to the ceiling. It is necessary to establish the position of ceiling joists and fix battens to these.

Panel sizes may have to be adjusted to enable joins to match the line of the battens; this may mean cutting panels and

mitreing the edges to provide a neat v-joint.

It is useful to have help when fixing ceiling panelling. Alternatively, you can make up an elongated T-shaped prop of 50mm × 25mm timber, with the upright slightly longer than the floor-to-ceiling height, to wedge the unsupported end of the panel while fixing. The cross-bar can be about 1m long. This device is sometimes called a 'dead man's hand'.

Making contact

Another way of fixing wood panels is with contact adhesive. This can be applied to any sound and level surface–though ir-regularities up to 6mm can be accepted.

Make sure that walls are clean and dry. Gloss or emulsion-painted surfaces should be firm and free from flaking. Papered walls should be stripped back to the bare plaster.

Apply the adhesive to both the wall surface and the back of each panel with a knotched spreader and allow to dry. When the two surfaces are brought together they will instantly bond.

Therefore, take great care to position the panels accurately, as with most contact adhesives, the panel cannot subsequently be moved once the two surfaces have made contact.

An alternative method is to bond panels directly to a wall surface using a specially formulated, gap-filling adhesive, contain-ing synthetic rubber, called Gun-O-Prene.

For 'secret' fixings, nail pins at an angle through the tongue and punch down

Use an old chisel as a cramp to ensure each plank tightly butts to neighbour

This is applied with a special gun, available on loan.

The adhesive is in cartridge form; applied at the correct temperature, one covers a single standard panel. Walls must be clean and dry and stripped back.

Once the panels have been cut and arranged in order of fixing, apply the adhesive to the back of the first panel, using a steady pumping pressure on the trigger mechanism, to ensure an even extrusion of adhesive.

Draw the nozzle in a line round the outside of the panel, about 50mm in from the edge and across the width, at 460mm centres.

Next, offer the panel to the wall, check for position and press firmly into place, using hand pressure. If the wall surface is slightly uneven, the adhesive will take up gaps. Where there is no skirting board and the panel is entirely un-supported, it may be necessary to pin the panel temporarily until adhesion has taken place.

Warped panels may be fixed using this adhesive. The adhesive is applied to the panel as for a normal fixing, the panel is offered to the wall, pressed firmly into place then removed. Enough adhesive to produce a honeycombed effect will be left on the wall. Leave for 10 minutes, then reposition the panel to make the final bond.

Battens can also be fixed with adhesive. It is applied to the wall surface at 400mm centres and used in conjunction with masonry-nail fixing at high spots.

External corners
These can be mitred along the abutting edges with a plane so that they fit snugly together, but this has to be done very accurately. It is easier – and produces a successful corner – to butt the external edges of panels against a vertical strip of timber fixed at the angle.

First, batten up to the corners, so that one vertical batten overlaps the other, presenting a solid timber edge. Select the timber edge strip, which should be about 50mm wide by 6mm thick, and either match the panelling or be of a contrast wood finish, and pin this on the face edge of the angle. Punch down the heads of the pins and fill the holes.

The two panel edges can then be butted neatly against the edge strip and pinned.

Once inserted, the tongue of the next plank completely conceals the fixing pin

Piece of scrap wood can be used as a template to cut corner plank accurately.

Internal corners
No special treatment is involved. Place two adjacent vertical battens alongside, butt the two panels at right angles together and pin.

Timber planking
Solid, timber lining in the form of wood strips, also provides a pleasing, decorative timber finish. There is a wide range of colours obtainable in both soft and hard woods and in various profiles.

One of the most popular is tongued-and-grooved board. Usually 75mm–150mm wide and 13mm and 25mm thick, this may have v-patterned grooves at the plank edges.

Timber plank cladding can be fixed vertically, horizontally or diagonally, dependent on the situation and finished effect required. It is easier to clad a ceiling with planks of timber than with panels.

Preparation
The timber should be conditioned in a dry room, ideally where it is to be fixed, for at least seven days.

When using tongued-and-grooved or square-edged cladding, it is generally necessary to fix batten framework.

Battens may be horizontally or vertically fixed, dependent on the plane of the cladding. For vertical boarding, use horizontally fixed battens; for horizontal fixing, vertical battens.

Diagonally fixed cladding can be fixed to either type of batten fixing. Vertical battens are fixed at 460mm centres; horizontal at 610mm centres.

When cladding from ceiling to floor level, an existing skirting can be used as the lowest fixing point, so battens should not be thicker than the skirting. Alternatively, the skirting can be removed and battens fixed at floor level.

Mark out planking with a try-square and cutting knife and cut with a 8–10 point panel saw.

Fixing
Vertical cladding is started from one corner. Make sure that the first strip is level, as this acts as a datum point for the rest of the work.

Measure and cut each length slightly over size; fit the first plank the groove

side of the cladding firmly into the corner. If necessary, scribe this and cut to fit if the room verticals are out of true.

Allow a 6mm gap at tops and bottoms for ventilation. Where necessary, scribe the plank tops at the ceiling, trim off excess with a sharp plane with a fine set and remove roughened edges with fine glasspaper.

Tongued-and-grooved boards allow cladding to be fixed by the 'secret' nailing method. The first strip will have to be pinned through the face of the panel, the head punched below the surface and the hole filled. Use 32mm lost-head nails.

Subsequent strips can be put in place and fixed, at an angle, with lost-head nails through the back of the groove and the heads also punched down. The tongue of the next plank slots over this, hides the pin head and holds the plank in place.

Use a chisel to cramp each board. Drive the chisel point into the batten and pull it upright to squeeze the board tightly against the adjacent board. Cramp only on the tongued side of the board. If it is damaged or bruised, it will be covered by the next groove.

Nail and cramp three boards at a time, working from the ceiling downwards, then reverse the work direction, by cramping and nailing from the floor level upwards, for the next three planks.

The last two cannot be cramped and will have to be sprung into place. You may also have to cut the last board and plane a bevel along the cut edge. Cut the boards slightly oversize and fit; they will be slightly bowed.

To achieve a tight, flush fit, spring them into position with a sharp blow of the hand. Fix these planks by nailing through the face surface of the grooves, again punching down the heads and filling the holes.

Angles
Internal corners require no special treatment. External corners may be dealt with as follows: cut off the tongue or groove from one length, to square the edge, then glue and pin this flush with the corner. Repeat with the abutting plank. This will present a neat edge. The edges can then be touched on with a dye or matching colourizer.

When fixing diagonal planking to vertical battening, it is essential to fix top and bottom horizontal battens at floor and ceiling level. The first plank fitted is the longest. This is fitted from one corner, at an angle of 45°, to the ceiling or highest point of the area to be covered.

Subsequent planks are pinned on each side of the master plank and the edges cut at a 45° angle. The planks will have to be cut slightly longer to allow for the 45° angle to be cut at each end.

Use a bevel gauge and handyman knife to mark out each angle accurately and then saw. Planks are pinned to battens in the normal way, and, when using tongued-and-grooved board, may be secured by secret nailing. The final boards will also have to be 'sprung' into place.

A point to remember is that if shelving or other support is likely to be needed later, fix support battens behind the panelling where they will be required.

Build a set of 'separate tables'

A small occasional table is a useful item of furniture. Making this table, which is simple and functional in design, introduces the technique of making a mortise-and-tenon joint, one of the most useful in general woodworking. The table can be finished in a variety of ways–painted, stained with polyurethane varnish, tiled or laminated, to give some examples.

This type of small table can have a host of uses in the home. It can be varied in size to suit your needs, with a choice of tops–laminated, teak-veneered or tiled. Construction utilizes the mortise-and-tenon joint to give strength. It is not recommended, however, that the unit dimensions greatly exceed those given.

Additional tools needed are a 10mm mortise chisel, a mortise gauge and a mitre box.

Leg construction
All pieces of similar size are, in the normal way, marked out together in the vice. Cut four legs 32mm × 32mm and 345mm long from planed softwood and mark with a try-square and a marking knife. Square the lines lightly right across.

From one end line, measure down the thickness of the top, less about 3mm, so that the top of the leg ends slightly below the table surface. From this line, measure the width of the rail and lightly square another line across the surface of the four legs.

Mark lines 3mm in from these points and square lines across (Fig. 2). These lines mark the length of the mortise, which will be cut later. Take the four legs out of the vice and square the top and bottom cut lines round on all surfaces.

Table top
Next, cut the top of the table. Use 18mm Finnish birch ply blockboard, or plastic or timber-veneered chipboard, such as Contiplas or Contiboard. The dimensions are 550mm × 550mm.

If the top is to be tiled, it is necessary to use a 'balancer' laminate on the underside of the blockboard to counteract the pull of the tiles, or the surface may warp. A less satisfactory alternative is to apply several coats of paint as a balancer.

Edging pieces
Cut four edging pieces 25mm × 7mm × 565mm long. These should match the timber of the table frame. These can be either cut square or mitred. If mitred, make slightly over length and cut the mitre with a sharp tenon saw in a mitre box (Fig. 3).

Mitres must be cut at a true angle of 45° so that the two angles make an accurate 90°. The work should be clamped during cutting. It can be held with a 'G' cramp, cushioned by a piece of scrap timber, so that the strip is not bruised.

Some mitre boxes incorporate a clamp to hold the material steady. Put the timber front side up in the mitre box so that you cut the mitre the right way round.

Nail one mitred strip carefully in position along one edge of the table, lining this up carefully. Knock a pin half way in at each end, so that you can make any slight adjustments by withdrawing the pins and repositioning the strip. Once this is correct, the remaining mitres should line up.

Where butt joints are used, you will have an overlap. Trim this off and plane the edges smooth with a block plane once the glue has dried.

Use the outside dimensions of this top, if different from 565mm, as the working dimensions.

If you tile the top, stick the tiles in place with resinous adhesive, which allows for movement of the wood. When set, grout the tiles in the usual way.

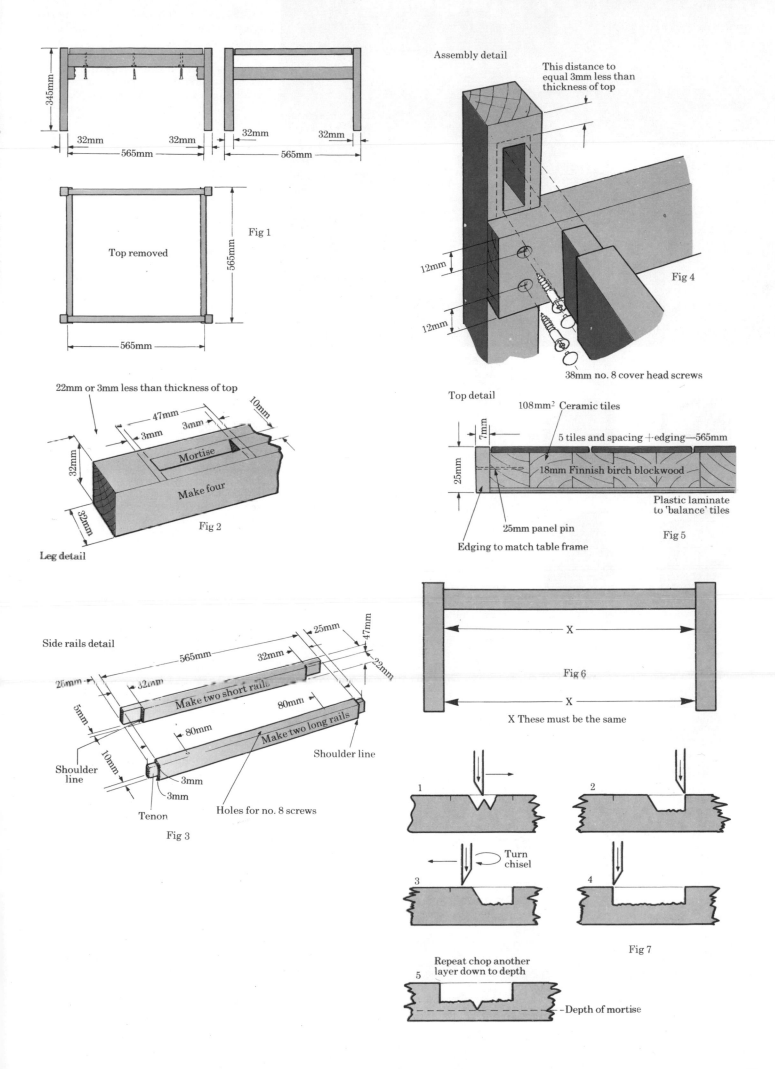

345mm

32mm 32mm 32mm 32mm

565mm 565mm

Top removed

565mm

565mm

Fig 1

Assembly detail

This distance to equal 3mm less than thickness of top

12mm

12mm

Fig 4

38mm no. 8 cover head screws

22mm or 3mm less than thickness of top

47mm

3mm 3mm 10mm

32mm

Mortise

32mm

Make four

Fig 2

Leg detail

Top detail

108mm² Ceramic tiles

7mm

5 tiles and spacing + edging—565mm

25mm

18mm Finnish birch blockwood

Plastic laminate to 'balance' tiles

25mm panel pin

Edging to match table frame

Fig 5

Side rails detail

25mm 47mm

565mm 32mm 22mm

25mm 32mm

5mm

Make two short rails

80mm

80mm

Make two long rails

3mm

3mm

Shoulder line

10mm

Shoulder line

Tenon

Holes for no. 8 screws

Fig 3

Fig 6

X

X

X These must be the same

1 2

Turn chisel

3 4

Fig 7

Repeat chop another layer down to depth

5

Depth of mortise

13

to the exact width of a 10mm mortise chisel (Fig. 7) by holding the chisel against the spurs.

The spurs are set to mark two lines on the legs between the prepared lines (Fig. 2). These should be the same distance from each edge of the leg. Check that they are correct by marking lightly from both edges.

If the lines coincide, the gauge is set correctly; if they do not, re-adjust the gauge and check again. When correctly set, place the timber upright in the vice and mark the lines (Fig. 2).

Without altering the set of the spurs, mark the tenons on the longer rails (Fig. 3). Once these are marked, set the gauge to 3mm, and mark the outer lines.

Cut the two shorter rails to length, plus 2mm, and reset the marking gauge to 5mm. Gauge the lines from the outside (best) surface for the recess (Fig. 4).

The four rails may now be sawn to shape. Keep the wood upright in the vice and saw so that the line to which you are working is easily visible.

The stages of cutting the tenon are shown in Fig. 8. Cut the lap joint on the end of the shorter rails in a similar manner.

Side rails

Cut the four side rails–two 565mm and two 615mm long–from 47mm × 22mm planed timber and place these on edge in the vice, keeping each pair together. The longer rails must overlap the shorter evenly at each end.

Square a line 25mm in from one end across and from this measure the overall length of the completed top and square another line across at this point. From this line, measure outwards another 25mm and square a further line (Fig. 3).

From the two inner lines at each end, measure 32mm back towards the centre and mark these points. This gives the inner shoulder lines on the two lower side rails. Take these four rails out of the vice and square the end lines on each piece right round on all four surfaces.

On the two shorter rails, square the inner shoulder lines across the outer surface and only lightly across the two edges. Avoid knife marking lines other than where they will be sawn as these will be difficult to clean off the surface.

On the two longer rails, square the shoulder lines right round the rails (Fig. 3). Always use the stock of the try-square from the face edge. You will find, if you work carefully, that the lines will join all the way round. This should be aimed at for accurate work.

Cut the two longer rails to length. Set the spurs, or points, on the marking gauge

Mortise cutting

Working with the mortise marking uppermost and the leg firmly cramped to the bench with a 'G' cramp, and a piece of scrap wood between to prevent bruising, cut the mortise. Work between the marked lines, starting in the centre.

Chop out a 'v' of wood about 10mm deep and follow the stages in Fig. 7. Stand behind your chisel and keep it vertical while you are chopping into the timber.

If you are anxious about going too deeply into your wood, a piece of adhesive tape round the chisel makes a good depth indicator. When all the mortises are cut, test, by trial assembly, and number each pair of joints for order of correct assembly.

Drill and countersink screw holes for No. 8 screws in the ends of the shorter rails. Drill the holes through the other two rails for securing the top. Countersink these to a depth of 10mm to accommodate the heads of 10mm No. 8 screws.

Mortise cutting can be facilitated by use of a jig, such as the Copydex Jointmaster.

Finishing

Clean up each piece and wax polish or polyurethane. Do not get any of these on the surfaces which are to be glued. When dry, glue up the two mortise and tenoned frames and cramp with a sash cramp.

Check that the legs are the same distance apart all the way down (Fig. 6). Sight across the legs to make sure that they are in the same plane. If not, loosen the cramp, adjust the legs, tighten again and check. Repeat until correct.

Once these frames are dry, screw and glue the lower rails in position (Fig. 4). Check diagonals for squareness.

Finally, plane off the ends level with the legs and screw the top in position from beneath.

Sawing order for right handed person

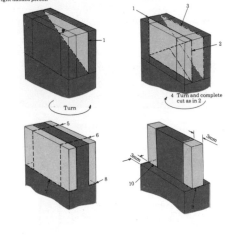

Turn

4 Turn and complete cut as in 2

3mm

3mm

3mm

Marking gauge lines

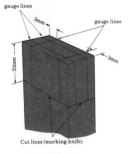

gauge lines

gauge lines

3mm

3mm

32mm

Cut lines (marking knife)

Cutting list – all mm sizes

Planed finished sizes	Qty.	Length	Width	Thickness
Legs	4	345mm	32mm	32mm
Rails	2	565mm	47mm	22mm
Rails	2	615mm	47mm	22mm
Edging pieces	4	565mm	25mm	7mm
Top	1	550mm	550mm	18mm
Plastic laminate	1	550mm	550mm	2mm
Coverhead screws	8	32mm × No. 8		
C/S Steel screws	6	50mm × No. 8		
'Domes of silence'	4	12mm diam.		
Ceramic tiles × 108m²	25			

These are finished sizes–allow a little extra length for marking out and cutting.

Timber may be hard or softwood, dependent upon finish required.

Shelving and storage –stylishly

Storage for larger items and display sections for ornaments are coupled in this multi-purpose storage system. Based on simple construction principles, it can easily be extended along or upwards; in fact, tailored exactly to the size of the room and the capacity required. Laminated chipboard shelves and doors provide an attractive wipe-clean surface, the softwood timber uprights providing a contrasting feature of the design.

This shelving and storage system is simply made, using planed softwood framework with doors and shelving of Contiplas laminated chipboard. The doors can be omitted, if wished, to make this an 'open' unit. The length can be varied to choice, and the unit even extended to ceiling height.

The cupboard sections can be moved from the bottom to the centre position, and a wider spacing could be adopted between shelves, for large books or big display items.

While the unit is capable of an infinite number of variations, the basic principles of construction remain unaltered.

Man-made boards will not take heavy loads without sagging, if the distance between supports is too large. Here, the shelves are supported at regular intervals of 710mm. The support timbers are a feature of the design.

Construction
Shelves
First, cut the four Contiplas shelves to an exact length of 2 286mm and the two end panels to 896mm, using a fine-toothed hand saw. Saw carefully and cut to a squared line. As a general rule, do not accept ends of any material as being completely square–always check for squareness and for damage, cutting the ends square if necessary.

Vertical supports
The eight vertical supports in this design are cut from standard 50mm × 25mm softwood. When planed, this reduces to 47mm × 22mm in size.

Place the eight lengths together in the vice, and secure them with a 'G' cramp. Mark out with a marking knife and square the dimensions (Fig. 2). Cut eight lengths 910mm long; this allows a little for waste at both ends.

The 'housings' or grooves must be marked out to an exact size to correspond with the thickness of the laminated chipboard. If there is any slight variation from the standard 16mm board size, make suitable allowance for this. A really tight fit between the board and the groove should be aimed at.

Choose the best side of your timber to show on the outside and square the marked lines, using a knife and try-square, across the inside face and down the other edge.

Set a marking gauge to 6mm (Fig. 2) and gauge the depth of the groove between each pair of cut lines, working from the inside face. Then, with a tenon saw, cut these grooves to depth and clean out each groove with a 12mm bevel-edged chisel, or use a router plane.

Mark the four corner supports 'back', 'front', 'left' and 'right' and put these temporarily aside. To avoid any mistakes, mark a pencil line down each one at the position of the rebate. It is very easy to cut the rebate on the wrong edge, and you will then end up with corner supports which will only fit on at the same end!

With a rebate plane, or a rabbeter attachment to an electric drill, cut the rebate (Fig. 5). These rebates are 16mm wide and as deep as the prepared housings (6mm).

Once these are cut, mark the positions of the screw holes on the vertical support. These must be in the centre of the groove and also in the centre of the support.

'Dot' punch these positions and, with a drill suitable for a No. 8 screw, bore holes, keeping the drill vertical in both directions. Countersink each hole.

With a tenon saw, cut off the surplus at the top and bottom of each support. Take care to keep the ends square and, with a smoothing plane, carefully clean up each one.

Use one of these supports to mark the positions of the shelves on to the end panels and square pencil lines across the surface.

In the centre, between the pairs of shelf lines, mark another line to indicate the positions of the screws. Set a marking gauge to 75mm and, working from both edges, mark the screw holes (Figs. 6 and 7).

'Dot' punch these positions, drill for No. 8 screw and countersink. With the gauge at the same setting, mark the corresponding screw holes on the ends of the shelves. Then reset the gauge to 8mm, half the shelf thickness, and mark a line across the first lines.

This gives the exact position for the fibre plugs which are fitted and glued into the end of each shelf to take the screws.

Next, dot punch each plug position and, with a drill suitable for a No. 8 plug, drill twice into the end of each shelf to a depth of 32mm. Fit and glue a No. 8 plug into each hole.

Clean up each support carefully with fine glasspaper and give each a coating of polyurethane. Dilute the first coat by about 20 per cent with white spirit. When dry, rub down and apply a second coat of 'neat' polyurethane and leave this to dry.

Assembly
Place the four shelves together, on edge, and secure with a 'G' cramp. With a pencil, square lines across the edges of the shelves, indicating the positions of the verticals. Work to the dimensions in Fig. 1.

Should there be any slight variation, it is important to keep the three spaces between the supports equal. When you are satisfied that the spacings are correct, square these lines across the boards and into the other edges. This will ensure that the back supports line up with the front ones.

Place the shelves on edge on the floor. It is almost essential to have help at this

stage. Place the four rear supports in position.

Drill through the holes in these supports into the edges of the shelves. Remove the supports and glue 32mm No. 8 fibre plugs into the drilled holes. Replace the supports in position and put in the four corresponding screws (Fig. 4).

Repeat this on all the supports. Turn the shelves over and repeat on the front edge. This time, insert screws which will accept decorative screw cappings.

Iron on laminate edging strip to the top of the end panels and trim this to size, following manufacturer's instructions. Place the end panels in position and screw these in place, using 'coverhead' screws (Fig. 7).

Back panels Cut the back panels from 380mm laminated chipboard to an exact fit between the vertical supports and mark these for the position of the securing screws (Fig. 8). Countersink and fix the

screws in place.

Cut 50mm strips for the second shelf, and, using the same screw spacing as before, screw these backs into place (Fig. 9).

The doors are fitted using 50mm flush hinges. This type of hinge requires no complicated fitting procedure. It fits on to the surface of both the vertical support and the door.

Screws which match the countersinking in these hinges accurately are essential. Any slight screw projection will stop the door from closing properly. It may be advisable to increase the amount of countersinking on the hinge. This is simply done by using a countersink bit in a hand drill to deepen the countersinking in the hinge face.

Make allowance for both the thickness of the hinge and to allow a gap between the door (Fig. 1). Measure the distance between the supports and divide this in half. From this measurement, subtract

4mm and cut each door to this size.

Veneer the cut edges with edging strip and trim to size. Screw the hinges on to the doors, 40mm from the tops and the bottom edges, using chipboard screws. These are special screws, designed to hold well in chipboard and are readily obtainable.

Place the door on the cabinet and mark the position of the hinge. Open the door and place the leaf of the hinge against this marked position. Now put in the screws.

Glasspaper, or if necessary, plane off the tops of each vertical support and coat with polyurethane varnish.

Fix the screw-head covers into position and mark the positions of the handles on each door. Drill the required holes and fit the handles.

There is a wide variety of door catches available. Magnetic catches are among the easiest to fit. One set should be used on each door.

This pattern of concealed hinge gives a flush, 'hingeless' appearance to doors

Brass dome caps, fitted over screwheads, are neat and serve to conceal fixings

Contiplas is marked out with try square for slots to accept the unit uprights

Slot can be cut roughly to shape with a pad or keyhole saw, jig or coping saw

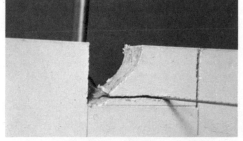

Finally, the joint is cleaned up with a chisel, so that upright is neatly jointed

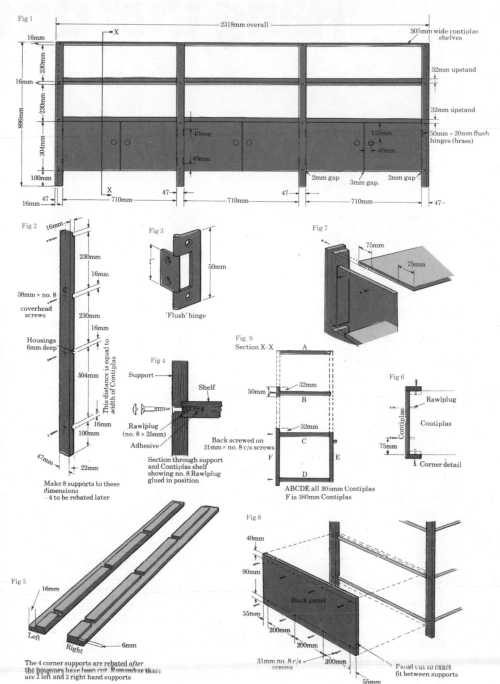

Fig 1

2318mm overall

305mm wide contiplas shelves

16mm
230mm
16mm
230mm
896mm
32mm upstand
32mm upstand
304mm
40mm
125mm
50mm × 20mm flush hinges (brass)
40mm
100mm
2mm gap
3mm gap.
2mm gap
16mm 47
710mm 47 710mm 47 710mm 47

Fig 2
16mm
230mm
16mm
38mm × no. 8 coverhead screws
230mm
16mm
Housings 6mm deep
This distance is equal to width of Contiplas
304mm
16mm
100mm
47mm 22mm

Make 8 supports to these dimensions – 4 to be rebated later

Fig 3
'Flush' hinge
50mm

Fig 4
Support
Shelf
Rawlplug (no. 8 × 25mm)
Adhesive
Section through support and Contiplas shelf showing no. 8 Rawlplug glued in position
Back screwed on 31mm × no. 8 c/s screws

Fig 7
75mm
75mm

Fig. 9
Section X–X
A
50mm 32mm
B
32mm
C
F E
D
ABCDE all 305mm Contiplas
F is 380mm Contiplas

Fig 6
Rawlplug
Contiplas
Contiplas
75mm
Corner detail

Fig 5
16mm
Left
Right
6mm
The 4 corner supports are rebated *after* the housings have been cut. Remember there are 2 left and 2 right hand supports

Fig 8
40mm
90mm
55mm
Back panel
200mm
200mm
200mm
31mm no. 8 c/s screws
55mm
Panel cut to exact fit between supports

Cutting list – all mm sizes

Part	Qty.	Material	Length*	Width	Thickness
Shelves	4	Contiplas	2·44m	300	16
Ends	2	Contiplas	896mm	300	16
Doors	6	Contiplas	From 2·44m sheet	300	16
Backs	3	Contiplas	From 2·44m sheet	380	16
Back rails	3	Contiplas	From 2·44m sheet	150	16
Supports	8	Softwood	910	47	22
Hinges	12	Brass	50	19	
Knobs	6	Brass	19 dia.		
Magnetic catch	6	—	32		
Coverhead screws	32	Steel and brass	38 × No. 8		
Steel screws	16		38 × No. 8		
Steel screws	36		31 × No. 8		
Hinge screws	48		19 × No. 4		
Fibre wall plugs	48		38 × No. 8		

* To allow for cutting

Hang that door!

Doors that creak and do not hang properly can be the subject of much irritation. Whether rehanging an existing door or hanging a new one, a careful scheme of operation is necessary, or the door may not hang properly, catch and be difficult to close. A door should fit correctly, with the minimum of gap, particularly if it is an outside door.

Doors are usually hung so that when they open they screen the room from both view and draught. A door must have a clear, all-round allowance for expansion in wet weather.

For an outside door, leave a clearance around the top three sides and at least 3mm at the bottom. For an inside door, the average clearance is about 2mm at the top three sides and 6mm at the bottom.

Panelled, solid doors have more movement than doors using man-made boards, which are more inert. Leave a new door in a room for about 48 hours to adjust to humidity.

Cutting to size

To protect a door in storage and transit, the stiles, the long rails, are made over-length and project beyond the end of the door at top and bottom. These extension pieces are called 'horns' or 'joggles' and have to be cut off.

It is best to leave these on, to protect the door from damage, until you are ready to hang it. Lay the door across trestles and cut these off flush with a hacksaw, finishing with a block plane.

Most doors have to be adjusted to fit the door frame. This is done by planing or 'shooting' the door. A home-made support can be made up to hold the door while the edges are being planed, consisting of a piece of 75mm × 50mm timber about 510mm long with an angled notch about 40mm deep and 50mm wide in it. A large wedge, about 255mm long, secures the door when placed in the support.

An alternative to using trestles and the support is a unit such as the Workmate portable bench, which can double for both and provides lateral support when planing, since the bench contains an integral vice along its length.

When shooting the stiles and rails, use a long plane, such as a jack plane; shoot from either end, as this will ensure an accurate line, free from hollows.

If the frame is out of true when the door is offered up, the door may have to be scribed to fit. You may have to wedge the door up into position with plugs at the bottom while you are checking the fit.

Once the hanging stile is a good fit against the jamb, the opposed stile should be planed. This edge must have a slight bevel on the inside edge of the non-hinged or lock stile to fit properly. A door about 50mm thick requires a bevel of about 2mm.

Next, fit the head of the door, testing the fit with the hanging (hinged) stile in position. Allow a little less clearance above the lock stile than the hanging stile, since the doors tend to drop in time, partly because of wear on hinges.

Fitting at the bottom on an outside door depends on the type of step or whether draught extruders or weather seals are being fitted.

Exterior doors are best hung with what is called a 'kick'. This means that the door, when opened, is slightly out of vertical, which increases the clearance at the bottom.

This is often necessary for porch floors, which may have a slight fall in the direction of the door. The kick is achieved by slightly varying the amount by which the hinges are recessed.

Hinges

Most doors are hung on cast-iron butt hinges. These are made in a range of sizes; the best average size for doors is 400mm. For heavy doors, it is advisable to use three hinges. This also helps to prevent warping and spreads the load. Where three hinges are fitted on standard doors, slightly smaller hinges can be used.

Pressed-steel butts are less strong than cast-iron ones and are more likely to give trouble through rusting.

The top and bottom hinges should be fitted to line up visually with the edges of the rails.

Prop the door into the frame, again on wedges, to hold it steady. Make a mark on both the door and the frame 150mm from the top and 230mm from the bottom. These will then line up with standard top and bottom rails. If an intermediate hinge is being used, mark a position halfway between these points.

Remove the door, take a hinge and draw round one leaf with a marking knife, in turn on the stile and on the door frame. Position the hinges inside the marked pencil lines. Set the position so that the hinge knuckle just clears the door and the frame.

Next, set a marking gauge to the thickness of the hinge flap and mark the front surface of the door and the frame for depth.

Hinges are always hung on the door first, so first cut the slot for this recess. To fit a hinge, chisel along the marked lines on the door. Make a series of cuts across the grain, to the depth of the gauge line, then pare, with the grain, to remove the waste. Turn the chisel bevel-side downwards to chop diagonally, which makes it easier to remove waste wood.

The leaves of cast-iron butts are normally made to taper slightly. When the outer surfaces of the leaves are held parallel, there is a clearance space between them.

The bottom of the recess should slope slightly to correspond with any taper of the leaf of the hinge, so that this fits flush with the surface of the wood

The door should be placed in the opening so that the loose part of the hinge is on the inner surface of the frame. Position a wedge beneath the door and a piece of packing, just under 3mm, above the top rail. This brings the door up to its correct position.

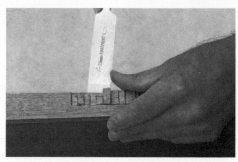

Next, slice crossways and pare away
waste timber to the depth of the hinge

The hole is then squared and cleaned
up with a wood chisel to accept the lock

Saw the protective horns or 'joggles'
from the end of the door and then plane

The joint is finally cleaned up to the
correct depth, using flat of the chisel

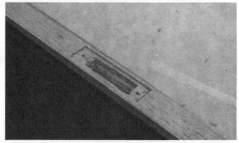

The recess for the lock plate is cut
out of the door edge, using a chisel

Try the door for fit. There should be
clearance of about 2mm at top and sides

The hinge should fit neatly into the
slot. Screw holes can now be drilled

The holes for the screws to secure the
lock in position can then be drilled out

Plane the door so that it fits snugly.
A hand or power plane can be used here

A marking gauge can be used to square
across the width of the lock shoulders

Marking gauge is again used to mark out
the depth of the latch and the spindle

Use the hinge as a template to mark out.
Cut out the profile with the chisel edge

The lock itself can be used to mark out
the width of the body of the lock

This is drilled out, again using a twist
bit. Check carefully that hole is accurate

Make a series of wedged cuts to the
depth of the hinge; keep within profile

A suitable twist bit may be used to
drill to the depth of the lock body

Latch position is marked on door jamb
from position of latch and chopped out

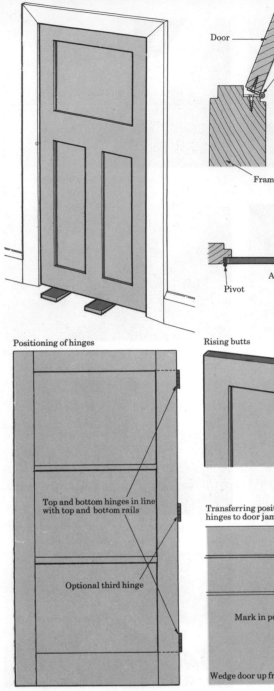

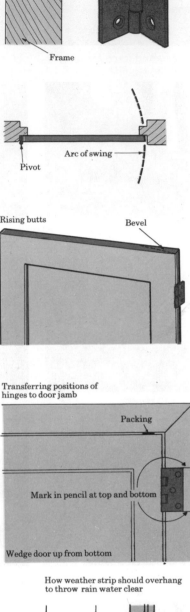

Positioning of hinges

Top and bottom hinges in line with top and bottom rails

Optional third hinge

Rising butts

Bevel

Transferring positions of hinges to door jamb

Packing

Mark in pencil at top and bottom

Wedge door up from bottom

Obtaining lift or 'kick'

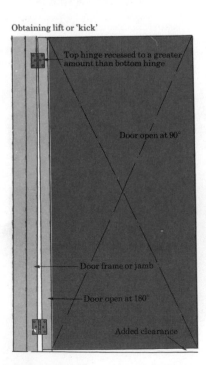

Top hinge recessed to a greater amount than bottom hinge

Door open at 90°

Door frame or jamb

Door open at 180°

Added clearance

How weather strip should overhang to throw rain water clear

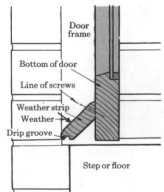

Door frame

Bottom of door

Line of screws

Weather strip
Weather

Drip groove

Step or floor

Door-holding block

Wedge

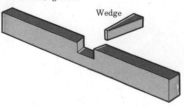

Door

Knuckle

Frame

Arc of swing

Pivot

Hang it!

Hang the door by inserting only one screw into the sides of each hinge. Make fixing position holes with a bradawl. Check the swing of the door and establish uniformity of clearance, then insert a second screw into each hinge and check again.

If adjustments are needed, these can be made by removing the door and chiselling the recesses as needed. If a recess is too deep, a packing piece made of thin card can be used to correct this. Make sure that the heads of screws are fully countersunk and offer no projections which affect the closing of the door.

If the door catches on the hinge side – because the hinge knuckle projects and causes it to swing wide – impart a slight bevel.

Rising butts are hinges which swing the door clear over carpets, by lifting progressively as it is opened. To provide initial clearance at the top of the door, the first 75mm or so of the top or head rail should be bevelled slightly on the inside edge.

A door should stay open in any position. If it does not, the screws are wrongly placed. To correct this fault, take off the door and adjust the screw positions slightly. If the door is badly out of true, you may have to reposition the leaf of the hinge; the existing screw holes should be plugged and new holes made.

Door furniture

Door furniture is fitted next. A wide variety is available in the general category of mortise locks and latches, rim and cylinder locks – the latter is a form of rim lock.

The height at which a door handle is fitted is a matter of choice, though it will look better if it has a definite relationship with any glazing bars. A midway position between two bars presents a neat appearance.

To fit a latch, square a line round the stile at the required height and gauge the distance of the latch on the stile face. With a bit and brace, bore a 15mm hole at this point to accept the spindle of the latch.

Next bore and chisel a slot in the edge of the door to accept the body or barrel of the lock. The size of this depends on the size and shape of the barrel; square the lines with a try-square and marking gauge. Use this as a template for accurate marking.

Drill a series of holes corresponding with, but slightly less than, the width of the body of the barrel of the lock and to the depth of the body; chisel these out squarely.

Insert the lock body and screw the end plate to the face of the stile through its fixing holes at the top and bottom. Attach the spindle and the door handle.

Determine the position of the striking plate by direct transfer from the latch when the door is closed. A small mortise can then be chopped through the hole in the plate with a chisel to accept the latch.

The action of the latch will be made smoother if the lead-in part of the striking plate is bent back slightly, into a small recess in the door frame.

Repairs to rickety stairs

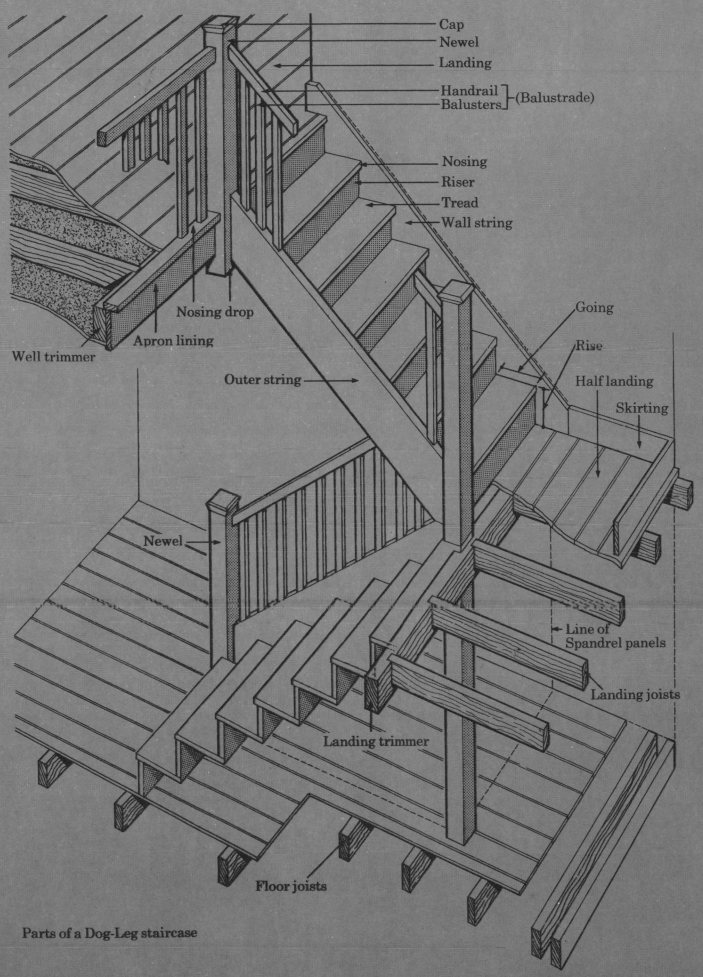

Cap
Newel
Landing
Handrail ⎤ (Balustrade)
Balusters ⎦
Nosing
Riser
Tread
Wall string
Going
Rise
Half landing
Skirting
Nosing drop
Apron lining
Well trimmer
Outer string
Newel
Line of Spandrel panels
Landing joists
Landing trimmer
Floor joists

Parts of a Dog-Leg staircase

Among the most annoying faults in the home are squeaky or loose stairs and floorboards. More often than not either can be quickly put right with hammer and nails or screwdriver, screws and glue; in other cases more work is involved. Gaps in floorboards are not only unsightly but may cause loss of heat and let in draughts.

Gaps in floorboards may be treated in three ways. They can be filled or caulked, taken up and recramped or covered over. Before starting work, first switch off the electricity mains to avoid any possibility of getting a shock if you should accidentally cut through wires beneath floorboards. Wires usually run lengthways – across the joists – under the centre of floorboards.

The position of joists can be found easily by the nail positions. Joists are usually located apart at centres or distances of 400mm and are about 50mm–75mm wide.

Holes and cracks

Holes and small cracks can be repaired with a proprietary filler. This can be rubbed smooth after it has set. If the floor is uncovered, a small amount of stain can be added to the filler material so that the repair matches the floor surface.

Wide cracks between floorboards can be filled by cutting slightly tapered wood strips. These should be coated with glue and lightly tapped in place with a soft-headed hammer or mallet. Any projections can be planed smooth after the glue has set.

First, establish the thickness of the gap, and then mark this on a section of oversized timber. Transfer this measurement, slightly oversized, to a marking gauge, mark the timber and then cut with a panel saw.

Slightly taper with a smoothing plane and knock this into place. Secure to joists, at intervals, with 40mm panel pins.

Gaps

Gaps can be filled with papier mâché when these are under 6mm in width. To make, tear newspaper up into pieces of postage-stamp size and mix in a bucket

with boiling water, a little at a time; pound the paper with a piece of timber until this becomes a thick paste.

Allow to cool for an hour and pour in a glue size. Once the mixture is cold it can be trowelled between boards with a scraper; push this well down. The floor can be rubbed smooth with an abrasive paper once dry.

If the floor surface is not covered, a soft, white, unprinted paper can be used, since newspaper papier mâché is greyish in colour. Prepare as before but bind to a thick paste using a cellulose-based wallpaper adhesive. The mixture can be coloured with a liquid dye to match floorboards.

Shrinkage

Timber flooring may shrink and gap considerably. Where there are serious gaps, the floorboards may be lifted and recramped to close up the gap. A pair of flooring cramps may be hired for this job.

First, loosen the boards and recramp and nail them in sequence. When you reach the last board, the gaps will have built up and be fairly wide. A wide strip of timber may be needed to finish off.

It is good practice not to lay strips of less than 75mm in width, since narrower ones may break under 'point' loading from heavy furniture.

To overcome this, the last board may have to be reduced in width so that a suitably dimensioned strip of timber flooring can be inserted. An alternative is to use a wider board to close the gap.

Cramping

You can make your own floor cramps and use the following technique to relay floorboards. Start lifting boards close to the skirting at one side but leave the board beneath the skirting in place. Plane off any tongue on the first board you take out.

Next, cut four softwood wedges from timber slightly thicker than the floorboards; these should be at least 455mm long, 50mm deep and taper to a point. A pair of these wedges must be placed at intervals of five floorboards.

Place the wedges together and temporarily fix, by half nailing, a piece of

scrap board tightly against the wedges as a support.

With two hammers, knock the wedges together, hammering from alternate ends: this forces the boards evenly together. You can now nail down the boards, using cut nails or screws.

Once you come to the skirting, use a chisel to lever the final board tightly against the others and nail down.

The gap between the board beneath the skirting and the final board may then be filled with a piece of matched boarding, cut to size. If you wish you may use a piece of tongued board, first cutting away the top of the tongue.

Patching up

Sometimes, a worn section of flooring cannot be patched up and must be replaced. This may be a simple matter of prising up and taking out a complete section of flooring; however, if only a short section is affected or it is easier to replace a small rather than a larger piece, it is best if you can cut through the board in the centre of a joist.

Check carefully that new sections of board are of the same width and thickness as the old. If the boards are merely butted together, the new section is simply nailed back in.

If you need access beneath the board to any services, the section should be screwed back. Drill and countersink the hole, so that the screw head is not proud of the surface.

Cutting out

Cutting is most easily done with a power saw. The depth of the cut should be carefully set to that of the thickness of the floorboards. Avoid cutting into the joist. First, pull out any nails so that the blade of the saw is not damaged.

It is better to make a bevelled joint, so set the blade to an angle of 45° for cutting out the old section and make sure that the new piece is also bevelled so that it fits snugly against the existing floorboard.

A faulty section may also be cut out by drilling a hole through the board close to the joist and then, using a pad saw or saw

Tap tapered strips of wood, cut slightly oversize, to fill gaps in floorboards

Section of floorboards can be lifted, supported on piece of wood then easily cut

Short length of board can be cut at angle with floorboard saw, padsaw or a jigsaw

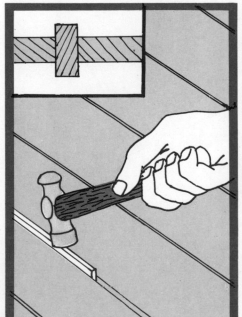

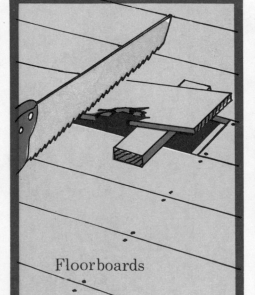

Floorboards

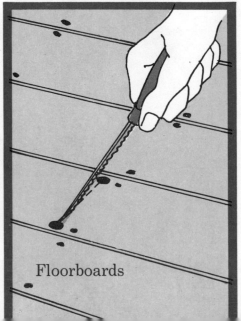

Floorboards

knife, sawing obliquely through to each edge of the board. This operation is repeated at the other end of the damaged section.

Tongued and grooved

Where the board is tongued and grooved, it is necessary to cut down one edge with a thin, broad chisel or a saw knife along a tongued section, which leaves the boards on either side with a tongue and groove respectively.

The bottom wall of the groove must be removed so that the top one rests on the tongue of the adjacent board. Make a cutting line on the outside of this wall, using a marking gauge.

Noggings

The replaced board and the original sound sections butting to it must be supported on either side with a fillet or 'nogging' nailed or screwed to the relevant joists.

These fillets must be at least 38mm thick and fixed with 64mm long nails. Fix each nogging with two nails into each joist.

Another method of lifting floorboards is with a cold chisel, bolster, or crowbar. These can be used to prise up the end of the board after punching in the nails. Take care, however, that you do not cause damage to adjacent boards. Once the board is raised sufficiently, slip a thick piece of wood beneath it to keep it up. The board can then be cut through beside the joist.

The claw of a hammer is intended to enable you to lever up floorboards. Insert the claw beneath the board to be lifted and tilt the handle, using the head of the hammer as a fulcrum on the joist.

Floor sanding

A proprietary floor sander can be hired and is an effective way to smooth an uneven floor, once boards are fixed down and nails and screws are punched below the surface. Remove layers of paint or varnish.

Use a coarse grade of paper; this fixes to a drum. Start at one corner of the room and work diagonally across; pull the machine backwards then re-sand along the same line.

Overlap each by about 75mm until the floor is sanded. If necessary, repeat in the opposite diagonal direction.

Change to a medium or fine paper and sand in one direction, along the boards, pull back and work over each strip twice.

Since you cannot get completely into corners, use a smaller rotary sander, orbital sander or sanding disc to finish these areas, with a fine grade of paper.

A safety tip: The fine sawdust becomes energized by the action of sanding and may flare up dangerously if burned afterwards.

Squeaky or loose treads

A loose or squeaky tread may be irritating but indicates little other than that a wedge beneath the stair tread has worked slightly loose. Wedges hold treads and risers firmly in place.

Another cause may be that glue blocks reinforcing the joint between treads and risers may be a little loose and need refixing. These are triangular in shape and are held in place by glue and screws, usually 75mm long.

The trouble is only serious if you can feel the tread move physically beneath your feet; it is time to cure the problem or serious trouble may occur, since wedges or blocks, or both, have become seriously loosened.

Access to wedges and glue blocks is beneath the stairs. If the underside of the stair is open, this is simply a matter of reglueing and refixing where necessary.

Wedges should be removed one at a time and then refitted. Any warped or broken ones must be discarded and new ones made. The original slope of the wedge should be exactly followed in the new.

Loose glue blocks should be reglued and screwed back firmly. Take care that all surfaces are first clean and dry or a poor joint may be the result.

Cracked treads should be reinforced with blocks of wood or corner-screwed steel angle brackets.

On older staircases, you may find that the underside is covered with a lath and plaster skin. This will first have to be removed, so you can obtain access.

It is unavoidably a dirty job and you should mask off, with dust sheets or poly-

thene sheet, as much of the surrounding area as you can.

Wear protective clothing and cover your head, then hack out the plaster work with as little dust as possible.

It is a good idea to replace the plaster with boarding or some other removable surface for easy future access.

Newel posts

Newel posts can become loosened – usually at the floor joist to which these are fixed. Usually, these only need rescrewing, but you will need to take up floorboards to do this.

If either the joist or post is damaged or split, use steel angle reinforcing brackets to make the repair.

These should be firmly screwed into place; glue or fit back damaged sections and support these with reinforcing blocks if needed.

Another problem is where the joint between the newel post and the outer strings becomes loosened, for this also loosens all the treads and risers. The post must be braced with woodblocks, 32mm square, which are glued and screwed into the inside corner.

Worn nosings

The rounded front part of a tread, the nosing, on conventional staircases, projects slightly and may become worn or damaged. This may happen on uncarpeted stairs, where the wear is usually in the middle of the nosing.

To replace a tread involves considerable work, but the nosing can be easily replaced with new timber. Make sure surfaces are clean and dry. Measure the amount of nosing to be removed and cut a section of hardwood to the corresponding width and thickness.

Mark the section accurately so that you cut it off completely flat. Next, cut away the worn section, just slightly forward of the riser, using a small saw.

Do not go completely back to the riser, as the joint, particularly if it is a tongued-and-grooved one, may be weakened.

The new section should be pinned and glued into place and allowed to dry thoroughly. Fixing pins should be punched below the surface of the wood and the small hole filled with a proprietary filler.

The nosing can be rounded with the spokeshave to correspond with the nosings on the staircase.

Worn steps

It is a simpler matter, on many staircases, to replace a worn bottom step; however, it is important to preserve both the height and width of the old one, since the 'going' or slope of the staircase should not be altered. This could be hazardous and cause someone to trip.

Squeaking can be caused by side friction between boards. The way to cure this is to dust the joints with a talcum powder or French chalk. Warped boards tend to lift nails slightly, allowing the boards to creak. These can be reinforced with countersunk screws, fixed at intervals.

Bearers nailed or screwed to joist give support for the boarding when replaced

Supporting Fillets
Joists

Common joints used in carpentry and joinery

for joining edges and particle board.

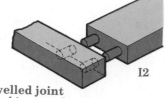

11 Tongued-and-grooved with loose tongue. The easiest tongued-and-grooved joint to make. The tongue may be made of plywood; the grooves must be deeper than half the width of the tongue.

Halved and lap joints
for general framing, carcase and light structural work. All may be pinned or screwed and glued.

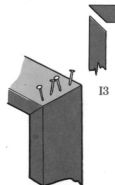

Dowelled joint
for cabinet work.

12 Hidden-dowel joint. Most common furniture joint. If dowel extends through 'A' it is a through dowel; simple to make and dowel ends may make a design feature.

1 Full lap T-joint.

2 T-halving joint or T-half lap.

3 Cross halving joint and cross halving cut on edge.

4 Dovetail halving joint. Used where 'A' has to carry weight or, if 'B' is vertical, it is likely to splay.

Mitred corner joint

13 Glued-and-pinned plain mitre. The simplest mitre joint most commonly used for picture framing.

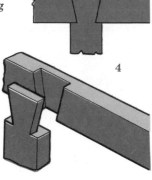

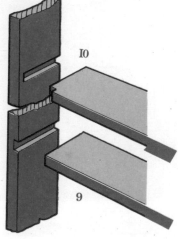

9 Simple, through-housing joint. For joinery and cabinet carcasing, e.g. shelving and stair treads.

10 Stopped housing joints; as 9 but has a neater finish.

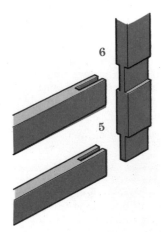

Rebate and housing joints
for neat, simple joinery.

7 End rebate joint; for carcasing e.g. bookcases.

8 Rebate housing or barefaced, tongued-and-grooved joints. General carcasing e.g. bookcases.

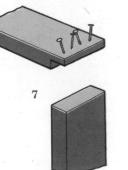

Bridle or open mortise joints
for framing and carcasing.

5 Corner-bridle joint; can be used for joining chair arms and legs.

6 Through-bridle joint gives a stronger finish than the halving joint.

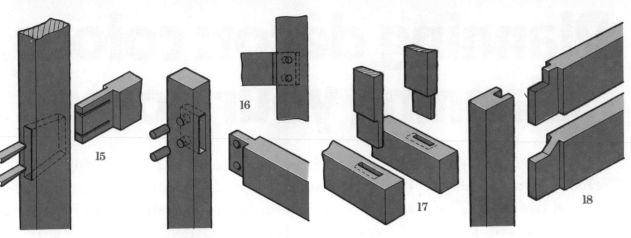

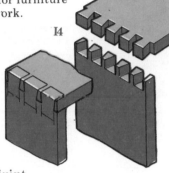

Mortise-and-tenon joints
the joint most commonly used where strength is required.

15 Wedged, through mortise and tenon. Tenon should extend 2mm beyond mortise to allow for trimming.

16 Stub mortise-and-tenon. In this case through dowelled. Note how holes are offset to allow dowels to draw up the tenon.

17 Barefaced tenon with single shoulders. Shoulders conceal any gaps in the work.

18 Haunched mortise-and-tenon and secret-haunched tenon; for furniture and high-class cabinet work.

Dovetail joint
the strongest joint for corners.

14 Open-dovetail joint; most suitable for boxes, but if well cut, can be effective decoration.

Lengthening joints

19 Simple scarf joint. May be glued for light work, otherwise it should either be screwed or bolted together with metal fish plates.

20 Fish-plate joint. A strong joint. Plates may be either plywood or mild steel.

Simple joints for man-made boards

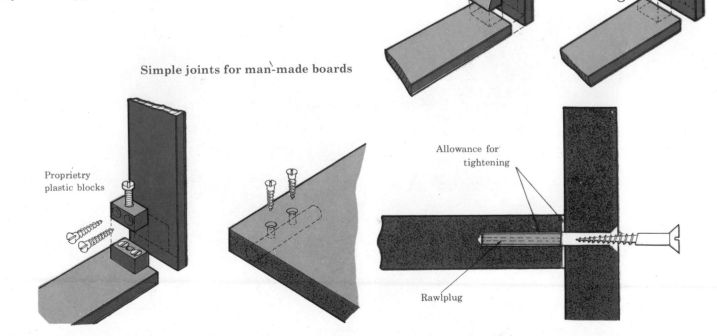

Proprietry plastic blocks

Allowance for tightening

Rawlplug

Planning décor: colour planning your home

Two homes, externally identical, may look totally different within – as a result of the varied use of colour, textures, furniture and fittings. The use of colour in home décor and furnishing schemes is a way of expressing individuality. Do not be too hesitant in experimenting with colour; while there must be rules, these should only be regarded as general guidelines.

Natural light, or white light, is composed of all the colours of the spectrum. The spectrum, or wheel of colours, is made up of all the colours of the rainbow. These are red, orange, yellow, green, blue, indigo and violet.

Primary colours

The colours red, yellow and blue are known as the primary colours. Strong, vibrant colours, especially red, cannot be produced by mixing any other colours together. If equal parts of red, yellow and blue are mixed together they will make a neutral shade of grey.

From this, two equal parts of yellow and blue mixed together will produce green and two equal parts of green and blue will produce blue-green.

Colour disc

Warm, advancing colours

Cool, receding colours

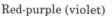

Yellow

Yellow-green

Orange-yellow

Green

Orange

Blue-green

Red-orange

Blue

Red

Blue-purple (violet)

Red-purple (violet)

Purple (violet)

It is possible to mix well over 2,000 distinct colours, using the primary colours in varying proportions.

Colour balance

When decorating a home, the object should be to try to achieve a balanced mixture of primary colours, shades and tints. Shades are produced by adding black; tints by adding white to the base colour.

White, black and grey are considered as 'non-colours'. White reflects light, black absorbs it and grey can be used to give a muted or receding effect. White is used extensively in modern décor to reflect light and colour, giving contrast and creating a sense of space.

Colour disc

In all this wealth of colour it may be difficult to decide on a harmonious colour scheme. A colour disc is the standard way of differentiating between the colours of the spectrum. Yellow is always placed at the top of the disc and grey in the middle, to give a reference point, when planning a colour scheme.

From yellow the colour range proceeds, clockwise, through the 'cool' colours on the right of the wheel to the 'warm' colours on the left.

Harmony

Colour can be used to produce harmony or disorder. It is better to use too few colours than to try to cope with too many.

There are some guide lines to follow when planning colour schemes. One method is to choose one colour and use it with shades and tones of that same colour.

This scheme can be difficult to achieve successfully, for unless carefully balanced it can produce a rather dull effect. Black, white and grey can be used to give added interest.

Two related colours, such as blue and blue green, can be used together if one colour is used in a greater proportion than the other. Again, white, black or grey can add interest. Opposite colours used in unequal proportions will give a visually interesting scheme. Used in equal proportions, opposite colours, orange and blue, for instance, will clash.

Another way is to use three different colours set at equal distances apart on the colour wheel – for example, orange, violet and green. There are, of course, different permutations of this scheme.

Other varied colour schemes can be devised by dividing the colour wheel into cool and warm colours. Take yellow-orange and red-orange, miss out orange between them and pair them with their opposite colours on the cool half of the disc. Here, the opposite colours are blue-violet and blue-green, blue being omitted.

Experimenting in colour

One needs to experiment with colours. Try, as far as you can, to see how colours will mix and blend. Obtain colour cards of paint colours, get samples of wallpaper and swatches of material to give you some idea of the finished effects of blending

colour. Look at the colours in artificial and natural light and appreciate the fact that some colours, in proximity with others, alter in hue. Colours may 'steal' from each other.

The aim should be to achieve a modulated blending or a complementary contrast but never discord. The latter can be difficult to live with and may create a cluttered, restless feeling.

Using colour

Red is a vibrant colour which should be used sparingly. It is suitable for use in such places as hallways, to give a bright, warm, welcoming feeling; in children's rooms; and in living areas, to highlight focal points.

Orange is another vibrant colour which creates a warm feeling, but it can be overpowering if used extensively – particularly in a small room.

Yellow mixes well with red but needs the contrast of a cool colour. Lemon-yellow contrasts well with greens and blues. Blue is a cold colour and may create an atmosphere of remoteness and chill. Blue and red tend to fight each other although they can, with skill, be used effectively together.

Purple is a rich colour but can be rather overpowering if used too extensively. Used sparingly, it can make a valid contribution to a décor scheme. Shades and tints of purple can make very attractive colour combinations. Black and white, though non-colours, are used as contrast mediums.

Contrast

Black contrasts well with white, yellow and pale tints. White is a very important 'colour'. Extremely versatile, it can be used for the main colour scheme with highlights in other colours. Alternatively, it becomes the contrast part of a scheme using colour.

All-white bedrooms are very popular – white walls, ceiling, fitted cupboards, carpet, bedspreads, blinds and so on. Colour may provide highlights in, for example, lampshades, cushions, occasional chair covers, a bedside rug or books on a shelf. To take another example, white used as a ceiling 'colour' and for woodwork, doors and window frames provides an effective contrast for carpets, furniture, soft-furnishing and ornaments in other colours, tints or shades.

If you want a restful scheme, you should include such colours as oatmeal, beige, gold, soft greens, browns and cream. More stimulating, but correspondingly less easy to live with, are colours such as orange, blue, purple, red, yellow and pink, contrasted with white or black.

Colour deception

Camouflage of unattractive or obtrusive features can be achieved by the clever use of colour. Grey mixed with any colour will cause that colour to recede. In this way, angular, ugly shapes that tend to intrude visually can be made to recede.

A number of doors breaking up a wall area can be made less obtrusive by painting the doors and frame in the same

shade as the surrounding wall. If you are using wallpaper, take a non-dominant, receding colour from the paper and paint the doors and frames in this. In this way, the door will blend into the back-ground. Radiators and pipes can also be similarly disguised. Paint them the same colour as the walls behind them.

Shapes within a room that are angular, such as chimney breasts, tend to be less attractive as features than rounded recesses.

To lessen their impact, paint or decorate them with receding colours and use bright focal colours or pastel shades, adjacent to the object, to draw the eye. The converse works if you wish to highlight a particular feature.

Colour can be used to deceive the eye and help to redress the balance of badly proportioned rooms. This needs additional planning, but much can be done with colour alone.

Proportions

In a narrow room, where one exists, leave the picture rail and bring the ceiling right down to it. Concentrate colour on the lower part of the walls; this will bring the eye down to the colour level and give an impression of width.

Paint the long walls in cool, receding colours and the short walls in a warm colour. Cool colours, like blue and green, make the walls appear further apart. The room will appear to be wider and shallower.

Flooring can also add to this illusion. Patterned carpet, lino, tiles or woodblock flooring should be laid with the lines running across the width of the room. Alternatively, a carpet with a diagonal pattern or carpet tiles arranged in this way will also make the room appear wider.

Another widening trick is to paint the ceiling in a colour that tones with the flooring and paint the walls white. The eye is drawn to the walls which gives an immediate impression of width.

One problem may be that the room needs an illusion of height. The eye needs to be drawn upwards; one way of doing this is to use vertical striped wallpaper. A plain floor covering in a matching or toning colour should then be used.

As cool colours recede and give an impression of depth and space, they can be used to make a wide room look narrower. The long walls should have a warm-coloured finish, while the shorter walls should be painted in a receding colour.

The floor covering should be laid with the pattern running from the front to the back of the room, emphasizing any lines on the walls.

A large floor that appears too spacious can be stained or painted. Highlight the centre with a bright rug or carpet. The carpet becomes the focal point and the surrounding area merges into the background.

Grand illusion

Conversely, fitted carpet gives an illusion of space. This illusion can be carried further by painting the skirting board in a colour that matches the carpet. In a small house, it may be possible to use the same-colour carpet throughout one floor. Qualities may vary, dependent upon the usage required in differing rooms, but when doors are open one will get the impression of an endless vista.

If this is not possible, carpet or floor-covering colours should be linked. Think of the visual assault of ill-matching carpets meeting in a hall or landing. Any linking hall or landing carpet should attempt to continue the adjacent colours.

Carpets are an expensive item and should be chosen to blend with schemes of décor and make a positive contribution to the overall effect.

Carpets and colours

Whether to have patterned or plain carpet is often debated. From the standpoint of colour scheming, plain carpets may be easier to furnish around. A costly item that may have to last for years, a carpet is less easily changed than the more versatile curtains and other soft furnishings.

However, plain carpets, especially if pale, do show specks and mark more easily than patterned carpets. The latter may be better in rooms where there are children or pets.

If in doubt when choosing a carpet colour, choose one that will blend well with several décor schemes. Colours such as brown, grey, moss green and beige might be suitable.

The carpet colour should be one shade darker than the walls – if they are the same colour, or used to give stability, a darker shade of the main furnishing colour – this will help to unify the scheme.

A room can be made to appear larger than it is by using a fitted, plain carpet in a receding colour and texture, or a carpet with a subdued pattern and colour.

Patterned carpets, in strong colours, will make the room look smaller but the danger here is a conflict between the carpet, the rest of the décor scheme, and the furniture, which may produce a cluttered effect. Soft furnishings, particularly, need to be chosen with great care.

Texture can be introduced through carpets and a textured carpet or a shaggy rug may provide a focal point to a room. Again, there is a danger of introducing too many textures in flooring, upholstery and soft furnishings. Nothing is worse than a multitude of textures, fighting it out together.

Well used, texture can add interest to a room. Textured wallpaper, such as hessian or woodchip, may make an attractive background against which to display pictures or ornaments.

Colour and texture

Colour is affected by texture. On a flat surface some colours will seem dull, while the same colours used on a textured surface will seem interesting and alive.

Smooth surfaces reflect light, while a rough surface absorbs light and gives a darker tone. A dark, matt surface absorbs light but a light, matt surface reflects light and is, therefore, suitable for use in rooms that lack a great deal of natural light.

Patterned fabric looks attractive against a white or cool background. Strong pattern tends to dominate and should be used sparingly. Less-definite patterns tend to merge into the background and are easier to live with.

Pattern, too, combined with the choice of colour, can be used to disguise problem features. Intrusive doors can be papered to match the wallpaper, matching wallpaper and fabric can help rectify a badly proportioned or ugly window.

Small, fussy windows can be hidden behind a wall of curtaining, or made to look quite stately by using long patterned floor-length curtains.

Patterned material can also be used to co-ordinate areas of a room – for example, in linking together curtains, bedspread, furniture covers and cushions.

Furniture can be used to help correct the proportions of a room. Try to avoid a cluttered room that is neither comfortable to live in nor pleasing to look at.

A long, low room can be quite depressing. Look at the entire area as one and then subdivide it, using colour, modular storage divider units or tall pieces of furniture. These units should reach the ceiling to give an illusion of height. Long curtains will also help to create a sensation of vertical height.

Tall furniture tends to give a feeling of height, while furniture arranged at a lower level brings focus down in a high-ceilinged room.

Space project

Many people want to create an impression of space in their homes. Much can be done with colour, pattern and texture but actual physical proportions, furniture and soft furnishings play an important part in the overall effect.

In other areas, modular furniture can be used, leaving floor space free. Wall units and shelves can be made of light material, so that they do not dominate the wall area. For example, glass shelves mounted on light brackets merge into the background. Picture rails can be removed, low radiators or skirting radiators can be used.

Often, two small rooms can usefully be combined into one living area. Instead of two cluttered boxes, one can have two functional areas, linked by flooring and décor colouring.

Dark walls need not necessarily make areas look small if they are combined with plenty of white on the ceiling and floor and in the furnishings.

Glazed look

Mirrors can be used to give an added dimension and feeling of spaciousness. A mirror backing a recessed alcove reflects light and gives a sense of space.

To widen a narrow hallway use mirrors or mirror tiles on one side. Use wall to wall carpeting and extend the colour of the carpet by 50mm or so up the wall.

Hallways, can afford to be decorated in bright colours. They need to be welcoming entrances, well lit and inviting.

Around the home

Homes are usually divided into particular activity areas. One room, where one may spend much of one's leisure time is the living room. This is a room that should be restful enough for relaxation yet stimulating enough for entertaining.

It is important when choosing colour schemes, particularly for a living area, to visualize the scheme under natural and artificial light. In fact, if you do a lot of entertaining, a colour scheme that looks its best in artificial light may be more successful.

Fluorescent light tends to bleach out colour, while ordinary tungsten lamps give a warmer glow to most colours.

Unless there is the opportunity to start from scratch, most décor schemes have to be built around existing furniture and flooring. There are two ways of doing this. The first is to take one predominating colour and create a colour scheme, using shades and tones of that colour.

The second is to use one fixed colour and a contrast. In the first case, an example is a blue-green carpet, complemented by varying shades and tones of green, used on the walls and soft furnishings.

A white ceiling would contrast the greens. Alone, this could be a boring scheme and would need to be livened up with splashes of colour in cushions and lampshades.

In the second instance, one fixed colour and a contrast can be used in a two-colour scheme. A scheme can be built up, using complementary colours. With green, one can add soft yellows, shades of orange and brown. The original colour might be echoed or repeated in window furnishings or carpets.

A natural woodblock floor, or a wood-panelled wall, rich in colour, could provide the basis of a natural-coloured, neutral-toned scheme. Here texture would play a big part in making a success of a scheme that is dependent on shades of oatmeal, black, grey and off-white. The whole scheme might need a focal point of more definite colour, perhaps in lampshades or cushion covers.

Aspect

Aspect affects the choice of room colour schemes. A room facing north will have a cold aspect with cold light. Orange, yellow, red, the warm colours, help to counteract any cold feeling and create a feeling of warmth.

On the other hand a west- or south-facing room, which will have a warmer light, can be decorated in cool greens, blues and greys.

Colour scheming tends to be rather subjective, so really it is a choice for the individual. Bedrooms are a personal choice and range from the feminine colour schemes, pale and pastel, to the very masculine room.

Children's rooms grow with them and while a pastel-shaded room is restful for a small baby, children enjoy the vibrant primary colours that adults may tend to find over-stimulating.

Teenagers tend to experiment with their own schemes, often achieving a discordant but successful clash of colours.

New paintwork, however carefully applied, is only as good as the surface beneath it. Careful preparation of the surface, whether exterior or interior, is essential. Paint can be applied to a variety of surfaces such as wood, metal, plaster, lining paper, plastic, polystyrene and stonework.

Preparation may count for three quarters of the time taken to do a job, but the result will be worthwhile. If work is rushed the result may be poor and not durable.

Surfaces to be painted must always be clean, dust and grease-free. Paint will stick to whatever is immediately below it. It will stick to dust and come away with it. If paint is applied to a greasy surface, the grease may combine with the oil present in the paint and lengthen the drying time.

If the surface is basically in good condition it may only need washing down with a paint cleaner, such as sugar soap or detergent. When washing down, particularly on walls and large areas, such as doors, start washing from the bottom and work upwards. In this way streaks of concentrated cleaning fluids will not run down the surface and form patchy areas which make for an uneven surface.

When the first wash is completed wash again, starting at the top, with clean water. This is to remove any remaining dirt and ensure that there is no residual

detergent left which might react with the chemical constituents of the paint. After washing, the surface must be allowed to dry completely before paint is applied. If necessary, rub down with a fine glasspaper and use a soft brush to remove any dust.

New plaster should always be allowed to dry out completely before a final decorative coat is applied. Some take anything up to a year to do this. If decorated during this time, use a water-based emulsion paint which will not seal the surface but will allow it to continue drying out.

In many cases, if old paint is in good condition and the new coat will marry with the old, it is not necessary to remove it. The surface may need rubbing down with a wet-and-dry paper, used wet. Rubbing down will slightly roughen the surface and provide a good key for the new undercoat.

Blistered or flaked paint must be scraped back to a firm edge. 'Feather' the edges with the abrasive paper until they are level with the surrounding surface.

Any indentations, cracks or joins in interior woodwork should be filled with cellulose filler before priming.

All distemper should be completely removed by being washed off thoroughly with warm water. Distemper and non-washable distemper used on ceilings, consisting of glue and whiting, are very hard to remove and difficult patches may have to be scraped away with a paint scraper.

Before applying a new coat of water-based paint, the surface should be sealed with a primer.

If the distemper is covering ceiling paper, the paper may need soaking two or three times. Scrape off the paper with a broad stripping knife. Take care not to dig too deeply, or you may gouge out a hole in the plaster.

Emulsion or any water-based paint should be sponged down with detergent and warm water. Again, work from the bottom upwards for the first wash and then wash down with clean water from the top.

If the surface feels rough when dry, rub it carefully down with fine glasspaper. Remember to dust down the surface before painting.

Other paints, such as enamel paints, oil paints, oil-based gloss paints and water-based gloss paints should also be washed down with detergent and warm water to remove grease and dirt.

After rinsing with clean water, allow the surface to dry and then smooth it with wet-abrasive paper, held over a sanding block or a conveniently sized piece of wood.

To remove very bad imperfections on woodwork, such as sags and runs, a soda block, which is very coarse, can be used to rub down the surface. After rubbing down with abrasive paper or soda block, finish with a fine glasspaper or a fine wet-and-dry paper.

Basically, the surfaces that need to be

painted can be divided into two categories: internal and external surfaces which may be old paint surfaces that need preparation and repainting; and new internal and external surfaces that need treatment. These surfaces may be wood, metal, plaster, stonework, rendering or paper.

Externally, paint is normally applied to wood, metal or rendering.

Unexposed wood or metal will soon deteriorate if left to the elements. It has to be protected from the action of frost and rain. New wood should be well seasoned and matured. Softwood needs planing as paint brings out the irregularities in the grain. Hardwood, used for sills and door thresholds, can be given a clear finish. Stop any joints or indentations with oil-based putty stained to match the wood.

Door and window frames made of softwood should be rubbed down or planed smooth. Patent knotting should be applied to knots and on resinous areas. Wood primer should then be applied, ensuring that it is well brushed in so that the grain is filled.

Hardwood window sills and door thresholds provide a good surface for paint.

Wood primer is oily. Some of the oil is absorbed into the wood and helps to give good adhesion. Oily wood primer should not be thinned unless it is being used on highly porous wood. This should saturate the pores of the timber. If this does not happen, air will be trapped in the pores by the thick primer.

As the temperature rises, the air expands, causing bubbles to rise in the primer and burst through the paintwork. To avoid this on porous wood use a thin saturation coat of primer, then when dry apply a second primer coat.

An aluminium sealer is effective. It prevents seepage of resin in highly resinous timbers and problems such as creosote bleeding through the surface. The ends of window sills and thresholds should be stopped to seal the open grains. This should be done before undercoating.

Sound wood surfaces that need repainting still need preparation. The surface should be washed down and lightly glass-papered. Brush down to remove dust. Often a coat of primer, well applied, may last several paintings without being renewed. Exterior wooden surfaces that have cracks or indentations should be filled with hard-stopping after priming, then rubbed down before either undercoat or finish coats are applied.

Metal door and window frames and lead pipes need preparation. They are liable to be dirty, and coated with rust. Large areas should be scraped or brushed down with a wire brush and emery paper. It is important to protect the eyes when brushing down metal as particles of rust may cause discomfort and even damage.

Next, use rust solvent to remove the rust particles, microscopic in size, which will cause further trouble. In difficult-to-reach areas a proprietary rust curative, a preparation that turns rust to iron-oxide, can be used. This can, on gutters, be painted over with bituminous-based paint. If the surface is good but smooth, it should be roughened to form a good key.

On window frames rust should be removed from metal with a wire brush. Rub down with emery paper and paint with a rust solvent. If the windows need reputtying, remove the old putty, treat the window frame for rust, prime the metal and then replace with metal glazing putty.

Walls can be protected against damp with cement or stone paints. Cement-based emulsion paints provide a damp-resistant layer but they are only as good as the wall beneath. This must also provide a waterproof barrier.

Before applying cement or stone paint the surface must be sound, dry and clean. If the rendering has blown (come away from the brickwork) it must be hacked back and re-rendered. Brush down the surface with a stiff brush and, if required, apply a clear sealant coat before covering with the decorative coats. Before applying an external wall cover coat, the wall should be quite dry.

Internally, surfaces that need preparation may be of wood, metal, plaster or paper on plaster. Plaster surfaces should be dry before painting. If painting a new wall, a water-based paint should be used to allow the plaster to dry out. Any cracks should be cut back and filled before painting or papering. Unless a papered surface is smooth it is advisable to remove the old paper before relining and repapering.

Wood surfaces, if sound, can be washed, rubbed down and painted. Badly pitted or blistered surfaces should be stripped back to the bare wood.

Where damage is only localized, treat the area separately—rubbing down and filling if necessary. If a complete change of colour is required, such as stripping a dark paint to repaint in a light colour, it is necessary to strip the paint back to the wood. Varnish should be removed before replacing with paint. It does not provide a good surface for new paint as adhesion, even after sanding down, is not good. Remove the varnish and treat as new wood.

Polish, wax and silicone adhering to a surface can be removed with white spirit. Rub off the wax or silicone with a rough cloth and sand down. If the paint separates, the surface is not clean enough. French polish can be removed with methylated spirit applied with a rough cloth.

There are three ways of stripping paint. It is a tedious job but the effort involved is worthwhile to achieve a good surface. Paint can be removed using heat, chemical or mechanical means.

Heat is most effectively applied to oil-based paints. You can use a blow-lamp or gas blow torch. A paraffin blow torch is quite difficult to use as it needs priming with methylated spirit. No form of heat should be used near glass, as this may cause it to crack. Heat should not be used near asbestos or plaster walls.

The modern blow torch may either be one that incorporates a replaceable canister of gas or an attachment joined by a flexible cord to a gas cylinder. The latter

Fill any cracks in interior woodwork with cellulose filler before priming

Where conventional, oil-based paint is to be used, bare timber should be primed

Rub down rusted metal with wire brush; treat chemically and apply metal primer

is useful for reaching awkward corners, but is not quite so portable.

Various fittings are available with gas blow torches, from pin-head to wide flames. A paint-stripping head, which spreads the flame, should be fitted to the blow torch. As the flame produced is non-luminous it is necessary to watch the work carefully. Used in conjunction with a stripping knife, the flame must be kept well ahead of the knife.

The flame should be played from side to side. At no time should the flame set the paint alight as this will char the wood. Hold the stripping knife at an angle so that the shreds of hot paint do not fall on the hand. Place something to catch the pieces. When stopping work turn the torch away from the surface to avoid accidental burning.

Start stripping at the bottom of the areas to be treated, covering only a small area at a time. Once the wood is completely bare, use glasspaper to smooth the surface, fill any indentations or cracks and then dust down carefully before priming. Electric strippers are slower and should not be used on damp surfaces.

Chemical strippers can be home-made or commercially produced. Simple strippers can be used on paints that dry by evaporation but not on bituminous cement or chlorinated rubber paints.

Methylated spirits will remove water-based paints, distemper or emulsion; ammonia dissolved in warm water will help remove the glue in non-washable distemper; cellulose coating can be removed by cellulose thinner.

Modern chemical strippers are spirit-based and should be brushed on to the surface with an old paint brush and left until the paint starts to bubble, when it can then be removed with a paint scraper. It is wise to wear protective clothes and old gloves when using chemical strippers, as these may irritate or burn the skin. If there are several layers of paint to be removed, more than one application of stripper may be needed.

A jelly-type stripper is easier to use than a liquid as it will stay in one place and not run down the surface. Never use a chemical stripper near a naked light as it gives off highly flammable vapour.

Always ensure adequate ventilation when working. Chemical strippers are very useful when stripping window frames –especially metal frames. Burn all the stripped waste. After the paint is stripped wipe down with white spirit and treat as new wood or metal.

There are various types of paint scraper. One has a double-sided blade, one side of which is serated to cut through the paint film. A shave-hook should be used for scraping mouldings. Using a paint scraper is a skilled job and takes time. It is also possible to sand off old paint using a hand block sander with fine, medium or coarse-grained glasspaper.

A sanding attachment to a power tool will make quick work of the old paint but has the disadvantage of producing clouds of fine dust. Always use with the window open and protect the eyes with goggles. There is also the danger that the wood may be scored too deeply and additional making good will be necessary. If using a sander on large areas it is advisable to use a sand belt or orbital sander.

Try to work in a dust-free room and use lead-free priming paint. In decorating any wooden surface, preparation may include the replacement of sections of wood. This may be due to wet or dry rot. Remove the sections of infected wood and treat the surrounding areas. If new sections of wood are used this wood must be knotted and primed before paint is applied.

There are several faults that appear in old paint surfaces. These include crazing, mould, cracks, flaking, blistering and bubbling, as well as the normal dents and chips of everyday wear.

Chips can be rectified by first removing the old paint, rubbing down or 'feathering' with glass paper and filling the hole with a cellulose filler. A hard-stopper would be used for external use, applied after the primer coat, and a soft-stopper used in-

ternally. This is allowed to harden and then rubbed down and primed.

When one coat of paint is applied over a coat of an entirely differently constituted paint the result may be crazing. The new and original coats of paint contract at different rates. If badly crazed, the entire surface must be stripped back to the bare wood which should be knotted and primed before painting. Small areas may be locally treated by rubbing down with a wet-and-dry paper before applying a new top coat.

A small area of blistering may be treated, by lifting the eruption with a knife, knotting the cavity, priming, filling with stopper and allowing to dry before rubbing down level with the surrounding surface. Once the surface has been allowed to dry the repaired areas can be primed.

Cracks in ceilings, walls and plaster according to size can be filled with plaster or cellulose filler. Make sure the crack to be filled is clean, clear out loose material and cut back if needed. Cracks should be dusted and damped before filling. Press the filler in and smooth off with a knife. Sand down to achieve a smooth surface.

If the plaster surface is to be painted it is a good idea to add a little of the chosen colour to the filler. This helps the filled area to blend under the colour coat.

Very wide or deep cracks should be cleared out and filled in layers, allowing each layer to dry before putting in the next.

Efflorescence, or the permeation of alkaline salts through the plaster, can only be cured if the wall is allowed to dry out. Use an alkaline-resistant primer and then redecorate.

Mould should be scraped off before redecorating. This can be caused by damp and lack of ventilation. Wash down with an anti-fungicidal preparation, allow to dry and then redecorate.

Primer and undercoating fulfil two functions: primer is used to seal a new or newly prepared surface; it is used on unpainted surfaces. Undercoat is used to fill in the wood before the top coats are added.

When repainting sound surfaces, rub with abrasive paper to remove 'bloom'

When using blow torch, play flame from side to side to avoid charring the wood

Patent knotting should be applied to knots in wood and on any resinous areas

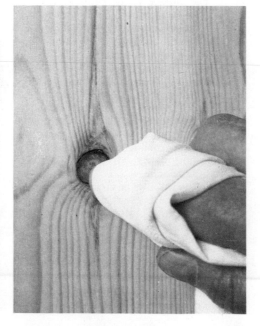

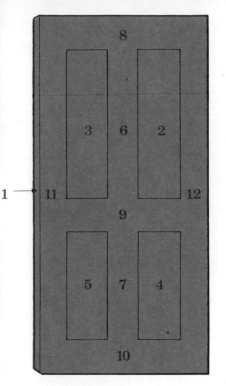

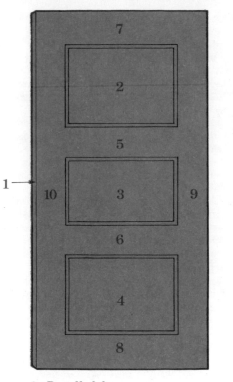

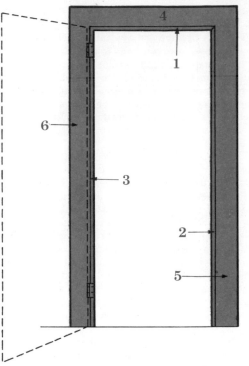

1. Cruciform door

Painting: order of sequence

2. Panelled door

3. Door surround; the faces of door stops are painted the colour of the outer face of the door

The finished effect in painting can only be as good as the work of preparation which went into it. Time spent in preparing the work and the careful choice of materials and 'tools', may possibly seem tedious but should enable you to achieve results of which you may be justly proud.

Preparation

Before beginning to paint, first clear the area as much as possible. Carpets should be rolled up and, if possible, removed. Curtains should be taken down and any furniture covered with dust sheets or paper.

Collect together all the equipment you will need. This includes brushes, paint kettles, clean rag, dusting brushes, a tack cloth and bigger items such as ladders, steps or trestles and, of course, the paint.

All equipment should be as clean as possible and dust-free. After pre-painting preparation there is likely to be quite a lot of dust in the air and on sills, picture rails and skirtings. A vacuum cleaner will remove the dust on the floor. Wipe down all doors, window sills, rails and skirtings. Before opening the paint tins, wipe the lids to remove dust. If the paint is not new, stand the tins upside down for a couple of days before using, to help loosen the settled pigment.

A well-ventilated environment is essential when painting as some paints have pungent odours. Unless it is very windy and dust is likely to be blown in, keep a window or door open to ensure circulation of air.

Paint, other than thixotropic paint (gell), should be stirred before use to mix together the pigment, thinners and bind-

ing agents in the correct proportions.

When opened, the paint should have a layer of oil or thinners on the top. If it is old paint, there may be a layer of skin which must be removed. Do not attempt to mix it in with the paint. Stir the paint from the bottom of the tin using a piece of clean wood or a paint-mixing attachment on a power tool.

The paint is at the right consistency when it flows evenly from the tip of the stirrer or stick without leaving lumps adhering. If lumps remain, the paint needs further stirring.

It is important to work with small amounts of fresh paint. To do this, paint can be dispensed from the tin into a paint kettle. Strain paint through a fine mesh, such as an old nylon stocking, into the kettle. Dispense about a 25mm depth of paint at a time. A kettle is easier to handle while working. Replace the lid of the main tin to keep the paint clean and prevent a skin forming.

Paint can be thinned with the solvent recommended for the particular type of paint. Usually, paint is supplied in the correct working consistency.

When painting a room, the areas are usually painted in the following sequence: picture rails, if any, window frames, skirtings and, lastly, doors.

If the surface is stripped bare or previously unpainted, a primer or sealer should be applied to the surface.

Separate primers are made for wood and metal. Some polyurethane paints can be applied straight on to wood surfaces, but metal must always be primed.

Obtain enough paint to complete the job. It is better to over-estimate as spare paint can always be used for touching in afterwards.

Painting should not be undertaken in a

moist or frosty atmosphere. Surfaces to be painted should always be dry. When painting outside do not prepare a greater area than can be painted in one day or spell of work.

Unprotected wood is particularly affected by rain, dew and frost and should be primed if left overnight. Primers do not weather well and ideally surfaces should be undercoated if they have to be left for any period.

Polyurethane paints have a limited 'wet-edge' time. If there is paint drag on the brush the remedy is to add a little paraffin to the paint.

Rubbing down between the coats of paint will give good inter-coat adhesion. If painting on to an existing gloss surface, this should be smoothed with a wet-and-dry abrasive paper or fine glasspaper to give a matt, slightly roughened, surface.

There are two methods of using top-coat paints. It is easier to use one coat of eggshell finish, followed by one gloss coat. Two gloss coats give a higher sheen but are slightly harder to apply.

Full gloss, semi-gloss, eggshell and flat-finish paints can be used on interior wood-work. Areas of paint that are subject to condensation and sunlight, such as sashes, window ledges, frames and reveals will last longer if a full-gloss paint is used.

External woodwork that has to stand up to weather should be painted with hard gloss paint, using the appropriate undercoat recommended by the manufacturer.

Undercoating

In general new paintwork on soft wood will last longer if a four-coat system of painting is used. This consists of one coat of primer, one or two coats of undercoat and one or two coats of top coat. A paint

How to do an undercover job

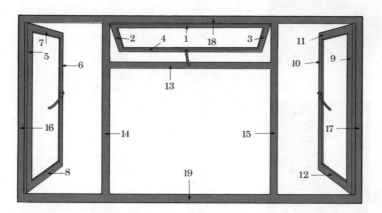

4. Casement window

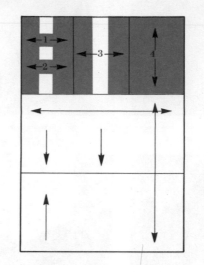

5. Large areas, such as a flush door. Divide the area into three. The colour indicates direction of brush strokes. Lay paint off well into previously painted areas

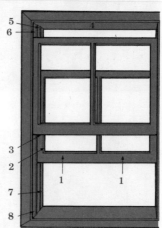

6. Sash window. Sashes should be temporarily fixed, at each stage of painting, with small wedges

system that is used internally should not contain a lead primer or any other toxic material, particularly where children may be present, since lead is poisonous. Avoid using lead-based paints on such surfaces as sills, stairways, nursery woodwork or furniture.

Undercoat should be applied after the primer coat has been allowed to dry for at least 48 hours. Before applying the undercoat, check that the primer is dry, but not too hard, and that any filling or stopping necessary is done. Lightly rub down the surface with a wet-abrasive paper, and then wipe off with a leather.

Once the surface is completely dry, apply the undercoat. Undercoat has more colour pigment than the top coat and should be similar to, but not match, the top coat.

The quality of the top coat is dependent on a sound undercoat. To achieve a dense base for the top coat, it is preferable to apply two undercoats. If there are uneven patches in the undercoat they will show through the top coat. This should be an opaque covercoat, free as far as possible, from brush marks.

Avoid putting on too much paint too lightly which could cause sagging or 'curtaining'. The skill comes in spreading the paint as far as possible, while keeping the density of colour. When the undercoat is completely dry, after about 16–20 hours, rub down lightly, clean with a tack cloth, and apply the top coat.

Wood

Use a brush slightly narrower than the area to be painted. Hold the brush in a flexible position. The movement of the brush is controlled by the wrist and hand and should be relaxed. Painting of detailed features such as beading requires the firm control of the forefinger, second finger and thumb. Any grip in painting should be relaxed, or the movement will be tiring and lead to fatigue.

Use of brushes

If you are using a new brush, first brush the bristles against the palm of your hand to remove any stray bristles or dust. Charge the brush by dipping the bristles into the paint for two-thirds of their length. Touch the bristles lightly against the side of the kettle to remove excess paint. After this initial dipping, it should not be necessary to dip the bristles more than a third of their length into the paint.

There are a number of aids to prevent the brush accidentally falling into the tin, from a magnetic device which fits on the side of the tin and is obtainable commercially, to a piece of string stretched across the top of the tin on which to rest the brush.

Work over an area of about 300mm² at a time. Brush firmly, but lightly, over the area. Brush up and down, then diagonally and finally across the grain to produce an even spread.

To obtain a clean, smooth finish 'lay off' across the grain one brush width at a time. If painting the stile of a door lay off with a downward stroke. Do not start to lay off in the centre of the area as brush marks will be left.

Work in a continuous sequence, and do not let one area become too dry before starting the next. If this happens the paint will not blend and a demarcation line will show. Painting in awkward areas such as corners is dealt with by jabbing the paint into the corner with the tip of the brush and then brushing the paint downwards.

It is important to work in a good light. Natural light is by far the best working light. Artificial light can cast shadows, particularly when using white gloss paint, since thin patches may be left which spoil the finished effect. If work has to be done under artificial light, use the best light available.

With many modern paints, brush marks will disappear when the paint dries.

While it is a great temptation to use one thick coat of paint, it is not wise as the paint is likely to run or 'curtain' and look unsightly. Two thinner coats give a better finish. Two topcoats are essential for external use, to give adequate protection.

Gloss topcoat is stiffer than undercoat and needs to be applied firmly. Most types of gloss paint take three to six hours to dry but will not dry completely for up to 24 hours.

Gelled (thixotropic) paints are used straight from the tin. The paint is only stirred if it is to be applied with a roller or has been stored for some time and a layer of oil has formed on the surface. When using a roller, stir the paint until it is really fluid before pouring it into a paint tray. If painting in the conventional way, stir up paint that has separated, replace the lid and allow to re-gell.

Gell paints have a good covering or obliterating quality. One coat is equivalent to one thin undercoat and one top coat of the conventional paint. Gell paint is applied and laid off in the same way as gloss paint. Less movement is required than when brushing gloss paint but the brush needs to be charged more frequently.

Old paint should be strained; discarded stocking makes a useful mesh for this

Piece of string stretched over top of a paint kettle provides rest for brush

Use masking tape or a piece of card to keep as much paint as possible off the glass

Using a rust inhibitor on a metal surface, then apply a metal primer

Paint one area in one movement and lay off immediately. Brush from left to right, then right to left in a slightly downwards movement. Without applying any more paint, brush up and down. This fourway movement gives an even spread of paint. Paint one area at a time, working towards edges and the wet edge. When painting stiles or panels, work towards the edge and lay off with a smaller brush.

Doors
First, remove window catches, stays, door handles and letter boxes. Once splashed with paint these are often difficult to clean.

Doors should be painted in a definite sequence. On conventional panelled doors first paint the mouldings and then the panelled area. The top panel should be painted first, avoiding the door edges and glazing beading. Then paint the lower panel or panels.

The wider sections dividing the panels are called stiles. These are painted next, again working down the door. The top, middle or lock rail, and the bottom rail are then painted in that order. Paint the inner panels then the stiles on each side.

The edge of the door showing from the painted side should then be painted in the same colour. If the door opens to the exterior the top and, if possible, the bottom edges as well should be painted to make the timber both weatherproof and waterproof. Water may collect under the door and, through capillary action, be absorbed into the wood which may cause the paint eventually to peel off.

Next, paint the architrave. This order of work helps to give an even coat and cuts down the risk of paint runs and visible lines of demarcation.

Flush doors present a large area which it is difficult to paint in one section. Divide the door horizontally, into three equal sections.

Using a 75mm brush, start in the top left hand corner of the door. First, paint a vertical strip, about 450mm wide, then paint another 450mm strip, parallel with the first. Cross brush the two strips evenly into each other and then lay off the paint vertically. This pattern is repeated for the entire door, section by section. Once the three sections are painted, finishing is completed by brushing lightly upwards and downwards to join the sections.

This method requires quick careful work, particularly with some of the quick-drying paints. Once started, the door must be completed in one operation.

Casement Windows
Windows should also be painted systematically. Casement windows may be fixed, or consist of a combination of fixed windows and windows that swing open or out. The closing surfaces of the opening windows should not be painted too thickly as this may cause difficulty in closing. This is most important on metal window frames.

Paint the least accessible parts first. Start with the glazing bead, then open the window and paint the top and bottom bar of the window, then the sides of the frame. The hinged upper surface should be painted at the same time as the top bar. Paint the inner faces of the surround to the frame next. Large, opening casement windows are similarly painted.

If the fanlight or long casement window is fixed, paint the glazing beads first, and then the part of the frame facing into the room. Paint the edges, top, bottom and sides, the horizontal bars, the vertical bars and the sill in that order.

When painting windows, use masking tape or a piece of card to keep as much paint as possible off the glass. The glazing putty should be covered with paint, especially on metal frames where moisture may seep between the putty and the frames, causing corrosion. Take the paint to the edge of the glass. If the paint dries on to the glass, use a paint scraper to remove the excess paint.

Sash windows
Start painting with the window closed. Paint the outer sash glazing beads at the top, bottom and sides. Then paint the side frame faces. Next, paint the parting beads but do not apply the paint too thickly. Open the sash and slide it down a little. Next paint the top bar, then slide the inner sash up and paint the lower bar beneath it.

Paint the inner sash in the same sequence as the outer sash, beginning with the beads. Complete the painting sequence as for a casement window. When painting the inner frame surround, first paint the outer mouldings then the upper and lower faces and then the two side faces. Finally, paint the sill.

When decorating a room first paint the skirting and picture rails. Make quite sure they are clean and dust-free and paint the top edge first. Take care not to brush the paint out too hard as the paint covering on the outer curve or edge of the moulding may work thin.

Metal
Metal window and door frames should be coated with metal primer. Before priming, make absolutely certain that all rust is removed and apply a rust inhibitor if necessary. Badly affected surfaces should be rubbed down first with a wire brush, to remove loose rust.

The choice of finishing coat is optional but as this is a vulnerable area a hard gloss paint would give good protection. Metal window frames and doors need to be maintained carefully and regularly. The protective coat should not be too porous. Alkyd undercoats and gloss paints are suitable.

If used externally, lead and copper are rarely painted. Internal plumbing pipes are often painted to improve appearance. After rubbing down with wet-and-dry abrasive paper, wipe down with white spirit to remove metal dust which can be poisonous. Lead pipes and gutterings can be painted with bituminous paint which imparts a rubberized protective surface.

Iron gates and railings should be rubbed down and cleaned off with white spirit. Do not wash them down before painting as water may be lodged in crevices and lead to fresh rusting.

TABLE 1

Material	Kind of Material	Primer
Timber	Ordinary softwoods used in building construction	Wood primer
	Most hardwoods used in furniture construction	Wood primer, slightly thinned with white spirit
	Porous wood such as oak	Wood primer thinned about 15% by white spirit followed by a normal coat
	Highly resinous wood, i.e. Columbia pine	Aluminium primer sealer
	Oily woods such as teak	Teak sealer
Building boards	Standard hardboard	Plaster primer, hardboard primer or emulsion paint thinned with the same quantity of water
	Tempered hardboard	Thinned emulsion paint
	Chipboard	Plaster primer
	Fire-resisting board	Alkali-resisting primer
	Plasterboard	Alkali-resisting primer
	Asbestos (when can be kept dry)	Alkali-resisting primer
Plaster	Old	Plaster primer
	New	Alkali-resisting primer
Metal	Iron and steel	Zinc chromate, red lead or zinc-rich primer
	New galvanized iron (showing bright silvery colour)	Calcium plumbate primer
	Old galvanized iron (showing a dull grey)	Zinc chromate or calcium plumbate primer
	Zinc-sheeting	As galvanized iron which actually is iron coated with zinc by a hot-dip process
	Aluminium	Zinc chromate primer
	Brass, copper, lead	No primer at all

TABLE 2

Surface	First choice	Second choice	Third choice
Walls and ceilings	Emulsion paint	Washable distemper (water paint)	Eggshell or matt alkyd-resin paint
Wood	Gloss alkyd-resin paint	Eggshell alkyd-resin paint	Matt alkyd-resin paint
Metal (including guttering)	Gloss alkyd-resin paint	Bituminous paint	Cellulose paint (small surfaces only)
Concrete and cement rendering	Stone paint, nylon-fibre based emulsion	Outdoor-grade emulsion paint (not waterproof)	Cement paint (waterproof)
Stucco	Deoresinous or vegetable oil paint	Limewash	
Asbestos (gutters and sheds)	Outdoor-grade emulsion paint (not waterproof)	Bituminous paint (waterproof)	
Wooden fences	Proprietary wood preservative	Creosote	Bituminous or gloss alkyd-resin paint
Where there is a steamy atmosphere such as in bath-rooms and kitchens	Gloss alkyd-resin paint	Outdoor-grade emulsion paint	Eggshell alkyd-resin paint (on no account matt or distemper)
Kitchen and bath-room furniture	Gloss polyurethane paint	Matt polyurethane paint	Gloss alkyd-resin paint
Nurseries	Use lead-free paints throughout		

TABLE 3

Paint type	Coverage m²
Alkali-resisting primer	8·36
Undercoat	7·50
Co-polymer acrylic	90
Emulsion paint	95
Thixotropic paint	55
Oil-based paint	100
Whitewash, limewash, distemper	90
Quantities all 500ml (millilitres)	

Harris 4 inch

Wallpaper can be a costly decorative material and to achieve a finished result of which you are justifiably proud, careful attention should be paid to the preparation of the wall surfaces. This is necessary to ensure a good base for the decorative paper. Estimating the amount of paper needed, choice of paper and the techniques of preparatory lining are important aspects of this highly popular handyman job.

Paperhanging: preparing to do a good job

When choosing wallpaper it is important to choose a paper of good quality; cheap papers are expensive in the long run as they tend to tear easily, fade and stretch. If the wall surface shows irregularities a thicker paper will cover blemishes and conceal minor defects.

The job of paper-hanging falls into three sections:

● Preparation of surfaces;

● Lining the wall;

● Final paper-hanging and finishing off.

The right tools for the job make progress smooth and the task much easier.

Preparation
Equipment needed
Two step ladders or a trestle; two scaffold boards at least 1830mm long and 230mm wide; some dust sheets, old newspaper or polythene sheeting; an old distemper brush; bucket and sponge or a coarse cloth; stripping knife; filling knife; scraper; waterproof abrasive paper, glasspaper or a hand sander.

As walls are rarely true, it is also useful to have a spirit level to check the verticals.

An 'extra' that saves time and effort is an apron, with large pockets to carry the small tools.

It will save time and muddle if the floor area is covered before work starts. Use old newspaper when stripping wallpaper, then, as the work progresses, the stripped paper can be rolled up in the newspaper and disposed of.

Polythene dust sheets are useful as the job of stripping paper is inclined to be wet and messy.

All clear
Working is easier if the space is clear. If all the furniture cannot be removed, stack it in the centre of the room and cover with a dust sheet. Roll up the carpets or cover fitted carpets with polythene dust sheets.

The room should be warm, clean and as dust-free as possible. Choose the best working light available.

Surface preparation
Good surface preparation is essential to achieve a perfect, finished job. Newly plastered wall surfaces should not be papered. The surface should be allowed to dry out for at least six months. If a decorative finish is required sooner than this, a porous paint finish, such as an emulsion, should be applied.

A prematurely papered wall will be unsatisfactory. The moisture in the plaster weakens the adhesive properties of the adhesive used and alkali salts, present in plaster, may stain the surface of the paper.

Walls that have been decorated with emulsion or washable distemper, once the drying-out process has stopped, can be papered over. This is not possible over non-washable distemper, which should be removed before papering.

Sound surfaces
A surface should be sound. If any areas are crumbly or flaking, scrape them clean and then wash down. Finish by rubbing over with glass-paper.

Oil-based paint surfaces, which are non-porous, can be papered but the area must be rubbed first with a wet, waterproof abrasive paper. Rub down bare plaster with a coarse, damp cloth to remove any surface deposits and then coat with a weak solution of glue size if the paste to be used is water-based.

A cellulose paste requires a thinned coat of cellulose used as a size. Size is used to seal the surface and provide a smooth area on which to slide the paper.

When preparing a surface that has been previously painted with an oil-based paint, add about a handful of whiting to a basinful of size.

Filling
If an old plaster surface is cracked, the cracks must be filled before the surface is papered. Cut back the unstable plaster to a v-shape, using a scraper. Damp the area and fill with a non-shrink cellulose filler. This must be allowed to dry and then

Tools and equipment

1 Paste and brush
2 Paste pail
3 Sponge
4 Adhesive
5 Spirit level
6 Chalk-o-Matic
7 Cutting wheel
8 Cutting knife
9 Plumb bob
10 Steel tape
11 Boxwood rule
12 Seam roller
13 Smoothing brush
14 Lining and wall paper
15 Shears
16 Paste table

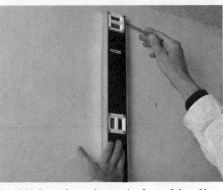

Establish and mark vertical working line. Ideally, start hanging near a window

Poor wall surfaces should be covered by lining paper. Cross-line very bad walls

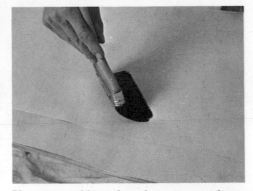

Use paste table and apply paste evenly to paper. Paste at angle out to edges

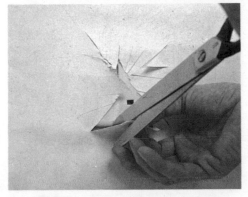

When papering round obstacles, make star-shaped cut and trim paper to fit

rubbed down lightly with glass-paper.

Where large areas of the plaster are unstable – if these sound hollow, when tapped, plaster has 'blown' and has no adhesion to the wall behind – the entire area must be hacked back and replastered. Wallpaper will not retain unstable plaster.

Let's strip
It is never wise to hang new paper over a previous covering. The two layers of adhesive may react together, causing both layers of paper to peel off. Also old joins may show through the new paper.

While there are commercially produced paper-strippers that hasten the job, most wallpaper can be removed after it has been thoroughly soaked with water. Start at the bottom of the area, and, with a distemper brush, scrub and soak the paper.

As work progresses, the area first treated should become removable. Repeated treatment may be necessary on thick papers or where adhesion is strong. The soaking-off process can be helped, on washable or particularly tough surfaces, by scoring the surface to allow the water to soak in. Over large areas it may be worth while to hire a steam-stripper.

Stripping is done with a broad-bladed stripping knife. Care should be taken not to dig the knife into the plaster as blemishes will need filling. Once the wall is stripped, wash it with a sponge and warm water and allow the area to dry. Before starting the next stage, ensure that any rough projections are rubbed down with glass-paper.

Wallpaper
A roll of wallpaper is 10m long by 520mm wide. Continental papers may be narrower and special papers are available in non-standard sizes.

A standard roll of paper will cover an

area of 5m². More paper must be allowed for pattern matching and cutting in. Machine-printed papers are usually supplied ready trimmed. If not, the unprinted 'selvedge' on each side should be cut off with a trimming knife and a metal-edged ruler. These papers can usually be trimmed when purchasing as most decorating shops have a trimming machine which will trim the paper in minutes.

Estimating
When calculating the amount of paper that will be needed for an area, always allow extra to ensure that there will be enough to complete the job. For large patterns this could add 610mm to the length of each run.

With a very expensive paper, it is necessary to measure accurately the precise amount of paper that will be needed. Divide the walls into 520mm widths round the room. Count the number of widths and multiply this figure by the height of the paper required. When using this method, remember to allow for pattern matching.

An alternative is to measure the entire distance round the room, including doors and windows. While less detailed, this allows for wastage in pattern matching.

First, measure the height of the room from the skirting board to ceiling. Divide the length of a roll of paper (10m) by the height of the room. A room with a height of 2440mm will allow four lengths to a roll.

Measure the distance all round the room and divide the total figure by the width of a roll. Divide this figure by the number of lengths to give the total number of rolls needed.

Rooms with ceilings that may differ in height over the area, or stairwells, should be measured by the first method, establishing the differing heights and adding the totals to find the paper required.

Colour matching
During printing, papers of the same batch may vary slightly, in colour and tone, from roll to roll or even from one edge to the other, within a roll. Before attempting to cut any paper, unroll short lengths from each roll and look for differences in tone value of colour.

When using plain paper or one with a small overall pattern, edge-to-edge variations may be overcome by hanging every other length upside down. In this way light edges will abut light edges.

On floral patterns there may be shadowing on the underside of the pattern. These should always be placed to the bottom. A length that does vary in shade or tone should be used at a corner over a door or under a window where it will blend in and be less obvious to the eye.

Pattern matching
Pattern matching is most important. There are two types of pattern: a set pattern where the pattern is repeated horizontally; and a drop pattern in which the design runs diagonally.

The bigger the pattern sequence, the greater will be the paper wastage. Patterns which match diagonally are more extravagant than horizontal patterns.

When hanging paper from left to right the left edge of the second piece of paper should line up with the right edge of the first piece and so on along the area. The converse applies when working in the reverse direction.

It is important that a paper with a definite pattern should match. While, with fairly muted overall patterns or plain paper, work should start from a window area and proceed inwards, when using a defined pattern, on a feature such as a chimney breast, the hanging sequence

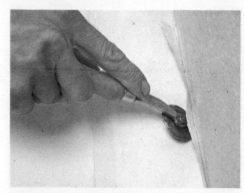

Wheel cutter has advantage of trimming paper closely to the contours of walls

Cut paper slightly longer than needed. With patterns, match 'repeat' carefully

To cut paper neatly, square up the edges and then fold down to a sharp crease

Paper can then be cut along line of the crease, using a pair of cutting shears

An alternative is to fold paper flat and slit along crease line with sharp blade

A knife and straight edge can be used. Paper can be torn neatly along steel edge

alters. The centre of the main design must start at the centre of the chimney breast or focal feature to prevent the room looking out of balance.

Cutting

Cutting a plain, striped or textured paper presents no problems of pattern matching. Cut sufficient lengths to paper at least half the room. (Some people advocate cutting all the lengths, including shorter lengths to go over doors, fireplaces and over and under windows.) When cutting each length, allow between 50mm and 75mm at each end for trimming.

A paper with a definite pattern needs cutting carefully. Place a length of paper, design upright, on the paste table and find the main motif or pattern. Cut the paper 75mm above this pattern, measure the length required and then add on an extra 75mm at the bottom. This gives the standard pattern drop.

Move this paper across the table, unroll the paper again and match up the next length to be cut. If the pattern has a big 'drop' there will be some wastage. It may be more economical to take another roll and match the next length from that, taking alternate lengths from two rolls. Manufacturers normally give guidance on the particular pattern drop for each design.

Adhesives

It is important to use the adhesive specified by the manufacturer, for the type of wall covering to be used. Paste should be mixed exactly as specified and used while it is still fresh. Generally, the thicker the paper the thicker the paste.

There are two main types of paste:

starch flour paste, which is mixed with hot or cold water; or water-soluble cellulose paste. Tub paste, sold in containers, comes into the latter category and is thinned with cold water. Cellulose pastes are easier to use and if accidentally spilt on the paper surface, will dry out without marking.

Unless you are using a vinyl paper or special wall-covering material, the paste should be allowed to soak in. The time allowed for this, as a general guide line, is the time taken to repeat the pasting sequence with the next length of paper.

While starch flour or cellulose pastes are suitable for most normal papers, these should not be used in kitchens or bathrooms.

In kitchens and bathrooms, where there may be high condensation, vinyls and washable papers, which have an impervious or nearly impervious finish, should be hung with a fungicidal paste. There are various heavy-duty fungicidal pastes available.

Tools
Paper-hanging

The following equipment is needed: A bucket, a plum bob or long spirit level, a pasting brush, a sponge, a stripping knife, a trimming knife, a boxwood seam roller, a pair of 305mm long scissors or paperhanger's shears at least 255mm long, a steel straight edge, a sharp pencil and a smoothing brush.

Other items needed: A paste table and access equipment—either a trestle or two step ladders and a suitable plank to act as a catwalk.

Lining paper

To achieve a high-quality surface finish

when hanging wallpaper, it is important to use lining paper. This is available in varying weights, and qualities, and provides an even surface of the correct porosity for maximum adhesion.

On good wall surfaces, a lightweight paper will be satisfactory. If the surface is uneven, a thicker lining paper will help to cover minor blemishes and irregularities in the plaster surface. When using a thick wallpaper, choose a corresponding lining paper. Lining paper can be used to line a porous wall.

When used purely as an under-paper, lining paper should be laid horizontally so that at no time will the joins align with the vertical joins of the decorative paper. The joins should be butt-jointed. Lining paper is pasted and concertina-folded before hanging.

Wall surfaces that are badly covered with hairline cracks should be lined twice, using heavy brown or white glazed lining paper. The first lining paper is applied horizontally, the second vertically.

Where cross lining, with long lengths of paper, lay the beginning of the length on the pasting table, leaving the rest to hang over one edge. Paste the exposed length carefully, ensuring that all the paper is covered to within 25mm of the end.

Take the end and fold back the paper, with paste to paste, making a fold or pleat of about 380mm in length. Continue pasting and folding in the same way until the entire length is pasted and folded into a 'concertina'.

Starting at one end of the room, hold the concertina section in one hand and, releasing a fold at a time, apply the lining paper with a roller or brush to smooth it out. All joins should be butt-jointed and excess paper at ceilings and skirtings trimmed.

There is more to paperhanging than meets the eye if you wish to achieve first-class results. Care at every stage of work, using a few sound rules, is the recipe for success. 'Awkward' areas, such as reveals, chimney breasts and papering around fittings may seem a problem, but, tackled systematically, are not necessarily difficult.

The art of paperhanging

Pasting
Stand the pasting table near the light source. Good light is important when checking pattern matching, measuring and ensuring an even spread of paste.

A plastic bucket is a suitable paste container. A piece of string, stretched tautly between the handle sockets, will be useful for wiping surplus paste from the brush.

When you have measured the length of the drop, cut, in one operation, several strips of the same length; this will save you time. Use a pair of scissors or a metal straight-edge and knife, or tear the paper along the straight-edge. This gives a neat, quick, accurate cut.

Paperhanging
Place the first length of paper, pattern side down, on the paste table. Line up the far end of the paper with the end of the table, allowing a slight overlap. At the other end, let the excess paper fall on to the floor.

Dip the paste brush into the adhesive until the paste is one third of the way up the bristles, wipe it against the string and start pasting, working from the centre of the paper outwards to the far edge.

Ensure that the paste is spread evenly. Never brush in from the edges as the paste will seep under the paper and on to the patterned surface.

Next, move the paper towards the near edge of the table and brush the paste towards you. Half the length is now pasted. Take hold of the pasted end of the paper and loop it over to the centre, paste to paste, making sure the top and bottom edges match. Do not fold in a crease which will mark the paper.

Move the folded loop along the table so that the loop overhangs the end. Apply paste to the other section in the same way. When this is completed, loop this end over to the centre so that the two looped edges meet.

Checking verticals
Start working at a window area. Take a point about 900mm from the window and mark in a vertical line. Use a chalked plumb-bob or vertical spirit level to mark the vertical from ceiling or picture rail height to the skirting.

Hold the bob firmly in one hand and 'twang' the chalked string so that it marks the wall, or use the level as a straight edge and pencil in the line. This marking should be repeated at every corner of the room.

Begin work at one side of the window, dividing the room into two sections. Hang the paper in sequence on both sides of the room, working towards the door. The advantage of this method is that joins and overlaps that occur will be in shadow and not so obvious to the eye.

This hanging sequence is suitable for plain or overall patterned wall coverings. Where a bold motif is used, the paper should first be applied to room features, such as chimney breasts and alcoves.

Hanging technique
Lift the looped, pasted paper over one arm and carry it to the wall. With the pasted inner side facing the wall, offer the top end to the wall at the junction of the wall and ceiling or picture rail.

Allowing about 50mm overlap at the top, slide the paper into position. Line it up with the chalk line, marking the perpendicular. Supporting the rest of the paper with the knee, brush down the centre of the paper and then outwards towards the edges to push out any entrapped air.

Open out the bottom loop and smooth this into position, using a similar brushing sequence – leaving a 50mm overlap at the skirting edge.

Trimming
With the back of the shears, press the paper into the angle between ceiling or picture rail and wall to ensure a neat fit. This will give a crease line at the point of trimming.

Gently pull the paper away from the wall and, from the back, cut away the surplus along this line, then push back the paper; a similar trimming method is used at the skirting edge.

If the paper appears wrinkled, this means the air has not been brushed out.

Peel the paper back gently, re-position and brush out that section. Any surplus paste on skirting or picture rails should be wiped off.

Butt joints
Butt joints should be used when hanging paper. The two edges should meet exactly. This is done by brushing the side of the piece of paper being hung into line with the last piece of paper. When the paper has been hung for ten minutes gently roll the seams with a boxwood roller.

Small or awkwardly shaped pieces of paper, needed for filling in odd widths, can be measured and cut on the flat surface of the paste table.

Corners
There are two types of corners to be papered:

● A projecting corner
● An inner corner.

Corners are not difficult to paper but do not attempt to hang a whole width round or into the corner. Irregular walls will almost certainly give an unsightly result.

Projecting corners
Measure the distance between the last full length hung and the corner, adding 25mm to this measurement. Cut off the paper, making sure that the edge is cut straight.

Hang the wider part of the length first, trim top and bottom and then position the overlap trim and brush out. This overlap will butt joint to the remainder of the length, which is hung next.

After pasting, loosely fold one end of the sheet of paper into the middle

Brush paper well into the wall at both the ceiling and at the skirting level

Make joints above a door or window where it is less obtrusive on pattern join

Similarly fold in half way from other end. Paper can now be taken to wall and hung

Back of shears can be used to mark the cutting line at ceiling and at skirting

Cut in around light fittings and trim; Plate can be removed to aid neatness

Unroll top half of fold and support the paper with a foot while you position it

Butt second length to first. Allow top and bottom overlap; check pattern match

At window, paper into vertical reveal. Space above is filled with matched piece

Inner corners

Inner corners can be treated in two ways. One is to offer the paper to the corner, and mark the position of the corner crease with the back of the shears. Cut the paper along this line; paste the two sections and draw together to make a butt joint.

In the second method, measure the distance between the last complete length and the corner, adding a 25mm overlap. Mark the next length to be hung. Cut off the excess and hang the first piece of paper so that the overlap turns the corner; trim top and bottom. Hang the remainder of the length to match the pattern and to be perpendicular.

In all cases, the paper should be pasted before cutting to fit round or into corners. The only exception is when using pre-pasted papers. These should be cut before the paste is activated.

Door frames

A neat fit round a door is achieved in the following way. The last full width is pasted and hung, then trimmed roughly, leaving a 25mm overlap at the top and frame side edge.

Make a diagonal cut, about 6mm long, in the paper, at the top corner of the door frame. Use the smoothing brush to press the paper into the angle between the wall and the door frame. Score along the top and bottom of the length with the shears and the top and bottom of the frame.

Peel back the paper carefully, cut off excess, then press it back. On a wide opening it will be necessary to match in a short length of paper over the centre of the door.

Windows

When papering round an obstacle, such

as a window, a long narrow gap is often left. Measure the length and breadth of this strip, taking the measurement of the gap from the last complete width hung to the window frame.

Place the paper, pattern uppermost, on the table and cut off a strip of the required size, adding 50mm to the length, to allow for pattern matching.

Paste the paper and butt-joint it to the last piece of hung paper. Excess paper at the trim should be cut off and the paper pushed into place. To camouflage the joins at top and bottom, tear off the excess paper to give a feathered edge and gently brush the paper in.

Light fittings

Before papering round any light fitting, such as a switch, it is wise to turn off the electricity at the mains.

Light switches may be either flush or projecting. Unless the fitting cover is removed, paper over a flush switch. Use scissors to make a hole in the centre of the switch position and cut diagonal lines beyond each corner. Crease the paper, on all four sides, with the back of the shears, and trim off the excess. Press the paper into position.

With a projecting light switch, hang the paper over the switch; this will cause a bulge in the paper, marking the outline of the switch. Next, make a small hole in the centre of the switch area, then peel back the paper.

Cut vertically and diagonally; make each cut about twice the length and radius of the fitting. Replace the paper, and crease round the fitting, peel the petal-like strips back gently again, and cut round these marks. Finally, press the paper back into position round the fitting.

Chimney breasts

A paper with a bold pattern should be hung centrally on a chimney breast. The centre of a pattern in wallpaper will either be on the paper edge or somewhere within the width of the pattern. Measure to find the central position of the chimney breast, then mark in the vertical.

Where the pattern is on the edge of a length, paste the paper then hang it with the pattern centre, flush with the vertical. Trim top and bottom and hang the second length on the other side of the centre line.

If the pattern centre is not on the paper edge, the method of hanging is slightly different. Mark in the centre vertical on the chimney breast, then measure on the paper the distance between the pattern centre and the left-hand edge of the paper.

Transfer that measurement to the chimney breast, and mark in the new vertical the measured distance on the left of the centre line.

The first piece of paper is hung to the right of this line. Butt-joint the second piece to the left of the line, flush with the first length.

Recessed areas

A bay window which presents a recessed area is dealt with when the wall above is papered. Do not attempt to fold the whole paper width round the corner, into the reveal; separate cut pieces will be needed.

There are two ways to paper a reveal: either outwards from the reveal or inwards. This depends on whether work is progressively towards or away from the reveal.

In working outwards from the reveal, measure, in one operation, from the inner edge of the reveal and round the corner.

Allow for trimming if the uprights are not true. Align the outer edge of a length

Hold paper with one hand and untuck the bottom fold and smooth down into place

After brushing out and trimming, smooth the joints flush with the seam roller

Leave gap and paper into the top of the reveal next to this unpapered section

Hang paper to vertical line on wall. Slide it finally into place to adjust

When hanging paper round door, cut out wedge so that paper can be fitted

Tear in trimmed piece of paper, 6mm above angle, to disguise line of join

Brush paper outwards at angle to remove air bubbles; check correct alignment

Paper can then be trimmed into the architrave with shears or the cutting wheel

Similarly, tear in around projections, such as the edges of window sills

of paper vertically and mark a working line down the wall.

Paste and hang the length, then cut the paper to the depth of the reveal, allowing about 6mm above. Smooth the paper into the reveal and trim the vertical edge as necessary.

A slight overlap will be left at the top of the reveal. Trim carefully round window sills or boards and the bottom horizontal edge of the reveal.

When working inwards, hang the paper in the normal way, butt-jointed to the adjacent section. Cut the top and bottom of the paper so that the paper butts into the reveal, where the vertical edge can be trimmed. Again, allow a 6mm gap above the reveal.

The procedure, whether working inwards or outwards, is the same for the next section. Cut a further length, making sure that any pattern matches, to fit to the length of the wall drop and reveal, and allow for trimming.

Hang this vertically and smooth into the reveal. Finally, cut an oversize piece of wallpaper to fill the gap alongside. Trim this to fit accurately into the reveal but overlapping at the front by 25mm.

Tear the overlap edge carefully; this will leave a ragged edge and conceal the join when pasted into position. Check carefully that the pattern is matched when cutting the infill piece.

Since the point above a door or window is often unobtrusive, any pattern disparity, caused by falling short of a complete length or width, may occur here.

Stair wells

Papering a stair well should logically start at the light source – either the front door or a stair-well window. This presents problems when the join of the stair-well wall and the head wall, which returns across the stairs, is reached.

Cutting this length would be difficult and the length of paper required would be unwieldy to handle. Therefore, start on the stair-well wall adjacent to the head wall.

Mark the vertical line on the stair-well wall. Hang the first length of paper, allowing a 50mm overlap on to the head wall. This will give room for adjustment if the wall is not true. A 50mm overlap should be allowed at the top and bottom of the length for trimming.

At the stair edge it may be a good idea to trim the paper roughly at the cutting angle, to prevent the weight of paper pulling at the pasted length and causing stretching.

As this is a long length of paper the normal double-looping method of folding paper will not do. Paste and fold as for lining paper in concertina form.

Hanging a long length is a two-handed job as the weight of the paper below requires support. If allowed to drop, it may tear or stretch.

The papering sequence radiates out from the first length. Work towards the landing, up the stairs, across the head wall, across the stairs and along the landing wall, keeping to the vertical.

Wallpaper repairs

It is possible to effect minor repairs to wallpaper.

On ordinary wallpaper an 'invisible' patch can be applied. A piece of matching paper cut larger than the damaged paper area will be needed. To soften the edges of the repair patch tear round them.

Check to see that the patch matches the surrounding pattern exactly. Peel back about 3mm of the backing paper

from the edges of the patch. Tear off the loose damaged paper.

Paste and insert the patch, matching the pattern all round. When the paste has started to dry, use the seam roller to smooth out from the centre to the edges.

On some wall coverings, such as hessian or vinyl, it is not possible to tear a patch. A patch repair, which is less unobtrusive than the previous method, can be applied in the following way:

Cut a matching repair patch larger than the damaged area. Place this over the damaged paper and cut a square through both pieces of paper. Remove the old paper, paste and insert the repair patch. Again, use the roller.

If the paper is not damaged, but there is bubbling of the surface, caused by incomplete adhesion or the wrong type of glue, it is possible to repair isolated areas by one of the two following methods.

Cutting or injecting

This is necessary when entrapped air has left a bubble and the paper can no longer be lifted. Make horizontal and vertical cuts, with a sharp knife, at the position of the bubble. Take the cuts back a little further than the bubble area.

Ease the four corners back and repaste, allowing the paste to soak in. After soaking, press the flaps gently back into position and roll lightly.

The other method is to inject the bubble with fresh paste, using a syringe. Let the paste soak in, then roll lightly.

Uneven adhesion at joins can be remedied by peeling back the section that has failed to adhere and applying a thin film of multi-purpose adhesive. Press the edge back into place and roll lightly with the seam roller.

Handy hints on paperhanging

Crooked top edge No room is built with mechanical precision, and where the picture rail–or, if no picture rail, the angle between wall and ceiling–are considerably off horizontal, do not use a large-patterned paper because the design at the top of each length will accentuate the imperfection. Use a plain paper or one with a less-pronounced pattern.

When to size and seal If in doubt whether to size a surface before papering it, dampen a finger and press it to the wall. A surface that is 'hot' will soak up the moisture immediately and will require size. Never size an emulsion-painted surface because size has a contracting action which could loosen the bond between the emulsion and wall plaster. The adhesive of a paper would do the same damage. Seal the emulsion coating with an oil-penetrating primer or coat of oil paint, thinned with the same quantity of white spirit. Seal hardboard with hardboard primer before papering.

Awkward joins If your supply of paper runs short, use off-cuts over a door or under a window. People seldom look over the top of a door when leaving, and curtains and furniture will detract from the window area. In any case, it will be relatively shaded there and imperfections will not be readily seen.

Stains on a chimney breast Wall stains that 'bleed' through wallpaper should be sealed in with two coats of aluminium primer sealer before hanging the paper. Then add a small quantity of whiting or finely powdered pumice to the paste to give more grip to such an impervious surface. Where stains are very pronounced, metal-backed lining paper may have to be used.

Where not to use vinyl Where a wall is uneven or pitted and cannot easily be made good, use ordinary wallpaper, not vinyl, as the latter will show up every mark.

Papering new walls Allow several months to elapse for new walls to dry out before papering, because damp will bring forward alkali salts which interfere with the chemical constituents of adhesives and could also cause colour change of greens and blues, or even staining.

Adhesive problems A growing number of papers are prepasted. Where you have to do your own pasting, remember that cellulose pastes, though they may not stain the surface, do not soak papers so evenly as starch and flour pastes. Heavy papers should, therefore, soak for eight minutes and then be repasted with an almost dry brush and hung immediately; otherwise blisters may form. With lightweight papers, paste one length and put it on one side. Paste a second length and then hang the first.

Painting over old wallpaper Use emulsion, not oil paint, because oil causes the fibres in paper to disintegrate.

Patching up To patch over an indelible mark on a paper, place a small new piece over the mark, with patterns matching, and cut round it with a sharp knife, penetrating new and old papers, down to the substrate. Then scrape off the old paper up to the knife cut and the new piece will fit exactly.
    Another way is to tear the patching piece away from the printed side to 'feather out' the edge. Treat a polystyrene lining that has been inadvertently damaged in stripping an old paper, by the first method.

Avoiding hazard Before hanging wallpaper, always fold pasted pieces inwards and put these under the pasting table, out of the way. Pasted paper is slippery and could cause a nasty accident.

Seam rollering with safety Rollering the joins on wallpaper, particularly heavy varieties, ensures adequate adhesion of otherwise vulnerable edges; though, by laying

the fibres of the paper, rollering could cause a 'polish' mark to show. To prevent this, insert a strip of ordinary paper (toilet paper will do) under the roller.

Surmounting shading difficulties As you open rolls of paper and compare them, you may be disappointed in the difference in tone from edge to edge or from roll to roll. This is a fault of the printing process and, if pronounced, will show when the paper is hung. If the paper is plain or a random pattern you can often overcome the edge-to-edge difference by inverting every other length you hang. Where the difference is not from edge to edge but down the length –though not so likely– see if another roll has the same difference. If so, cut one length from one part of one roll and the adjoining length from the same part of the second roll.
    Where half the rolls are printed on the light side and the remainder on the dark side, hang light-toned rolls on side walls and those that are darker on the wall facing the window. Light striking the latter will even out the tone and the difference at the corner of the room where the papers abut will not be noticed.

Recipe for an ideal kitchen

KITCHEN

The kitchen has been called the hub or workshop of the home. It should be well planned, attractive, easy to clean and pleasant to work in. While this is the ideal, even the mostly unlikely and awkwardly shaped kitchen can, with careful thought, be satisfactorily redesigned as an effective work-unit.

Any kitchen redesign will be limited by the size and shape of the room and the demands on that room by a particular family situation.

Types of kitchen
There are three main types of kitchen:

The galley-type, usually in a small area where the work units are placed along one or two sides of the room, with the minimum width required for door opening between them. This provides for economy of movement and enables maximum use to be made of the storage space available.

A 'U'-shaped arrangement, usually in a larger area, consisting of storage units on three sides of a square.

The third arrangement is best in the larger kitchen. This utilizes a peninsular unit – a section of units and worktop area which may house cooking discs, placed at right angles to the main run of units.

This can act as a room divider and is useful where the room is large and is combined as a dining room and kitchen.

Scale plan
It is a good idea to make a scale plan of the kitchen on graph paper using 25mm to 300mm (1in. to the ft.) Cut out, to the same scale, pieces of paper or thin card to represent any units or appliances you may have such as washing machine, cooker or refrigerator, and any proposed new units; 'juggle' these about on the paper until you come up with a satisfactory combination.

Planning
Making the best use of your kitchen area needs careful planning. First – and this depends upon the space available – decide whether the kitchen is to be purely a work area or work and dining area combined.

A kitchen should be labour-saving, not only from the viewpoint of cleaning but also designed to cut down on unnecessary walking.

Adequate storage facilities must be incorporated in specialized work areas. The three main areas are for food preparation, cooking and washing up.

Washing up demands three working areas: one for stacking dirty dishes, the sink, and an area to receive clean dishes for drying and stacking away.

It is also essential to have a flat surface on which to place hot dishes from the oven.

These areas need to be fairly close together.

It is a good rule to have one flat area of working surface between each major appliance which does not possess a flat surface. Working surface is essential, particularly near the cooker and sink.

Ideally, doors should not face each other as this splits up the kitchen. Start

Galley

'U' shape

Basic types of kitchen
Peninsular

the layout design from the sink, to avoid, where possible, re-routing plumbing.

When planning, remember that cupboard doors need to open, cookers should not be directly under windows (because heat may crack glass) and that you must also allow for the opening of room doors.

At this stage, re-hanging doors or repositioning windows may provide extra usable space.

Working heights
The standard height for pre-made kitchen units, from ground to working-surface level, is between 750mm and 900mm, with a depth of 535mm.

Kitchen units are available in pre-assembled whitewood, pre-finished, or as self-assembly units, which are either pre- or unfinished. Alternatively, you may prefer to make your own units, which can be tailored to fit a non-standard sized kitchen.

Unfinished units may be painted or stained, polyurethaned or laminated, to name a few treatment possibilities, to merge with your colour schemes.

Focal interest
Domestic chores are more acceptable if there is a focal point of interest outside the kitchen.

Ideally, the sink should be near or beneath a window. If the outlook is dull—for instance a drab wall—consider brightening it up with a coat of light paint. This will not only enliven the view but also reflect light back into the kitchen.

Colour
Colours are a matter of personal choice, but a useful guide is to decide the effect you want—cold and clinical or warm and homely.

Colours in the blue, green, yellow

spectrum will make the kitchen look colder than warmer colours such as brown, red and orange.

Lighting
All main working areas should be well lit. Fluorescent lighting gives shadowless working light. Spotlights can be used to provide extra light or localized light—for instance, over the cooker.

Storage
Access to storage is important, and to allow for unnecessary expenditure of energy, store the most frequently wanted items just above or below worktop level and those less needed either lower or higher than this.

Wall cupboards are best positioned about 300mm above working surface level up to a maximum of 1830mm. Open shelving is another form of storage.

Particularly in larger areas the peninsular kitchen has many advantages. This cuts down the walking distances between working areas. Built in hobs and cooker provide neat and streamlined features. A central hood over the cooking area enables effective extraction of smells.

For many homes, the U-shaped kitchen is the choice, particularly where the overall kitchen size is small. This arrangement allows a large amount of work top area. Timber panelling, stainless-steel tiles, ceramic floor tiles and laminated worktops all provide easy-to-clean surfaces.

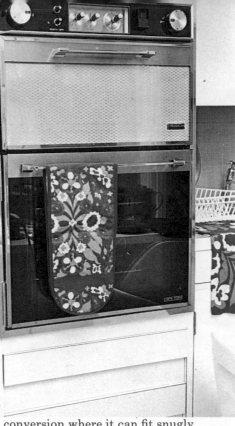

A space-saving concept where this is at a premium is an alcove kitchen. This has particular applications for a house

There is no advantage in having shelving that is too deep and 300mm is probably the deepest normally needed and then only suitable for storing larger items.

A shelf of between 150mm to 200mm is quite deep enough for most kitchen cartons, boxes and jars. Drawers with a depth of 150mm are useful for storing cutlery and kitchen utensils. Drawers which are very deep are only useful for storing bulk items and large cooking utensils.

Food

Storage of food safely and hygienically is important. Perishable food is best kept in a refrigerator.

Doubling up

Many kitchens double as a laundry room, with a washing machine and spin-dryer often sharing the same plumbing services. Ideally, the area used for washing clothes should be as far as possible from the cooking area. In a large kitchen you might partition off an area as a laundry.

A space as small as 1520mm × 1220mm, with a sliding door and a window, will take a front-loading washing machine, laundry basket, as well as shelves for washing powder. A slightly bigger area would also house brooms, mops and cleaning materials.

Appliances

When thinking of appliances, not only do you have to provide for the appliances, you have to try to anticipate future acquisitions. Washing machines, electric cookers and refrigerators are now considered almost standard equipment in many homes. You may add a food mixer, coffee grinder, toaster, home freezer, dishwasher, waste-eliminator, extractor fans and so on.

conversion where it can fit snugly between the chimney-breast walls and the end of a room.

Plug sockets

Plug sockets should be at working-top level, spaced roughly at 1830mm intervals round the room. No plug sockets should be within 1830mm of the sink. Sockets for 'fixed' appliances such as cookers, refrigerators and washing machines may be fixed lower down.

Before adding extra sockets, check that your wiring is able to cope with the potential extra load and renew and augment as necessary. Always remember, if you are in any doubt consult a qualified electrician.

Refuse disposal

Refuse disposal is always a problem in the kitchen. One of the most hygienic ways to dispose of food wastage is by means of a waste-eliminator.

The pedal bin with plastic liner bag, foot operated, is a less-sophisticated means of disposal. Some disposal-bag systems are designed to fit on the wall or back of base-unit doors.

Cooking smells

Unwanted cooking smells can easily permeate the house, caused by the natural convection of hot air. As it is difficult to keep a kitchen door closed at all times, an automatic door closer will help to solve the problem. Smells will be contained and steam will not spread out into the rest of the home.

A more effective way of combating cooking odours and condensation is to install a powerful extractor fan, or an air cleaner, sited near the cooker; these can either be wall or window mounted.

It is better to use a fan than to open a window as natural ventilation tends to blow the steam and smells back into the room while a fan draws them out.

It is possible to fit a cooker hood which incorporates an extractor fan. A simple

version draws up fume-laden air and the smells are neutralized by passing through a charcoal filter pad. These pads are renewable.

More complicated extractors have a powerful fan which pulls the fumes out, through a tunnel, connecting the cooker hood with an outside vent.

Condensation

Condensation occurs when steam reaches a cold surface, and turns back into droplets of water. Windows, cold spots, such as lintels over doors, and cold wall surfaces are vulnerable areas.

Adequate heating, by means of a radiator from a central-heating system, a high-level infra-red heater, or heat from a domestic boiler, will help to raise the temperature.

Polystyrene tiles or sheeting, which should be fire-retardant, can be applied to the ceiling. These are now made in many decorative effects. Not only do these help to provide thermal insulation, but they also raise the touch temperature of the ceiling surface which reduces condensation.

Wall finishes

Wall coverings vary from paint to washable vinyl kitchen wallpapers in a multitude of designs. Wood panelling, ceramic and stainless-steel tiles and cork are other possibilities.

When deciding on wall surfaces, there are two main considerations: cost and durability. If you like to change your décor scheme frequently, wallpaper or paint is probably best. Wood panelling, stainless steel or ceramic tiles are more expensive but provide a durable and virtually maintenance-free surface.

Flooring

Flooring should also be hard wearing, warm, easy to clean and attractive. The choice of flooring ranges from linoleum to thermo-plastic tiles or sheeting, vinyl, foam-backed sheeting, ceramic floor tiles, loose-lay kitchen carpet tiles to kitchen carpeting.

There is a wide range according to cost, colour, texture, design and finish required.

Final touches

The proportion of kitchen window space should be about 20 per cent of the floor area.

Finishing touches to a kitchen come in the window furnishings. Picture windows provide a good vista but limit privacy. A roller blind, either pre-made or in kit form, is a good solution. Rolled up out of sight during the day it provides privacy at night.

Roller blinds are also quite acceptable on doors. Most kitchen blinds are plasticized and only need to be wiped clean. Blinds are made in a wide variety of colours and designs.

Venetian blinds, with plain or coloured slats, have the advantage of enabling outward vision while retaining privacy. These need a little more care and cleaning.

Tiling: how to be versatile in ceramics

One of the oldest decorative surface treatments, ceramic tiles are now made in vibrant colours, patterns and textured surfaces. These have many applications within and outside the home. Tiling techniques are not difficult, and the results provide an attractive durable decorative finish for floors and walls.

Glazed ceramic tiles are made in a wide range of colours and effects. These range from simple plain colours to sculptured, patterned and decorative tiles.

For use out of doors, many manufacturers can supply tiles which have been treated to make them frost-resistant. Many plain, coloured tiles can be accurately matched with bathroom fittings. Floor tiles, which are thicker than wall tiles, are also available in complementary colours.

Types of tile
There are three main types of ceramic tile. The main 'bulk' or 'field' tile usually has spacer lugs on the outer edge, which provides a neat 2mm gap between tiles. These gaps are later filled with a grout, a compressible, white material, mixed with water to a paste, which gives an overall patterned appearance.

The RE, or round-edged tile, is used for edging or for part tiling, to give a rounded-off finish, and for external corners of window reveals.

Tiles with two adjacent round edges are known as REX tiles. These are used for purposes such as splashbacks and as top corner tiles in part tiling.

Ceramic tiles are made in three main sizes – 108mm² × 4mm thick and 152mm² × 6mm thick – corresponding with the Imperial 4¼in and 6in sizes – or in panels of 50 mosaic tiles, measuring 55mm × 25mm × 4mm, mounted on a scrim backing.

Calculating the amount
When calculating the number of tiles needed, allow around five per cent of the total for breakages and waste on the tiles you have to cut. With 108mm² tiles, allow a row of three full tiles for every 430mm² of wall, and 72 tiles for every 900mm² of wall. In each case allow for two cut tiles per row. Similarly, with 152mm² tiles, allow six full tiles to the running metre or 36 tiles for an area of 900mm².

To calculate the number of RE tiles needed, measure the length of the area to be tiled, allowing three 108mm² or two 152mm² tiles for each run of 305mm.

Materials

Adhesives
This is supplied, ready constituted, in cans, or in powder form, to which you add water. Reconstituted adhesives usually have a limited life and you should mix no more than you can apply in a given time.

There are adhesives for internal and external use and for various types of surface and conditions, such as where dampness may occur.

Thick-bed adhesives are made to enable uneven surfaces to be evenly covered – though you should always prepare the surface to be as even as possible.

A can of 4·50 litres covers an area of roughly 5 m².

Grouting
This is a white powder mixed with water to a fairly stiff paste. A quantity of 1kg is sufficient for an area of 4m².

Tools
Essential tools are a notched spreader, a small trowel, pincers, a tile cutter, a spirit level or plumb bob, lath or batten, sponge or tiler's squeegee.

Additional items which may prove useful are a radius cutter, to make large holes in tiles, a tungsten-tipped drill, for small holes, and a carborundum block or carborundum file, for smoothing rough edges on cut tiles.

Notched spreader
Plastic spreaders may be supplied with the adhesive, or you can buy a notched trowel. If you have any quantity of tiling to do, the latter is a worthwhile investment. The ridges in the adhesive created by the notches in the spreader or trowel give the tile greater adhesion.

Pincers
These are used to nip out small sections of tile to fit, or to go round oddly shaped corners.

Tile cutters
These are of various types, ranging from a simple scriber with tungsten-carbide tip, to tile-cutting kits, consisting of a platform, small try-square and a wheel cutter.

Spirit level or plumb bob
Either can be used to establish an accurate vertical working line. The spirit level is used to establish the horizontal working line and to check work as you progress.

Lath or batten
This consists of a straight piece of timber, of the same length as the longest area to be tiled.

Sponge or squeegee
Either can be used to apply grout between

the tile joints; surplus is rubbed off when dry.

Surface preparation

Surfaces should be clean and free from grease. Irregularities should be smoothed down, cracks filled in and any screws, nails or other projections removed. If you are planning to tile on to new plaster, make sure that the surface is dry and free from dust. Apply a sealant to porous surfaces, to prevent the absorption of adhesive.

A painted surface, if sound, provides a good tiling surface, but gloss paint should be scored to assist adhesion. Any unstable paint should be removed by rubbing down with a medium grade of glasspaper.

Old tiles, where these present a firm,

even surface, may be tiled over. These tiles are often 13mm thick, on an equally thick mortar backing. A bulky effect can be produced, particularly where the original consisted of half-wall tiling.

It is worthwhile to consider removing thick tiling. These may be chipped off with a club hammer and a bolster. Over a large area, a faster way of removal is to hire an electric rotary hammer, with a combing attachment.

Dry partition surfaces may also be tiled, provided these are rigid. It may be necessary to remove surface coverings, in order to reinforce framework or studding, to provide the necessary rigidity.

Plasterboard, plywood and chipboard should be fixed on battens of 75mm × 50mm timber, spaced at intervals of about 300mm, both horizontally and vertically.

Tile on to the 'rough' side of any board and seal the reverse side with a specified sealant for the material, though ordinary paint undercoat should prevent moisture seepage.

Expanded metal, if fixed at intervals of about 300mm, is also suitable to support rendering for tiling.

Setting out

Because floor levels vary and few corners or angles of rooms are accurate, some care is needed in setting out tiling, otherwise the results may appear uneven and irregular.

Matching tiles on sills and window reveals provide a neat 'all-over' look

First, establish an accurate working reference or datum, then take a tile and place this at your lowest tiling level – the floor or the skirting board.

Mark the height, including the spacer lug, on the wall and use the spirit level to mark a straight horizontal line. Fix the top of the lath or batten accurately along this line, over the full length of the area to be tiled. As the batten is later removed, it should be fixed with the nail heads protruding, so that these can be pulled out easily.

Check that the batten level is accurate and stand one tile on end and run it alongside the floor beside the batten, to make sure that this is neither too high nor low.

Mark out batten into even tile widths; this avoids uneven cuts at wall ends

Fix a temporary batten to the wall at height of one tile; true with level

To support tiles above a reveal, fix a temporary batten, lined up with level

Use a plumb bob or spirit level to find true vertical, one tile in on each side

When tiling around fittings and obstructions, also use a tile-support batten

Fix temporary vertical battens one tile width in, or work to marked pencil line

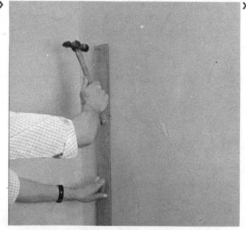

After tiling, fill the joints with a grouting and polish the tiles when dry

From the centre point of the wall, mark the tile widths along the batten. This will ensure that equal cut tiles appear at the ends and help to avoid short awkward cuts. At each end, use a plumb bob or the spirit level to mark the verticals; these correspond with the point of each last full tile.

This procedure is repeated on any walls which adjoin the first. If the wall space does not allow an even number of tiles, it is better to increase the space between them slightly, to avoid having two cut pieces abutting in the same corner.

Applying adhesive

Adhesive should be applied to the surface to be covered rather than to the individual tiles, as this provides even adhesion. Spread adhesive to a thickness of about 3mm and cover only 1m² at a time.

The serrated edge of the spreader forms ridges which give good suction and adhesion. Press down firmly, so that the teeth of the spreader are in contact with the wall surface.

Tiling

Start tiling at the left-hand intersection of the batten and vertical line. Begin with the bottom row and work upwards.

Tiles should be pressed firmly into place. Never slide a tile into position as this weakens adhesion. Any adhesive left on the tile surface can be wiped off before it dries. Tiles tend to 'creep', so verticals should be checked frequently.

Constantly check that horizontal lines are also accurate and that tiles are firmly bedded and not proud of the adjacent tile surfaces. Omit, at this stage, tiling where obstructions, such as sinks and window reveals, require the cutting in of individual tiles.

Where difficult areas have to be tiled or part tiles are used, the backs of these can be individually 'buttered' with adhesive, spread to a depth of about 3mm, using a small trowel.

Allow several hours for the tiles to set, then remove the batten and fill the remaining spaces with tiles cut to fit, individually 'buttering' the backs.

Fixed objects and reveals

When tiling round a bath or hand basin, there may be less than a full tile above these items. First tile alongside the bath or basin and omit the tiling above the units.

Fix a batten above the unit to correspond with the line of the tiles on either side and tile on to the batten, which should be horizontally accurate. Once the tiles have set, remove this batten and fill in below with cut tiles.

A similar technique is used in tiling round door or window angles. RE tiles should be used on the reveal side of window and door openings–not on the face side of the wall. Tiles on the inside top of reveals should be kept in place by a long section of batten, propped up by vertical pieces of timber.

Contrast can be provided by tiling one wall plain and the other in a pattern

Bathroom accessories, such as soap dishes, are fixed in the same way as tiles. During general tiling, fix an ordinary tile loosely in the place of the soap dish.

When tiling is completed, remove the loose tile, apply a 3mm-thick layer of adhesive to the back of the accessory and press it firmly into place. While the adhesive is setting, support the accessory with adhesive tape.

Cutting tiles

A felt-tipped pen is useful for marking the line of a cut on a tile. To make a straight cut, draw a tile cutter tip firmly across the glazed face of the tile surface. There is no need to do more than just score the glaze.

Apply adhesive evenly with a notched spreader; work area of 1m² at a time

Place each tile firmly into place; never slide a tile as it may not bed properly

Walls are seldom even, so top, bottom and tiles at side must be cut in later

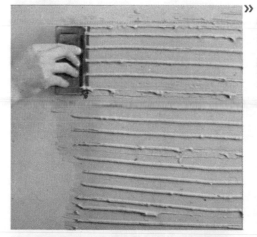

Use a straight edge when scoring tiles; press firmly with cutter to break glaze

Place matchstick beneath the cut line and press evenly on each side to snap

Awkward shapes can be cut out by carefully nibbling away tile with pliers

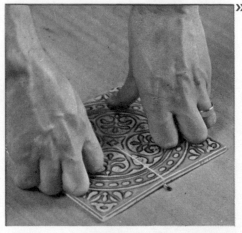

Place a small piece of wood, such as a matchstick, under the tile, and with the glazed side upwards, exert downward thumb pressure on both corners. The tile should snap evenly along the scored line. Very narrow cuts may have to be 'nibbled' away with pincers.

On a shaped cut, mark the area to be cut away and use the pincers to nibble away small sections of tile at a time. Even with care, this may lead to some false starts. For very difficult cuts, it is a good idea to cross-hatch, or score, the glazed surface of the portion to be cut away. A carborundum block or file can be used to trim up and smooth rough edges, once cut.

A round hole can be made at the edge of a tile. Place a coin on the tile and score round its outside. Next, cross-hatch a series of score marks inside the circle then carefully nibble away with pincers.

Using a slow speed, holes can be drilled in tiles with a masonry bit. The back of the tile should be firmly supported, or it may break.

An alternative to drilling a large hole with a radius hole cutter is, after marking the position of the hole, to cut the tile in half, and use pincers carefully to trim out two semi-circles. When assembled again, the join between the two pieces will scarcely show.

Grouting

Grouting should be left until the tiles are firmly set – for at least 12 hours. Using a sponge or squeegee, rub the grout firmly into the tile joints. Remove any surplus grout with a damp sponge. Once the grout has dried, rub off any powder on the tile surface with a duster and run a pointed, slightly rounded stick between the joints to give a neat joint line. Finally, polish the tile surface with a clean, dry cloth.

Mosaics

Mosaic tile sheets – roughly covering the area of five 108mm² tiles – are applied in a similar way to single tiles. Tile sheets can be regarded as a single large tile.

Check, as usual, accurate horizontal and vertical alignment and work as close as possible with each panel to the edge of the tiling surface. The backing scrim, to which the tiles are fixed, can be easily cut through with a handyman's knife; individual tiles can be detached and cut to fit.

In setting out the panels, try to avoid awkward cuts. The small size of the individual tiles will help to achieve this. The panels are simply placed on to the adhesive – and not slid into position – in the same way as a standard tile, and pressed down firmly.

The tiles are grouted similarly to standard tiles, once the adhesive has dried thoroughly. A white, plastic edge strip can be used for finishing.

An interesting application for mosaic tiles is the making of pictures or designs, by removing tiles of various colours from their backing. Unless the motif is very simple, it is best to draw the picture or design on to graph paper first, to provide an accurate design to work to.

Tiles are versatile! They can be used to provide decorative surfaces almost anywhere in the home. These examples show not only their 'conventional' use in kitchens and bathrooms, but also elsewhere in the home – as a decorative surround to a fireplace. Tiles present a clean and permanent form of wall covering

The new look for old in bathrooms

If you decide on a refit for the bathroom, careful thought is needed as to the present and future requirements of those using it. Space may be better utilized by a general rearrangement. Modern, matching colours in surfaces and appliances, and a wide range of wall and floor finishes can be used to update the bathroom and make this a décor success.

Any bathroom should be planned to suit the needs of the people using it. Requirements of, say, a young married couple, a growing family, or older and possibly infirm people, will obviously vary.

The amount of traffic, and the times of demand on hot water supplies, all need to be taken into account, for nothing disturbs the routine of a house more than a congested washing and bathing area at times of heavy demand.

The amount of equipment in an average bathroom varies but the usual minimum is a bath and a wash handbasin.

WCs may be included or be separated from the bathroom. Obviously many bathrooms are not large enough to take extra fittings such as showers, bidets or an additional wash-handbasin, but, with careful planning, a great deal can often be achieved.

The position of bathroom fitments normally depends on the siting of plumbing outlets. It may be possible to reroute pipes and waste outlets on existing systems to achieve a more workable arrangement.

Fittings are made in a wide range of colours.

Hot and cold
It is as important to take as much care when choosing taps as choosing bigger bathroom fittings. Taps should be well designed—and easy to operate and clean.

Modern taps may be made of chromed brassware, gold plated if you prefer the opulent touch, or made of tough plastic.

The upstand of the tap should stand well clear of the bath or basin. If the upstand is not high enough it is difficult to clean the tap and the area beneath.

Taps should not be mounted too near to the wall so as to pinch or bark the fingers when the tap is turned. The screw-on screw-off tap is most often used though some are foot operated.

Baths and basins
Basins are made in a wide range of shapes and sizes, in vitreous china, fireclay, enamelled sheet metal, plastic and glassfibre. Fixings vary but basins are usually

Above: A colourful tiled arrangement in a bathroom, in which the sanitary ware, flooring and fittings all complement each other.

mounted on a matching pedestal, wall mounted, or fitted in a vanitory unit which can also provide useful storage.

A basin should fulfil certain basic requirements. It should be shaped to hold a good depth of water without wastage, enough to immerse both hands below the overflow level.

You should be able to wash your face without hitting your nose on the taps! The water should run away quickly and there should be a 'soap-sinking' deep enough to hold the soap.

Baths also vary greatly in design. They are made of enamelled cast iron, enamelled pressed steel, moulded plastics or glass-fibre. The latter materials have the advantage of being light and easy to handle.

Usually, baths are rectangular, with one end slightly sloping. Taps may be fixed at the end or the side of the bath, dependent on design. The best way to test a bath is, before buying, to lie in it and see if it is comfortable.

Most modern baths have matching side and end panels to provide a neat appearance, hide the plumbing and yet provide access where needed.

If elderly people or small children are to use the bath it is possible to fit a bath with a dipped side to allow easy access. Also an integrated hand grip is desirable. If this is not available, a wall-mounted hand grip will give safe support.

Some baths have a specially designed non-slip base. If the base is smooth, keep a rubber mat in the bath for use by the elderly or very young.

In cases where bathroom and WC are combined, it is sometimes possible to separate these two areas.

Where space is limited, the cut off could be a studded partition, decorated to match the walls, or in a bigger area a system of storage such as open shelving, cupboards or drawer units could be considered.

If the WC area is not too small, it may be possible to plumb in an additional small wash-handbasin. These can be very compact and may be recessed into the wall, surface-fixed or corner-mounted.

The 'loo'

The height of a WC is usually 410mm from the ground plus the thickness of the seat. Research has suggested that 355mm is medically a better height. In a small area, a low-level cistern may look neater and take up less head room than a high-level type.

It is desirable to locate a WC beneath a window.

You can install a slim-line cistern where space is limited. WC cisterns can be chain, lever or foot-pedal operated. On hygienic grounds, the latter is desirable.

WC pans are usually made of vitreous china or fireclay. Most seats are now made of plastic rather than wood. These are available in a wide range of colours and patterns. Padded vinyl and even heated seats are also made.

Boxing in

Pipework for baths, handbasins, showers, WCs and so on is best hidden. Try to make pipe runs neat and conceal them as much as possible. Exposed pipework can be boxed in with a simple framework and hardboard structure, but access must be left for any maintenance work that may be necessary.

Allowing for access fixing points, the covering can be painted, tiled and so on to blend with the general décor scheme.

Lighting

If the bathroom has a high ceiling, it may be possible to recess lighting above a false ceiling. Some shaving mirrors have lights incorporated. Strip lights can be concealed behind curtain pelmets or under cupboards.

All lights must be controlled by pull switches. Wall switches are illegal in bathrooms. If elderly or infirm people or small children use the bathroom, it is desirable to incorporate a low-wattage light fitting which can be left on all night.

Surfaces

All surfaces in the bathroom should be easy to clean as well as decorative. Wall surfaces are available in a choice including plain and decorative ceramic tiles, wood panelling, cork sheeting, cork tiles, washable wallpaper, laminate and paint.

Walls can be decorated with washable or waterproof wallpapers. These are hard-wearing, easily cleaned and decorative.

Cork panels or cork tiles provide attractive finishes and also possess some insulant value, are warm to the touch and help absorb sound, often a problem in the bathroom. A coating of clear polyurethane varnish will seal the cork which, particularly in panel form, may crumble and be vulnerable to small fingers.

Ceramic tiles may be plain, veined, marbled, textured or patterned, many in standard colours. It is not always necessary to use all-patterned tiles; attractive schemes can be evolved using mainly plain tiles with featured effects—such as splashbacks, bath surrounds, mosaic panels, isolated textured tiles and so on.

Laminates, plain or patterned and available in a wide range of colours, also provide pleasing and easily cleaned wall surfaces. They are also suitable for shelf coverings, cupboard facing or lining and as surrounds to vanity units or wash handbasins.

Flooring

Bathroom floors need to satisfy a variety of conditions. They should be warm to the touch, non-slippery when wet, easily cleaned and attractive to the eye—conditions fulfilled by cork flooring. Cork tiles, sealed with polyurethane, are available in shades from dark brown to gold. Cork is easily cleaned.

Thermoplastic tiles, and vinyl sheeting

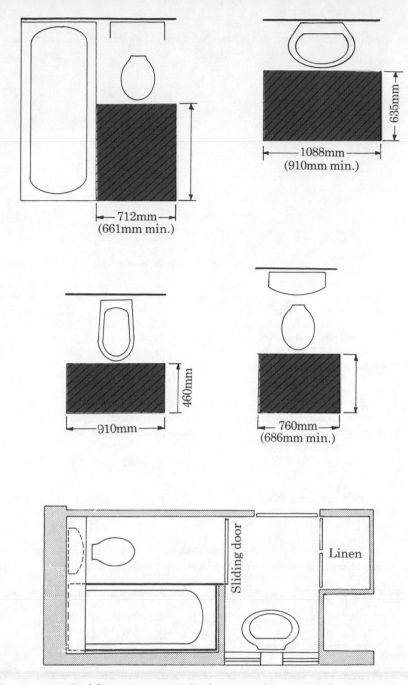

Sliding door

Linen

Basic areas required for movement in bathroom and a compact bathroom area

Heating and hot water

Heating may be provided by means of a heated towel rail or clip-on rail above the radiator. Localized heating may consist of electrical radiant wall-mounted heaters.

These heaters, controlled by a pull switch, should be mounted high on the wall and well away from the bath and directed at the drying area. They must be of an enclosed pattern suitable for bathrooms.

Hot water is a vital part of the successful bathroom. This may be provided by the general domestic hot-water system or by an instantaneous hot-water heater. These heaters work by gas or electricity. When using any form of gas water heater you must have a flue outlet and adequate ventilation.

Storage

If there are children in the house cleaning materials should be kept in a locked cupboard, as should any medicines kept in the bathroom.

Bathroom cabinets may be white wood cupboards which can be painted, laminated, or supplied ready painted or finished. Cabinets may have a mirror incorporated.

Some units incorporate lighting strips, which must be of a safe pattern, and shaver points. Provision for a shaver point, of the double-insulated pattern, is desirable.

Always avoid placing shelving over baths or handbasins as heavy objects falling may cause damage.

Windows

Windows are very important. At least one fanlight window should open to allow adequate ventilation. If there is no opening window a wall or window-mounted extractor fan should be used. In a completely enclosed bathroom, a system of ducted ventilation is essential.

Windows with louvres give privacy and ventilation. Opaque decorative glass can be used. Apart from good natural lighting, adequate artificial lighting is also important. The bathroom should be evenly lit.

Finishing touches

Window furnishings may be curtaining, of possibly plastic or towelling material, venetian or roller blinds. Venetian blinds usually consist of metal slats coated with plastic, though timber slats are available. These are made in a variety of colours and offer privacy while allowing light into the room.

Roller blinds are made in a wide range of colours and patterns. Maximum light can enter the bathroom by day, by raising these fully.

Much can be done with décor finishing by choosing accessories carefully. Towels, and bathmats, in matching colours, help to give a unified look. It is in choosing these items that one can experiment and add a touch of individuality.

---

are available in many colours, textures and patterns. These are also easy to clean but may be slippery when wet. Linoleum in bathrooms can also be slippery.

Nylon carpet, self-adhesive or loose-lay carpet tiles are also possible bathroom floor coverings. Loose-lay tiles have the added advantage of being easy to wash and can also be moved around to equalize wear.

Ceramic floor tiles are made to match wall tiles. The floor tiles are thicker than those for walls. Mosaic floor tiles or standard ceramic tiles should be fixed with waterproof adhesive and grouted with waterproof grouting. As ceramic tiles are cold to the touch a bathroom where they are used needs to be well heated to prevent surface condensation.

All floors should be laid on a firm, level surface. Flooring is part of the décor scheme and should complement the other fittings and furnishings.

Mirrors

Mirrors are valuable in the bathroom, particularly as an aid when shaving.

They may have plain or magnifying glass. Some mirrors have an incorporated light which helps to heat the mirror and cuts down condensation.

Lightweight mirrors, consisting of a plastic film, with a metallic coating, are not liable to condensation but scratch rather easily, and are, consequently, not suitable in bathrooms used by small children.

Mirrors can provide an added sense of dimension, particularly in the small bathroom.

Cutting condensation

As bathrooms are subject to condensation, thin polystyrene sheeting applied behind the wallpaper or panelling will help to insulate the walls, raising the touch temperature and so reduce condensation.

Emulsion paint can be used on the walls and ceilings to help prevent condensation. Ceilings may be decorated with polystyrene tiles or veneer. These materials are decorative, absorb sound and moisture and provide extra insulation.

What to do if your plaster cracks up

Cracks and holes not only look unsightly, but are signs of deterioration in the fabric of the home–and should be quickly put right. Plastering techniques are a matter of some practice, with the careful and systematic application of the methods involved. Choice of plaster materials is also important in relation to the type of surface, in order to achieve good results.

Plaster cracks are usually caused by slight settlement or traffic vibration, a heavy knock or, sometimes, by damp penetration or even impurities in the original plaster mix. There are two types of crack: check cracking, due to shrinkage of plaster which is usually slight and of minor importance, and map cracking, which is deeper and wider and may be due to settlement of a building or possibly caused by timber shrinkage.

Plaster types

Plaster is applied basically to two types of surface–those to which some type of key is attached, such as wooden laths or expanded metal, and solid surfaces, such as brick, building blocks or concrete.

On solid surfaces two coats of rendering, known as the floating coat and the setting or finishing coat, are usually applied. When almost hard, the floating coat is keyed by scratching the surface; this ensures a good grip for the finishing coat.

When plaster is applied to lathing an extra coat, known as a backing coat (or pricking-up coat, when applied to metal lath) may be necessary.

Plaster may be bought ready mixed in bags; only the addition of water is required to make it workable–or traditional mixtures of sand, lime and Portland cement or plaster of Paris may be prepared.

The type of plaster you decide to use will largely depend upon the existing surface you are making good. If it is a soft finish, such as lime-hair plaster, found in many old houses, then a proprietary ready-mix, soft plaster, called a retarded hemi-hydrate, will best suit the work.

If, however, the surface is hard and grey in colour then a slow-setting hard plaster over a backing coat of cement: sand: lime is preferable.

There are different types of soft plaster, for various background surfaces: solid, with normal absorption, a grade for high absorption, and grades containing anti-rust agents and bonding fibres for applying to metal lath, wood-wool slabs and expanded polystyrene. There is a bonding coat for hard, low-absorption surfaces, a grade for heavier surfaces, and a setting coat, suitable for all backing coats.

The harder, anhydrous plasters, which are grey, pink or white in colour, should not be applied over a soft, hemi-hydrate backing coat or to patch soft plaster; either will produce cracking.

A suitable backing coat for anhydrous plasters is white hydrated lime (obtainable in 25kg and 50kg bags), Portland cement (obtainable in 50kg bags), and good-quality fine building sand in the proportions 1:1:6 by volume.

For filling cracks and small abrasions, use one of the cellulose-based fillers. Cellulose fillers have the advantage over the older gypsum-based fillers that they do not shrink.

Setting times

Anhydrous plasters have a gradual and continuous setting time of two to three hours; towards the latter end of this time they may be softened with water and any irregularities polished out with a steel finishing trowel.

Retarded hemi-hydrates have a 'final-set' time of about $1\frac{1}{2}$ hours. Only during the first 60 to 70 minutes can the plaster be worked, and it is not possible to soften it once the hardening process starts, although a little water, as a lubricant for the trowel, may be used during the final polish.

You may find, due to the short setting time, that hemi-hydrate plasters are difficult to work over large areas; on the other hand, they are ready mixed, lighter and cleaner to work with. It is worthwhile persevering as, once the technique is mastered, they are in fact easier to use than anhydrous plasters.

If you do use ready-mixed plaster only mix up the quantity you need and do not 'over-mix'–that is do not add more plaster to water than recommended.

Mixing

The way in which plaster is mixed is critical to achieving a good finish. When-

ever possible, follow manufacturers' instructions exactly. When mixing up sanded mixes, make sure that the gauge box (or measuring container) is kept clean, and that the quantities are exact. Turn the dry materials over thoroughly until an even colour is produced.

Finishing plasters can most easily be mixed in a bucket. Fill a clean bucket half-full with clean water and sprinkle the plaster into this until plaster settles on the surface, then stir briskly until a creamy mixture is obtained.

Should you wish to use lime plaster, rather than a lightweight mix to repair an existing surface, first make a lime putty, by mixing hydrated lime to water until a creamy mix is achieved. Let this stand for 24 hours, then tip some on to the spotboard in the form of a ring.

Pour some water into the ring and into this pour plaster of Paris (casting plaster) until all the water is soaked up. Mix thoroughly with a gauging trowel. Always use clean water and tools, otherwise the plaster may be weakened.

Estimating quantities

For general gap filling with cellulose fillers, a large carton will usually be more than enough for a room. For estimating the coverage of soft plaster allow, dependent upon background, the following:

Backing coats:
Normal absorption
11mm thick   6·5m² to 7·4m² per 50kg.

High absorption
11mm thick   6·5m² to 7·5m² per 50kg

Metal lath (metal)
8mm thick   6·5m² to 7·8m² per 50kg

Metal lath (wood wool, polystyrene)
11mm thick   3·3m² to 5·0m² per 50kg

Bonding grade: Hard surfaces
11mm thick   5·3m² to 8·3m² per 50kg

Heavier surfaces
8mm thick   7·0m² to 7·5m² per 50kg

Finish
2mm thick   20·5m² to 24·7m² per 50kg

When estimating a sanded floating-coat mix, calculate according to the quantity of sand needed. Roughly 380mm³ of sand mixed with lime and cement to proportion 1:1:6 by volume will cover a 30m² wall. The 380mm³ of sand should be mixed with 100kg cement and 50kg lime. Pink cement 3mm thick will cover 11·5m² per 50kg. Grey cement 3mm thick will cover 13m² per 50kg.

Include about 10 per cent for wastage on all calculations.

Tools for the job

Preparation:
- **Putty knife** or old **screwdriver.** Used for scraping loose plaster from cracks.
- **Bolster, cold chisel** and **club hammer** for cutting out patches and trimming old plaster.
- **Paint brush** for damping backgrounds.

Mixing:
- **Two buckets,** preferably rubber or polythene, for mixing up plaster and holding water; it is important to clean these out thoroughly after each mix.
- **Spot board** This can be a piece of ply, preferably marine, about 270mm², to contain plaster. Plaster can also be placed in a light metal bath.
- **Gauging trowel** available in various sizes, but one of 15mm length will be most convenient; it is used for measuring (gauging) small quantities of materials and working small areas of plaster.

Application:
- **Laying-on trowel** has a steel blade of about 280mm × 120mm, reinforced by a steel or alloy tong attached to a handle. The banana shape is easier to hold as straight-turned handles are liable to slip.
- **Skimming (or hand) float;** made of wood measuring about 300mm by 115mm.
- **Angle trowel (or twitcher).** These can be for internal or external angles. The latter is more for convenience than necessity.
- **Small tools;** various shapes and sizes, the most common of which is the leaf and square. They are usually made of steel.
- **Scratcher;** used for keying backing coats. It can be made from a piece of ply through which nails are driven.

- **Devil float;** has a similar use to the scratcher, but is better on large areas as it smooths burrs as it keys.
- **Feather-edge rule.** A straight piece of wood with one edge chamfered to 6mm thick. Made from 125mm × 25mm timber about 1·5m long, it is used for working down backing coats and working angles.
- **Filling knife;** used for filling cracks. It should have a thin, springy blade.
- **Hawk.** Made of metal or wood, it has a working surface of about 300mm² and is for holding plaster up to the working area. Other general tools you need are a saw, a spirit level, a plumb line, a measuring rule, a claw hammer and, for mixing large quantities of cement, lime or plaster, a shovel.

Patching cracks and blemishes
First of all clear the crack of dust and loose plaster by scraping with a putty knife or old screwdriver. Where possible, undercut the edges to give better keying. Run a damp brush down the crack; this will help the filler to bond to the wall and, at the same time, clear the crack of dust. Some manufacturers of cellulose filler specifically tell you to omit this procedure, in which case brush the crack with a dry brush.

If the crack is more than 6mm deep, using a steel small tool, fill it with proprietary filler, mixed to manufacturer's instructions, to within 3mm of the surface. When this has set, damp down and fill to the surface with more fresh filler, flushing it off level with the surrounding surface using either a small tool or steel finishing float.

If gypsum, as opposed to cellulose-based fillers are used, they are liable to shrinkage, so fill the crack proud of the surface and smooth down when it has dried out.

Medium-sized holes in plasterboard
Where the holes are more than 13mm across, use anhydrous plaster and scrim cloth to fill the hole. First, enlarge the area round the hole with a cutting knife, by a further 13mm wide and 6mm deep. Cut a piece of scrim cloth to the size of the enlarged hole. If the hole is very large, two pieces may be overlapped.

Dampen the recessed area round the hole and place small blobs of plaster round the edge. Locate the scrim over the hole. The blobs of plaster will hold the scrim while the entire area is covered with a thin plaster coat. Once the surface begins to set, apply one or two more coats to bring the repair up to the level of the surrounding area. When the plaster coat has almost set, dampen with a brush and polish with a metal float.

Power sockets
Resiting a power socket may necessitate a minor replastering job, using a cellulose filler. Before starting work, switch off the power to the socket and remove the fixing-plate screws. Clean out the cavity and dampen the surrounding plaster before applying the first coat of filler with a pointed trowel.

If there is a gap at skirting level, crumple some chicken wire or use expanded metal to plug the hole, plaster over this, and allow the coat to set. Before applying the second and final coat, dampen the area, screw back the face-plate and polish the final coat with a metal float. Do not reconnect the power until the plaster is quite dry.

Lath-and-plaster repairs
Large holes in lath-and-plaster walls can be repaired, using expanded metal to support the repair area. Hack back loose plaster, undercut, and cut the mesh to size. Either nail it to existing timber uprights or bend it over the laths. Apply plaster with a pointed trowel, a little at a time, building up the surface with thin layers. Leave the first coat for at least 24 hours before damping down for the finish coat. Smooth and polish this with a metal float, damping down with a little water.

Smaller holes in lath and plaster can be repaired with a cellulose filler, provided the laths are intact, to support the new filler. Clean up the area by pulling away torn paper. Where the laths are broken, prepare a plug of paper, of roughly the size of the hole, soaked in plaster. Push this carefully into the hole below the surface, and cover with a thin coat of filler to within 2mm of the surface.

Once dry, dampen and apply a thin finish coat to bring the repair area level

On hair-line cracks, enlarge with a v-cut, or undercut with sharp implement

Damp down the crack with a paint brush to aid actions of suction and bonding

It is useful to mix a dilute water-PVA solution to aid bonding on shallow cracks

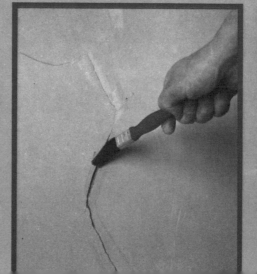

with the sound surface. To assist the repaired area to blend in with surrounding surfaces, go over the area with a damp brush to fuse the edges of the repair.

Patching large areas (solid walls)

Before decorating a room some filling will usually have to be done, but sometimes it is easier and better to put in a large patch, rather than to fill a lot of individual cracks. There are also hollow patches where the plaster has 'blown', that is, it is no longer bonded to the wall.

You can recognize 'blown' areas by tapping the wall gently; it will sound hollow. Unless these hollow spots are cut out, they will soon craze and, under extreme circumstances, cause wallpaper covering to split.

To prepare a large area for patching, the whole of the damaged plaster must be removed with a bolster, cold chisel and hammer.

First, cut a line around the extremities of the damage with the bolster, then remove the plaster within this area right back to the brickwork.

Then clean up the edge by cutting back a further 25mm; this edge may then be undercut with the corner of the bolster. Clean the area with a damp brush and apply the backing coat of plaster. To do this, mix up the plaster or sand base on the spot board; when it is ready, scrape a convenient amount on to the hawk; hold the hawk against the working area and, with the laying on trowel held at 35° to the horizontal, scrape the plaster from the hawk on to and up the wall. Work from the bottom to the top of the patch.

If the patch is 10mm deep or less, fill the hole level with the surrounding plaster. If more than 10mm, fill to half the depth and, when almost set, scratch the surface to give it a key. When dry, apply another (floating or straightening) coat up to the surrounding level.

Using the feather edge, rule off the plaster to the surrounding level, working from the bottom to the top and operating the board with a side-to-side scraping motion. If there are any hollows, fill them and rule off once more.

Where hemi-hydrate plaster is used, cut back the edges of the patch to about 3mm below the surface before it sets; this can be done with the corner of the trowel.

If a sand-based floating coat has been applied, then the whole of the new surface must be cut back to a depth of 2mm to 4mm. This is to allow for the finishing coat. This job is best done with a short rule, narrower than the patch, and it is for this reason that the initial cutting out must be done cleanly. Having cut back, go over the surface lightly with the scratcher, then smooth off the burrs with the wooden hand float.

Mix up the finishing coat and pour it on to the spot board; clean out the bucket ready for further use. Put some finishing plaster on to the hawk and, with the wooden float, skim the plaster over the surface of the work, keeping the strokes as vertical and as even as possible. When the surface is covered, repeat the procedure, this time with horizontal movements, pressing firmly.

Check this coat with the feather edge and, if too much plaster has been applied, rule it off to the required level. Wash the float and work over the plaster in a continuous circular motion, consolidating the plaster, particularly any seams.

Now, using the steel trowel with a little plaster slurry, work over the surface with a vertical pressing motion. During this operation the plaster might tend to drag slightly; if so, apply a little water with the brush to act as a lubricant.

Finally, as the plaster sets, polish it with the steel trowel and wash off the surrounding edges with a sponge.

Repairing corners

There are a number of ways of repairing damaged external corners; the method used depends on the degree of damage.

Small chips can merely be refilled with a cellulose filler, while larger, jagged edges may need reinforcing below the plaster coat. This can be done in one of two ways. The first, using aluminium or nylon strip, is best when the surface is to be papered, as the strips fit flush with the plaster. A stronger reinforcement is a round-nosed expanded metal corner piece, which can be plastered over.

To make good small chips, first remove any loose plaster and dust. Mix the filler to a fairly stiff consistency and apply to the corner, proud of the surface area. As the filler starts to set, use a finger to round the corner slightly. Wear rubber gloves. Once

the filler is dry, rub down with medium glasspaper to match the surrounding corner angle.

An expanded metal angle bead is fitted in the following way. Hack back about 125mm of plaster, using a bolster and club hammer, on both sides of the corner. Place blobs of plaster at 610mm intervals down both surfaces. Fix the expanded metal corner round the wall angle, checking the true vertical with a straight edge and spirit level, before pressing the edges of the metal into the plaster.

The straight edge is used to adjust the reinforcement, allowing 2mm for the thickness of the finish coat. Render both vertical surfaces to within 2mm for the final finish coat, applying this thinly over the corner nosing, slightly proud of the bead.

Another way involves using battens, but this type of repair will not give extra reinforcement. First, trim back the plaster and nail a batten to the brickwork, so that it protrudes by the thickness of the plaster. With a plumb line or spirit level, ensure that it is vertical. Use galvanized plaster nails to fix the batten and place them into the mortar between the bricks; remember to leave the heads proud for easy withdrawal.

Apply a floating coat between the plaster and the batten, rule off, cut back and key as necessary. When the plaster is dry, remove the batten, tapping it lightly to free it from the plaster before withdrawing the nails.

Next, fix it to the adjoining plane and apply a floating coat as before. When this coat is dry, remove the batten and, with a steel trowel, arris the corner. The finishing coat may then be applied.

In the case of hemi-hydrate finish, this may be applied to both sides simultaneously, taking care to apply the slurry evenly. With anhydrous plaster it will be advantageous to use the batten. Fix the batten to overlap one corner of the floating coat, by the amount it was cut back (2mm to 4mm). This time, the batten should be packed out with thin ply, stout card or hardboard, by the amount that it projects.

The finishing coat can then be applied to the corner. When this is polished and set, the batten may be removed, and the other side finished in the same way.

Leave for 24 hours and then round off the corner using fine glasspaper.

Fill using a broad filling knife. Finish proud with some fillers, flush with others

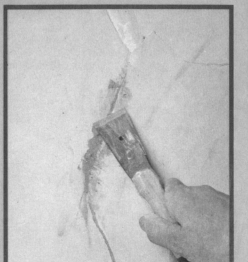

When dry, carefully rub down the filled crack, using a fine grade of glasspaper

With damaged corners, fix batten to one edge and work to this to finish square

Plastering: what you need to know

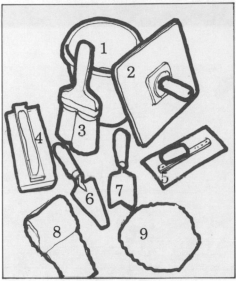

Tool and materials in plastering
1 Plastic bucket **2** Metal hawk **3** Two
knot damping brush **4** Wood float
5 Finishing trowel **6** Gauging trowel
7 Angle tool **8** Scrim **9** Plaster.

**To achieve a smooth, well-plastered
surface needs care and patience. Sometimes, the remedy for a badly cracked
wall or ceiling area is to hack off the
old plaster and start again. Alternatively, the surface may only need
simple patching. Textured finishes can
present an attractive 'face' and make
a pleasant ceiling surface.**

Ceiling repairs

Repairing larger cracks is slightly more
involved than repairing minor cracks. To
repair larger cracks in walls or ceilings,
you need a proprietary filler, medium-
grade glasspaper, a glasspaper block, a
filling knife or scraper, an old paint brush
and a spot board or hawk.

Use the scraper or filling knife to scrape
out the old plaster then brush out the dust.
Open out the crack, making an under or
V-cut, which will help to key the new
plaster in place. Brush out any further
dust.

The replacement filler can be a proprietary type; use a cellulose-based filler
for large cracks that have to withstand
stress or heat. Mix the filler on the plasterer's hawk with a little water to a workable
consistency. If the mix is too wet, it will
not stay in place. Mix enough for only an
hour's work.

Use the brush to dampen the area
around the crack and, with a pliable
filling knife, press the plaster into the
crack, leaving it slightly proud of the
sound surface. This can be rubbed down
when dry.

On deep cracks, apply the filler in
layers, allowing each layer to harden
before the next is applied. Level off the
final layer with a broad filling knife.

On an emulsioned ceiling, mix a little
of the colour with the filler. This will help
to make the crack disappear when the
area is repainted.

A filled surface crack can also be
painted with a dilute coat of the emulsion
before the area is repainted.

Where damage is extensive, the filler
should be mixed with equal parts of clean
sand. Fill in a layer at a time, allowing
each layer to harden and dry out before
the next is applied. Only the surface layer
should consist of proprietary filler.

Shrinkage cracks

Small, shrinkage cracks often appear
in the angle between the walls and ceiling
of new buildings. This type of shrinkage
is not normally serious but is unsightly.

Use a scraper to open up the crack to
2mm wide. Dampen the plaster along the
crack with clean water. Mix the filler to
a creamy consistency and use the finger
to press the mix into the gap. Allow this
to set slightly and then, using a damp brush

clean off the excess. Do not paint for at
least 24 hours.

Plastic surfaces

Where the ceiling is plastic surfaced,
use a filler formulated for use with this
for repair. Use a sharp cutting knife to
cut back all the loose surface paper. If the
plaster core of the plasterboard is exposed,
dampen this and then apply a thin layer
of a cold-water mix formulated for use on
plastic surfaces.

Special scrim paper tape should be
soaked, and then laid, using a paint
scraper, in strips over the damaged area.
Allow to dry for at least 12 hours. Next,
apply a second coat of filler evenly.

Use an applicator, which may be a proprietary type or simply made from a piece
of laminate 200mm × 115mm in size secured between two pieces of softwood
40mm × 13mm and 200mm long.

Damp round the repair area and apply,
with a brush, an even coat of filler. To
match the textured surface of the surrounding area, use a texturing tool.

This is a block of plywood, about 150mm
× 100mm with a handle. A sponge is fitted
to the block and covered with polythene
sheet secured round the handle with an
elastic band. The pad, which is textured, is
then applied to the ceiling to match in the
new surface with the old. Excess can be
removed with a damp brush.

Work to a timber rule when plastering reveals and corners; remove, then polish

Vertical timber rule is fixed slightly proud of surface and plastered flush

Wall rendering coat is 'devilled' with scratcher to provide key for finish coat

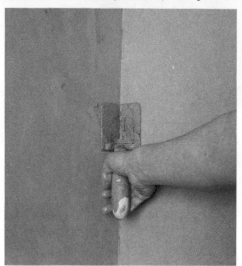

Edging tools are made to provide smooth finish to either inner or outer reveals

Lining paper

It is possible to disguise hair line cracks particularly on ceilings. The simplest and cheapest way is to cover the area with a lining paper and then paint the surface. If the surface is particularly uneven, embossed, chipwood or pebble-dash paper might be used, their textures camouflaging any irregularities.

More permanent finishes are the plastic type of textured finish. These are applied with special tools but are quite within the scope of the home handyman.

Polystyrene, either in veneer or tile form, also makes an attractive cladding material. It also has the added bonus of raising the surface temperature and helping in the battle against condensation.

Replastering

For replastering walls or ceilings you will need the following tools:

- Hawk,
- Spot board and suitable support; for this an old firm box of convenient height will do,
- Metal float,
- Angled trowel,
- Gauging trowel,
- Wooden float,
- Two-knot stock or a distemper brush,
- Scratcher; one can be simply made from nails, with their heads removed, driven into a piece of wood.

Prepare the wall by removing any loose materials and lightly brush down with a wet brush.

When patching, there is the benefit of surrounding plaster which limits the area covered and, at the same time, acts as a guide for plaster thickness when ruling off.

When plastering a whole wall there is no such guide and the first operation is to make one.

Mix up a small quantity of backing coat and apply a 150mm² 'dot' of this about 150mm from a side wall and the same distance from the ceiling. Make the dot about 12mm thick and keep it as even as possible.

Repeat with another dot 1·3m below this, using a rule and spirit level to check that the surfaces are vertical. Repeat once more just above floor level.

Check with a line—help will be needed here—that the three dots are in the same plane and amend them as necessary. Now repeat this whole process at the other end of the wall.

This done, place dots intermediately at about 1·3m centres across the wall.

Once you have checked that the surfaces of the dots are in the same plane the next step is to join them up with

screeds, first vertically and then horizontally.

Mix up a quantity of backing coat and, with the steel laying on trowel, screed between the dots from the floor right up to the ceiling. This done, rule off, preferably using a straight-edge rule about 1·8m long, and again check for verticals.

Repeat this process across and then up the wall so that the wall is divided up into convenient working areas.

The remaining areas of brickwork can now be treated in exactly the way as for applying a floating coat on a patched area.

Go over the whole wall with the devil float, wash down any adjacent surfaces and leave to dry out.

If a sanded floating coat is being used, allow at least 24 hours, but if a lightweight plaster is used, four to six hours is sufficient.

Before applying the finish plaster, test the surface for suction. This is extremely important if the floating coat has been left for longer than the times given. Brush water on to the surface; if it is sucked straight in there is too much suction which can not only weaken the final coat, but make it difficult to apply.

Dampening the wall well should overcome this problem, but if this fails, brush

Paint is well rolled out in the tray and then evenly applied to the ceiling

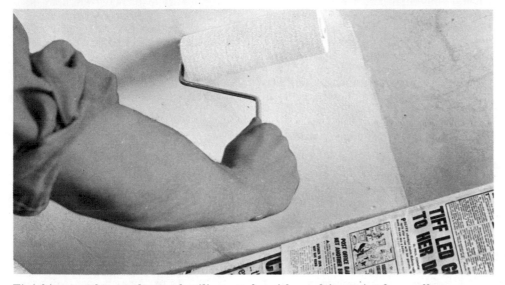

Finishing touches to plastered ceiling can be with emulsion paint from roller

on a bonding coat of PVA or wood adhesive (one part PVA to six parts water by volume). This should be done immediately before laying up the finish plaster.

Mix up the finish and skim on another coat with the laying trowel. Start with a band, about trowel width, immediately below the ceiling, then continue, with a vertical movement, over the whole wall, working from left to right if you are right handed or from the other direction if left handed.

Once the wall is covered, repeat the process with the wooden float. Then with the wooden float, apply a third thin coat horizontally. Make sure that any seams are well consolidated.

Apply the final coat of finish plaster with the steel trowel using long, firm, vertical strokes. Finally, polish the plaster using a sprinkling of water as a lubricant.

The angle trowel (or twitcher) should be used between operations to consolidate the corners.

After polishing, clean up adjacent walls and floor before the plaster sets hard.

Ceilings and walls, in older properties, may consist of lath and plaster. Once a ceiling has deteriorated badly it may be necessary to remove it completely rather than trying to do a patch-up job.

Stripping a ceiling is never a clean job, so before starting clear the room completely. Hang dust sheets over the doors to prevent dust travelling to other rooms, and cover the floor.

Use a club hammer and chisel to remove the old ceiling, taking care to clean the joints thoroughly. Punch down, or remove any projecting nails.

Modern ceilings usually consist of decorative plasterboard or plasterboard covered with a finish plaster coat. Plasterboard is composed of a gypsum core, sandwiched between paper lining.

It is available in various-sized sheets, but for most purposes 1·2m × 2·4m is a convenient size. There are two thicknesses – 10mm which should be used at standard 450mm centres – and 13mm for more widely spaced joists.

Plasterboard

Plasterboard is heavy and care must be taken to support edges where they abut the wall. Two methods are suitable for this job. The more satisfactory and stronger method is to plaster the board into the wall plaster surface.

Before starting to plaster the ceiling, cut back a 50mm wide strip along the top of the wall edge where it joins the ceiling. Butt the board tightly up to the unplastered wall surface. Strengthen the joint with scrim. Fill in the gap when applying the finish plaster coat.

The other method, which is not so strong, is to abut the board edge to the plaster surface of the wall and reinforce the right-angled joint between wall and ceiling with scrim.

At all times, use jute scrim unless the boards are not to be plastered. In this case, use cotton scrim.

Cutting

Plasterboard can be cut by scoring the face side, using a sharp knife held against a straight edge. Lay the board, face side upwards, on a bench or table, the cut edge aligning with the edge of the support surface.

The core is snapped by pressing down sharply on the overhanging edge. The board is turned over and the paper backing is cut through with a knife.

Plasterboards are nailed either across or along the joists, using either 30mm or 40mm galvanized plasterboard nails, dependent on the thickness of the board. Boards should be put up in both directions, particularly over a large area. This will avoid long joins which may cause later cracking of the finish coat.

Nailing should be at least at 150mm intervals and nails should be positioned no less than 13mm in from the edges. Nailing any closer will cause the boards to split at the edges. Drive the nails in firmly but without damaging the paper covering.

A 3mm gap should be left between the boards. This allows for scrimming, with 90mm-wide jute scrim, before plastering.

If you are working single handed, a device called a 'dead man's hand' will be necessary. This is a pole, or piece of straight-edged timber with a platform 600mm wide fixed to the top. The pole or timber support stands on the floor, with the platform resting beneath the ceiling supporting the plasterboard, leaving both hands free for working.

Measure out and cut the required lengths of scrim. Mix about half a bucketful of finish plaster. Transfer this to the hawk and, using a laying-on trowel, work along the joins between the boards. Press the plaster well into the gaps.

Position the scrim at one end of the joint and guide it into position over the gap, using the trowel to press it firmly into the plaster. Leave the joints between the ceiling and wall until last.

After scrimming, start laying on the plaster coat, treating each board as a separate area. Scrim a thin layer of plaster, using the steel trowel, up to but not over, the scrimmed joints.

Use the wood float to apply further plaster until the ceiling surface is covered to a depth of 5mm. With the steel trowel, lay on a small amount of fresh plaster to fill in gaps, and even off where necessary.

The strip between the wall and ceiling, if the plasterboard abuts the unplastered surface, is next filled in, using an angled trowel. It is smoothed off with a steel trowel.

Once the ceiling has started to set, smooth over the plaster with a clean trowel. A small amount of water, 'flicked' on from the brush, aids this process but do not make the surface too wet.

An angled trowel is used to smooth the corner between the walls and ceiling. Plaster is a quick-drying compound so the job, once started, must be finished rapidly.

Glazing: glass with care!

Choosing glass

Glass is made in a variety of thicknesses. The choice depends on the size of sheet and the degree of exposure to wind and consequent suction loads on the surface. Most domestic glazing uses glass 4mm thick.

Glass is now sold by thickness; it was formerly sold by weight. The main basic thicknesses are: 2mm, 3mm, 4mm, 5mm, 5·5mm and 6mm. Special glass is required for greenhouses, the 3mm grade being most suitable.

Types

There are two basic types of clear glass–sheet and float.

Sheet glass is made in three grades: OQ– ordinary quality; SQ–selected quality; SSQ–special selected quality. For general glazing purposes, the OQ grade is suitable.

Sheet glass used for normal glazing work is a clear drawn glass. Since the opposite sides of a pane are never perfectly flat and parallel, some degree of distortion is inevitable. Sheet glass is commonly used for domestic glazing and is available in thicknesses from 3mm to 6mm.

Float glass is made by floating the liquid glass over a surface of molten tin. This produces a glass similar to plate glass, which it has replaced. Float glasses are made in thicknesses from 5mm to 25mm. As this glass is free from distortion and is strong, it has many applications, including those of glazing large picture windows and for such things as glass table tops.

Float glass is also produced in plain or tinted decorative forms by using various processes, including acid etching, electro-floating and sandblasting. Additional decorative effects are obtained by the introduction of certain materials into the molten glass mix, to alter its light and heat-transmission characteristics.

Patterned glass includes glasses with several different decorative finishes and is frequently used for 'modesty' glazing in bathrooms and toilets.

A typical example is rough-cast glass, which is smooth on one side and obscured on the other. These glasses are usually produced by passing molten liquid glass through rollers, to produce patterns in plain and tinted versions. Thicknesses are generally between 3mm and 5mm. The degree of transparency and light diffusion depends largely on the type of pattern used.

Wired glass has a metal mesh embedded in it. This mesh helps to hold the glass together and reduces the risk of injury from falling glass.

It is also accepted as a fire-retardant material. The mesh may be square (Georgian) or diamond pattern. Such glass is often used in porches and garage roofs, but as it is difficult to cut if re-used it is best bought ready cut to size. It is made in 6mm thicknesses only.

Toughened glass Float, sheet and even some patterned glasses can be toughened by a special process which can increase the strength of the glass by four or five times. It is suitable for doors and similar areas where there is a danger of impact, since it shatters into granules instead of sharp splinters if broken.

Another type of glass is a strong, translucent glass used mainly outdoors for carports and the like, though it can be used indoors.

Solar-control glass reduces the transmission of heat, light and glare from sunlight. It is available in a range of colours in float, laminated, rough-cast and patterned form.

Mirrors are also made from float glass of SQ grade. This is moisture-proofed, silvered and edged in a variety of ways, by machine and by hand grinding.

Ordering

When you order figured glass, always give the height first and the width next. This is critical, for instance, in the case of ribbed glass, since the pattern should run from top to bottom. If you give the width first, the pane would end up with the ribs running from side to side.

In measuring up irregular openings, such as arched window frames, it is always safer to make up a template in hardboard or plywood. If the opening is to be glazed with figured glass, mark the side which is going to be towards the outside of the house 'face'. If this is not done, the 'wrong' side of the cut pane may become a dirt trap and be difficult to clean.

Storing

Glass should be stored vertically at an angle of 25° in a dry place. Lean the panes on two wooden slats propped against the wall and place rag or newspaper pads under the top edge of the panes to stop them from coming into direct contact with the wall. The surface of glass is easily spoiled by dust and moisture, before or after glass is fitted, so protection or regular cleaning is desirable if glass is to remain in the best condition.

Tools: T-square; tape; felt-pen; glass cutter; pliers; circle-arm cutter; oil box

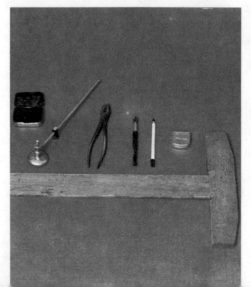

Double check measurements and mark the position on glass with felt-tipped pen

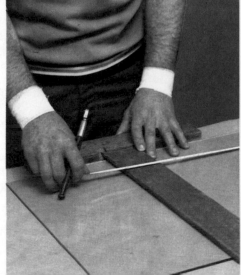

Press evenly with cutter to score; use a single stroke and do not back track

Choosing the right glass for your needs is as important as using the correct techniques to cut it. Glass comes in various grades and thicknesses, types and designs. It is both decorative and functional, since a window is an integral part of the structure of the home.

Handling and carrying

Gloves should always be worn when handling glass. These should not be too stiff, since it is important to be able to feel the glass to handle it safely. You can use folded newspapers or old pieces of inner tube as improvised 'laps' when carrying glass. Wrist bands are a further safety recommendation.

Always handle glass gently but firmly and never grip it tightly. To reduce dangers of breakage, carry glass vertically and not at the horizontal and never balanced on the head. When negotiating sharp corners or winding staircases, allow plenty of room for the glass behind you.

Small sheets of glass may be held under the arm, supported from beneath by the hand at the centre of balance. If the pane is too large to fit under the arm, hold the centre of the bottom edge with one hand and tilt the pane forward, holding the leading edge near the top corner with the other hand. Rest the upper portion of the sheet against the forearm and shoulder.

Large sheets should be carried by two people. The one in front should adopt the same position as a single person handling a large sheet. The one at the back should support the glass with one hand cupped around the lower corner holding the bottom edge, with the back edge against the shoulder. The top edge should be held with the other hand. Where people are carrying glass care must be taken to walk in step at a slow pace, particularly at any change of level and when turning corners.

Glass can be carried up ladders—supported by a second person for larger sheets, but this practice should be avoided as it can be very dangerous in the event of a gust of wind or if one slips.

Transporting glass

Smaller panes can be carried on the back seat of a car, but protect the upholstery with a blanket, lay the glass flat on the seat, and turn the blanket over the edges to prevent damage to the glass and to the car.

If you are carrying two or more panes, interleave these with newspaper. Glass carried in the boot should also be wrapped in a blanket, so that there is no direct contact with the car body.

Larger panes may be carried on a roof rack. First, lay a sheet of 19mm blockboard on the roof and cover this with a blanket, place the glass on the blanket and then fold it over the glass. The whole assembly should be lashed to the rack with a sash cord or a clothes line. Remember that sharp braking may throw the glass forward.

Tools for cutting glass

A steel glass cutter is adequate for most work and cheaper than the traditional glass cutter's diamond. If you can, choose a cutter on which the wheel is clearly visible when the tool is in use, as this promotes greater accuracy.

The back of a glass cutter has small notches cut out. These are not, as sometimes supposed, devices for notching off protrusions and edges but are gauges, so that you can gauge the thickness of glass correctly for the job in hand.

If you are doing any quantity of glass cutting, it is worth the trouble to make up or buy a T-square, to guide the cutter during its stroke. A 1220mm length of 76mm × 6mm ramin or oak, preferably chamfered at one edge, with a 305mm length of 51mm × 13mm placed at right-angles across one end, is satisfactory.

A notch should be let into the cross arm, adjacent to the chamfered edge on the long arm, to allow the cutter to run cleanly off the edge of the glass at the end of its stroke.

A pair of pliers, for trimming narrow strips of glass and uneven edges, a ruler or steel tape for measuring and a felt-tipped pen, or Chinagraph crayon, are other tools. A small empty tin, filled with felt and soaked with light machine oil enables you to lubricate the cutter.

Cutting

Preparation: Professional glass cutters wear protective wrist bands, since a splinter of glass could cause serious injury. It is advisable, then, either to wear wrist bands or to wrap your wrists with household bandages or something of that sort.

You will need a large, flat working surface to lay the glass on, such as a bench, kitchen or dining table. Place a blanket on the table to protect it and the surface of the glass from being scratched.

Where odd shapes must be cut, always make a template first from stiff card, carefully checking its accuracy. Make this about 3mm smaller all round than the actual measurements, to allow for the distance between the edge of the cutter and the cutting wheel.

Before cutting, clean the surface of the glass by wiping it with a proprietary glass cleaner or with methylated spirits. Mark the cutting line on the surface and re-check dimensions before cutting.

Lubricate the glass cutter before use by wiping it on the felt in the tin container. Hold the cutter so that the handle rests between the first and second fingers and

Place glass cutter under glass at the score line; press down evenly to break

Wear protective gloves when carrying glass; support it firmly as illustrated

Stand pane at angle on soft base, with front timber 'stop'; lean on soft 'laps'

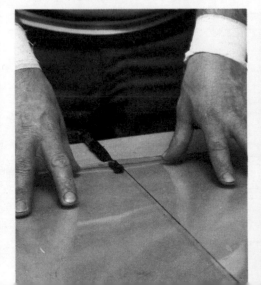

the bottom of the hand remains clear of the glass.

With the straight edge held 3mm from the marking line, to allow for the thickness of the wheel, score the surface of the glass along the line with the cutter, using a firm, smooth stroke. Draw your arm back while keeping the rest of the body stiff. Never back-track, as the glass may break at a point other than where you want.

Scoring should be completed as one operation. This is so as to score the glass evenly, enabling the piece to be snapped apart easily. Once the score mark is made, lift the glass and tap it gently from underneath along the length of the mark. Then position the edge of a small batten, about 50mm wide, directly under the cutting line or use the cutter as a fulcrum.

Place your hands on either side of the glass surface of the line and as close to it as possible, and press down slowly and firmly with your fingertips until you get a clean break along the cutting line.

Where it is necessary to remove small strips or pieces of glass, score the line as before and then, using the jaws of a pair of pliers, break off the waste pieces in small bits.

Curves and angles can also be cut by scoring the glass to the shape required by means of card templates. Once the glass has been scored to shape, tap it carefully from the underside and then, gripping the piece firmly on each side of the score marks, snap evenly downwards to break the glass.

Removing rough edges

After completion of cutting, rough edges can be smoothed away by using a carborundum stone. You will need two—a 121 fine and a 122 medium. You will also need a natural pumice stone, some pumice powder and a wood block. Both the carborundum and pumice should be kept wet at all times when being used.

The first stage is called arrising and is to remove the sharp edge. Use the medium stone at an angle of 45° and rub downwards in one direction. Once the edges have been arrised, the flat part of the edge can be ground with the face of the medium stone.

Rub it up and down, keeping it in contact with the glass at all times. Follow with the fine stone to produce a sheen.

Basic polishing can now be done with the pumice stone, but to get a really fine finish, use a wood block dressed with pumice powder.

Glass chart

Application	Suggested type of glass	Normal thickness	Other information
Windows			
Single glazing up to 2 m² between 2 m² and 3·3 m² over 3·3 m² up to 750 m² between 750 m² and 1·8 m²	Float or drawn sheet glass for clear vision Patterned glass for privacy	4mm 5mm or 6mm 6mm, 10mm or 12mm 3mm 5mm	Windows must withstand wind pressure, therefore in exposed sites thicker glass may be necessary.
Double glazing	Two panes float glass for clear vision One flat and one patterned for privacy One solar-control glass (tinted) and one float glass for protection from sun's heat	Hermetically sealed units vacuum or air spaces varying from 4mm to 12mm, or secondary sashed (fitted to existing windows)	All types of double glazing keep heat in during cold weather, reduce condensation and 'cold zones' near windows
Doors			
External All-glass Framed	Toughened glass Float or patterned	12mm 5mm or 6mm	Glass at low level might present a hazard, particularly to children. It is suggested that toughened glass be used. Framed doors, including patio doors, can be double glazed
Internal All-glass	Toughened glass or patterned	10mm	
Framed	Float or patterned	5mm or 6mm	
Partitions, room dividers	Patterned glass	5mm or 6mm	See above
Sliding doors for serving hatches, cupboards etc	Float or patterned glass	3mm, 5mm or 6mm	Large selection of patterns, including amber, blue and green tints
Table tops Large	Float glass	12mm, 15mm, 19mm or 25mm according to size	
Coffee tables	Float (clear, grey, green, bronze) or rough cast	10mm or 12mm	
Shelves	Float or rough cast	6mm, 10mm or 12mm	
Mirrors	Silvered float	6mm Verity range standard sizes or mirrors 'made to measure'	
Pictures	Diffuse reflection	2mm	Use on water-colours, prints and so on, to eliminate dazzle from lighting
Greenhouses, cold frames, cloches	Horticultural sheet glass	3mm or 4mm	A cheaper-quality glass with good light transmission necessary for growth
Windbreaks	Toughened glass, such as (Pilkington) Armourplate or Armourcast	6mm or 10mm	Ideal for terraces and swimming pools; no maintenance required
Fire-resistant glazing	Polished or rough-cast wired glass	6mm	Suitable for fire doors and partitions where up to one hour fire resistance is needed

The glazed look for doors and windows

A broken window is probably one of the most inconvenient things which can happen at home. It can also be dangerous because of broken and jagged pieces of glass, so should be quickly repaired; this is not a difficult task. Updating your glazing can bring more light into your home and give an opportunity to make use of some of the many interesting coloured and textured glasses which are made.

Glazing work is best carried out in warmer weather, as at lower temperatures glass becomes brittle. Avoid using old glass; this turns brittle with age, is difficult to cut satisfactorily and will tend to break.

Situations requiring glazing attention are door or window repairs or replacement, improvements where an ordinary clear glass is replaced by a patterned or textured glass, or where a timber door is replaced by complete glass or glass-panelled door, to let in more light.

In some cases it is advisable to remove frames, when glazing or reglazing, for safety or access reasons.

Wood frames

Glass is held in a channel called a rebate, usually with putty and special pins, called sprigs, but sometimes with panel pins. When handling glass, always wear thick protective gloves. Apart from the danger of injury from slivers of broken glass, new glass may have sharp edges.

Tools

You will need a glazier's hacking knife, or an old screwdriver, to remove the existing glass, a pair of pincers, to pull out glazing sprigs, and a Warrington-pattern hammer with a cross-pein head.

Techniques

An intact pane can, with care, be removed undamaged, though this is more difficult to do in cold weather or when glass is old.

Work from the top of the frame downwards when removing glass. First, loosen all the putty around the outside edge of the glass with the hacking knife. This will expose the sprigs or pins; these can be carefully pulled out with the pincers. Eventually the pane, or remnants, can be lifted out. Take care, however, that the glass does not fall out and shatter.

Old, hardened putty may have to be hacked out with a hammer and chisel. Any segments of glass remaining in the rebate can be prised out with pliers.

Next, remove all old putty down to the bare wood. Clean the rebate with medium glasspaper, apply a coat of wood primer and allow to dry. Drying takes about four hours.

Measure the rebate with a steel tape, from the inside edge of each rebate, taking each side top and bottom separately and then measure across the two diagonals. These measurements should be equal if the frame is square.

Glass must be cut slightly undersize to allow for expansion. For sheets of average size, allow around 1·5mm, but twice this where the pane is more than 370mm² in area.

Once you have cut the glass, it is wise to remove sharp edges with an oilstone lubricated with water, oil, turpentine or white spirit. So that the glass fits accurately in the frame, mark the outer face side; a wax pencil or crayon can be used.

Standard putty is used for glazing timber frames. A non-hardening mastic should be used when fitting sealed double-glazed units or glazing metal frames.

Putty

Roll the putty in the hands until it is soft and easy to work. If putty is too oily, it can be wrapped in newspaper to absorb the oil. Linseed oil can be added to standard glazing putty to soften it. Once the consistency is correct, lay a 3mm thick strip of putty, called the bedding putty, into the back of the rebate with the thumb.

Place the glass in the rebate. Set this in from the bottom, leaving an equal space on each side, and press the glass, firmly at the sides, into position against the putty; never press glass from the centre.

Press evenly around the edges until all surplus putty is squeezed out, leaving about 1·5mm between the back of the glass and rebate. Cut off excess putty with the putty knife.

Fix the glass into place by tacking the sprigs or pins into the frame, parallel with the face of the glass. Start the pins with the cross-pein head of the hammer. Keep the side of the hammer parallel with the face of the glass and on it while fixing; this will avoid hitting the glass and, possibly, cracking it. Space the sprigs at intervals of about 150mm.

A strip of weathering putty should now be evenly applied at an angle on the outside of the rebate.

Smooth the putty with the putty knife, keeping this lubricated with water to prevent putty from sticking to the blade. Hold the blade in one corner against the rebate, with the tip resting at an angle of about 45° on the glass, and draw the blade smoothly downwards.

This angle is important as it allows rain to run off and not collect. Trim away excess putty with an even pressure of the knife. Trim each area with one stroke to ensure a clean surface line. Make a neat mitre at each corner. Finally, go over all the putty surfaces with a damp, soft brush

Allow two or three weeks to elapse and then paint over the putty with an oil undercoat and then a finishing coat to match surrounding paintwork. Allow paint slightly to encroach, by about 3mm, on to the surface of the glass, to seal the join.

Wood beads
These can be used in place of weathering putty, but the glass should be set in bedding putty. Bead can be square, splayed or quarter-round softwood. It is fixed with 19mm–25mm panel pins and glazing felt. When using wood beads, a slightly thinner glass can be used.

Measure the sides and tops of the rebates and check the diagonals for squareness. The four beads should be cut slightly over size; mark these in pencil to show the respective positions. Mitre the ends, using a mitre box and dovetail saw. Paint the backs of the beads with a primer.

Lay the beads flat and gently tap two panel pins part of the way into the centre of the bead at about 25mm from the face of each mitre. This will establish the angle of entry for fixing into the frames. Remove the nails and drill holes; this prevents the beads from splitting. Drill further holes at about 15mm distances along each piece.

Put the beads into position and gently tap down the pins, just to the face of the beads.

These are not fixed permanently until all four are in position. Fix first the upright, next, the opposed bead and then top and bottom beads; check also that the glass remains accurately in position.

With a centre punch, tap the pins below the surface. The holes can then be filled with putty or a filler, and any inconsistencies in the mitres made good. Then the bead can be rubbed down, prepared and painted.

Glass vibration, which can be noisy and even cause glass to break, can be avoided by using adhesive glazing felt in place of bedding putty. This is cut to length and set into the rebate before fitting the glass.

Use stout protective gloves to remove segments of glass from a broken window

An old chisel or steel blade can be used to hack out old putty and glass

Next, carefully pull out old glazing sprigs or pins with a pair of pliers

Measure the rebate, both horizontally and vertically; double check

Check for squareness by measuring the diagonals; these should be equal

Hole for metal glazing clip; remove these carefully for reuse.

Locate pane of glass in the bedding putty and lever it gently into place

Place the hands on either side of the pane and press it evenly and firmly in

Fix glazing sprigs and then trim off surplus putty on inside of the rebate

With thicker glass or in larger areas, cups and screws can be used in place of panel pins. If made of brass or white metal these can look attractive, particularly on natural or varnished timber.

If cups are not used, the screw pilot must be recessed with a countersinking bit. First drill the pilot hole; this is unnecessary where cups are used.

Countersunk heads should be recessed below the surface of the beads. To fix, position one of the side beads and make a hole through the pilot hole into the frame with a bradawl, and fix in the order used for pinned beads.

Brass screws fixed through hardwood should first be lubricated with candlewax to prevent them from snapping off.

Metal frames

Though the procedure for glazing metal frames is largely the same as for wooden frames, a mastic glazing medium has to be used and added provision must be made for expansion.

Sprigs are not used; glass is held in place by spring clips, resembling a bent letter 's' which hook into the rebate. These press on to the glass face. When reglazing, carefully remove existing clips for re-use.

Metal frames require small plastic expansion pieces in the bottom frame rebate. These are set into the bedding mastic and their thickness must be allowed for when cutting glass.

Two causes of glass in metal frames

cracking are rust and distortion. In some cases you may have to contemplate fitting a new frame, if deterioration is considerable or the distortion cannot be corrected.

Any rust should be removed by cleaning the affected area with wire wool. It should then be treated with a rust inhibitor and primed.

In some cases, metal glazing beads are fixed to the outside of steel and aluminium windows with grub screws. Before removing these, first lubricate with a drop of penetrating oil; this facilitates removal.

In cases where, with any window or door, only surface putty needs renewing, simply remove the deteriorated putty and re-putty the rebate with new weathering putty.

Once the rebate is free of débris, next clean up the rebate with a dusting brush

On metal frames, the rebate should be prepared with a coat of metal priming

It is a sound idea to protect the eyes with protective goggles during glazing

Clip seen in place, holding glass firmly against facing putty

Bedding putty is applied evenly into the rebate and the pane of glass is inserted

Expansion pieces in the bottom rebate are necessary with metal window frames

Ball putty in the hand and evenly apply the facing putty to glass and the rebate

Use putty knife at angle. Keep putty moist so that knife does not make it drag

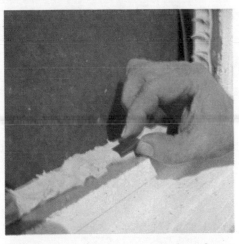

Finally, trim off surplus and mitre the corners; later apply protective paint

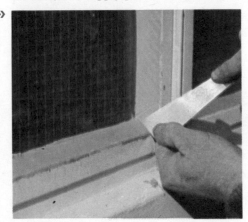

Be your own master glazier

Cutting holes or circles in glass, or drilling holes in mirrors, need not be a job only for the expert. With care, the right tools and some patience, the handyman is quite able to cope successfully with such tasks. Leaded window lights may, from time to time, need replacement of panes, or the frames may need repairing. If tackled systematically, this is no more difficult than other types of glazing.

Cutting holes and circles

To cut circles or holes you need a tool called a radius or circle-arm cutter. This is a cutting wheel, mounted on an adjustable arm, which revolves on a central pivot and suction cup.

The length of the arm can be adjusted to vary the radius of the circle. This tool is much easier to use on glass in a flat position, though it is possible, with care, to cut a circle from a fixed pane of glass.

To find the centre point, mark diagonals on the piece from corner to corner, with a felt-tipped pen or crayon. The intersection of the diagonals gives the centre.

If the circle is not to be cut in the middle of the glass, mark out a rectangle in the chosen area and work accordingly. Measure off, along one diagonal, the exact radius of the circle to be cut, from the point where the diagonals cross.

Fix the suction pad on the cutter on this central point and set the arm so that the cutting edge just reaches the length of the radius. Now scribe the circle, holding the cutter firmly and applying even pressure all round.

The pivot must be held down firmly on the glass while the cutter wheel is revolved.

Safety circle

Once this is completed, move the cutting edge about 20mm inwards and scribe a second circle. This is known as the 'safety circle', because it helps to keep the edges of the glass from splintering.

With the metal tip of the glass cutter, tap the underside of the glass upwards towards the cuts. Work slowly and carefully around both circles. The object is to 'open up' the cuts so that the removal of the waste glass is both clean and neat, without splintered edges. Tapping out could take 10 or 20 minutes–and there is no advantage in rushing it.

Next, divide the safety circle into wedge sections, using the ordinary glass cutter. Cross-hatch these wedges and, with the head of the glass cutter, tap out one small piece of glass from beneath, then carefully break out the glass in the safety circle with pliers.

Next, make radial v-cuts to the line of the outer circle. Take care not to mark over this line, or the glass may shatter. These score marks should be at intervals of about 25mm and are broken out with pliers. First tap and then break out glass until the whole of the opening is cleared.

Drilling

Drilling should be done using spade or spearpoint bits, which are made specially for glass drilling. A power drill can be used at a slow speed, but a more reliable method of drilling is by using a bit and brace. The speed of drilling should not exceed 350 revolutions per minute.

Holes should not be drilled closer than 13mm from the edge of a glazed surface and, if possible, keep this to 25mm. Where a masonry drill is not available, a tapered triangular piece of file may be used, with care, in a brace. The turning motion should be slow, steady and with even pressure.

The glass should be laid on an absolutely flat surface. Mark the drilling position by pressing the tip of the bit on to the glass. This is to fracture the surface, to prevent the bit from wandering while drilling.

When drilling a mirror, start on the non-reflective side, to prevent damage to the silvering. To find the drilling position, cross measure from the outside edge of the glass. Avoid too much downward pressure as this may fracture the glass.

Make a small well of putty around the drill hole and fill this with turpentine or white spirit; with mirrors use water as oils will cause staining beneath the glaze. When you begin drilling, the spirit will turn white with powdered glass; when this happens add more spirit.

Just before the hole breaks through the glass, stop for a moment and clean away débris. Proceed carefully as the bit nears the other side. Do not stop turning or you will run the risk of splintering the glass around the edge.

There is a danger that the drill may 'break out' a large sliver from the face side of the mirror if you drill only from one side.

It is a good idea to finish off by drilling from the face side just before the bit breaks through from the back. Again, mark accurately from the edges and drill with great care.

To find its centre point, mark out the
diagonals of the area of the circle

Radius-arm cutter has central suction
cap and adjustable glass-cutting head

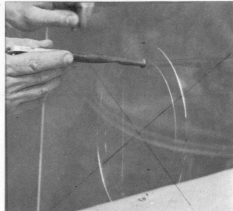

Scribe outer circle and inner 'safety'
circle; tap with cutter to spread out

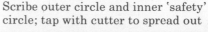

Score between inner and outer circle at
intervals to safeguard pane from breaking

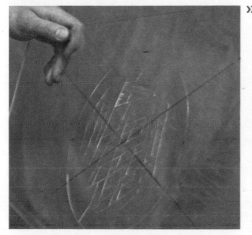

Carefully tap out the criss-crossed
section, using the head of the cutter

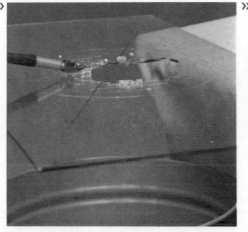

Tap cross cuts to 'spread' these and
remove safety circle with pliers

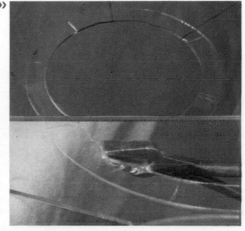

Cutting a circle is cutting a hole in
reverse. Score safety lines from edge

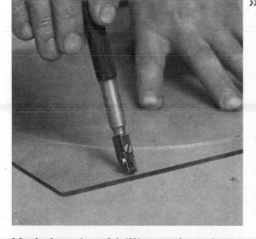

Tap beneath the glass in order to spread
the score marks made by the glass cutter

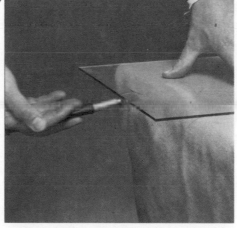

Using the pliers, gently break off the
outer segments to leave circle of glass

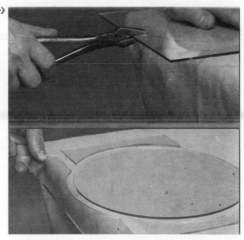

Mark the point of drilling, make a ring
of putty and pour the lubricant

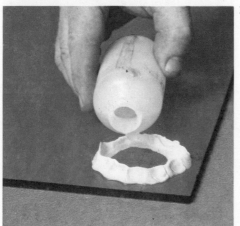

Mark starting point with tip of spade
drill; drill slowly and keep lubricated

Arris edges with carborundum block; this
is used at angle of 45° in one direction

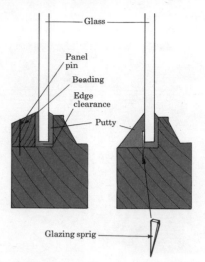

Glass

Panel
pin

Beading

Edge
clearance

Putty

Glazing sprig

The finishing touches in window glazing:
facing putty or wood beading

Repairing leaded lights

In the traditional leaded light, separate pieces of glass are held in a framework of specially shaped lead extrusions called 'cames'. The whole framework, called the light, is then inserted in the rebate of the window casement like a single pane of glass.

Tools needed are a glass cutter, a 6mm wood chisel, a soft brush, a putty knife, a hammer and a soldering iron.

Materials: gold-size putty cement, plumber's black, solder, flux and wire wool. Gold size is an addition to the putty which prevents cracking and should be mixed well into the putty. Gold size accelerates drying.

Even if only one or two pieces of glass are broken in a leaded light, it is likely that you will have to remove the whole light to replace them.

If you can repair the window in situ, do so. Leaded lights are easily distorted when removed from their frames. Where a window has bulged badly, however, take it out carefully.

Always work on the outside of a window so that any disfigurement of the cames cannot be seen from the inside.

Start by carefully cutting away the putty, avoiding damage to the outer lead cames. Remove the sprigs or oval brads—there are normally two to each edge of the frame.

Insert a wide chisel behind the light and ease it gently out of the rebate, working progressively along each of the edges in turn.

Lay the light on a flat surface and, with a knife, cut through the top of the cames, cutting diagonally into the corners to enable the edge of the lead to be prised up. Slip the blade between the lead and the glass and draw it along the came.

Repeat the process with the blade of a screwdriver until the lead is gradually lifted and bent back.

Continue until the glass is loose enough to draw out. Tap out the glass from the inside of the window. Collect the pieces and dispose of them. Clean out the grooves in the cames with a chisel, taking extra care to ensure that there is no débris left in the corners.

Brush round all the empty cames and then fill these with a soft, gold-size putty cement, pressed well down into the came. Cut the new glass carefully to size and insert this.

Support the light on a flat surface, such as a piece of hardboard, and press down the cames firmly with a putty knife, handle of a screwdriver or a wallpaper roller to ensure that they are all flat on the glass. Carefully trim off surplus putty from both sides of the glass with the putty knife.

Burnish the broken joints with an abrasive pad or medium-grade glasspaper or with fine wire wool.

The conventional way of sealing the corners is to solder them. Plumber's black is applied beyond the corner of each joint to limit the spread of solder. Check that the surface is clean, or the solder will not adhere.

Soft soldering is carried out at temperatures of between 120°C and 240°. An electric soldering iron is the best choice. Soft soldering is a relatively low-temperature process for joints which do not have to take a lot of weight or heat.

Apply flux and place a little solder on each broken joint with a moderately hot iron. To finish the joint neatly, to match the others, rub with the soldering iron, in a circular motion.

Alternatively, you can seal the corners with plastic repair materials. Clean the joints, knife the plastic into them and allow it to set hard.

Where leaking is caused by a fault in the putty, mark the leaking points with a wax crayon during wet weather.

When the weather is dry, open the cames up slightly, and scrape out the old putty. Replace it with new and press the cames firmly back into place. Check again during wet weather.

Use oyster knife to raise lead came to 90° angle; cut to lift at solder joints

Mark outline in pencil; use as template to cut glass. Nick off pane corners

Press on top surface with shaped piece of boxwood, keeping putty knife beneath

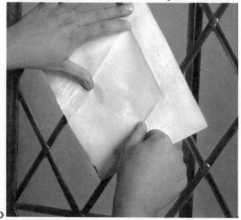

Take rubbing on piece of paper in order to establish size of glass needed

Insert new pane using putty knife. Hold knife under came when pressing this back

Finally, fork putty into the came. This is special soft putty for leaded lights

Restoring and refitting sash windows

Windows and doors are parts of the home where deterioration can set in very quickly. It is important to give these regular attention, to avoid the considerable expense of replacement and the damage which neglect can cause to the fabric of the home. Painting regularly is always the first line of defence against wear and weather.

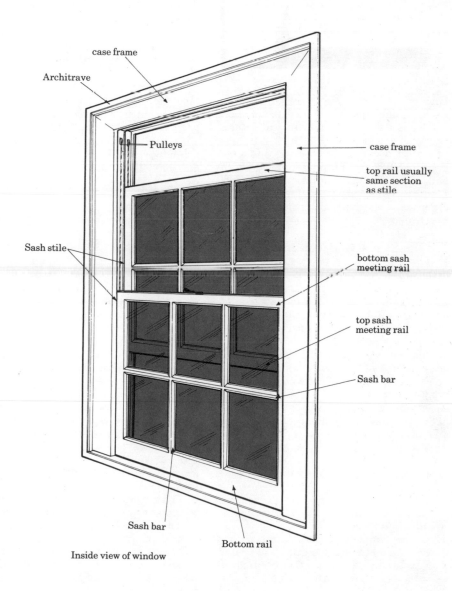

Angle blocks
Architrave
Inside lining
Pulley head
Parting bead
Axle pulleys
Outside lining
Pocket parting slip
Sash cord
Staff bead
Pulley stile
Jamb outside lining
Jamb inside lining
Removable pocket pieces for access to weights
Draught bead
Sill

Sash-window repairs

case frame
Architrave
Pulleys
case frame
top rail usually same section as stile
Sash stile
bottom sash meeting rail
top sash meeting rail
Sash bar
Sash bar
Bottom rail

Inside view of window

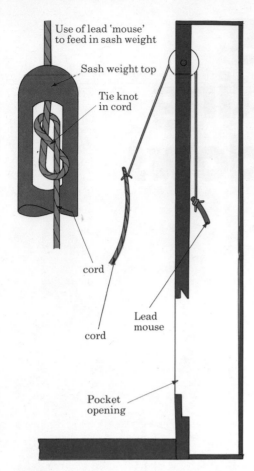

Use of lead 'mouse' to feed in sash weight

Sash weight top

Tie knot in cord

cord

cord

Lead mouse

Pocket opening

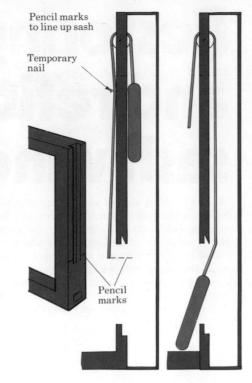

Pencil marks to line up sash

Temporary nail

Pencil marks

The lead mouse is used to weight the new sash cord and is later removed
Before taking out the lower sash mark the place where the ends of the sash cords come on the cord and on the frame

Properly maintained, windows and doors, both wood and metal, are unlikely to cause much trouble. Lack of or poor maintenance is the usual cause of deterioration. Frames may jam and not open properly; warping may occur, and glass crack or become loose; tenons may rot and break or glue joints come apart. Metal windows may rust and warp. In either case, the expensive solution may be new frames.

Paint fulfils a vital protective function. If it is not kept up to standard, it will deteriorate, flake away and allow timber to become saturated, causing it to swell up in wet weather. Wet rot may irreparably damage the fibre of timber.

Because damp is an all-pervading problem, repairs should ideally be tackled during dry weather. Apart from the inconvenience of removing doors and windows during cold and wet weather, timber remains swollen and problems are not easy to rectify.

If you have a number of doors and windows to repair, take out only one at a time. It is a good idea to tack a piece of 500-gauge polythene in place over the opening, fixing this to battening, so that it stays securely in place.

Windows and doors
There are two basic types of window–the casement and the double-hung sash. However, the movable part of any window's called a sash. There are various types of door–solid, panelled, ledged and braced, glazed, part-glazed, and doors with fixed or opening lights.

The principle of repairs is much the same for both doors and windows. However, it is the latter that tend to demand the greater attention, so reference is largely to repairs of windows.

A casement window that will not close properly is a problem. Sash windows may stick and be difficult to slide. Look, at this stage, at the sash cords, for these may have frayed and need to be replaced.

Order of repair
The main operations involved in repair and maintenance are: removal of windows; taking out glass; dismantling the frames; cleaning up joints; glueing and repegging joints; checking for squareness and alignment; removing old paint; repriming and repainting; reglazing; and, finally, rehanging. Broken or rotted tenons may also have to be replaced.

When removing an upstairs window without help, use a strong line to support the window before you loosen the hinges. This should prevent hazards such as a window falling out and being wrecked and, perhaps, injuring someone below.

If you are working alone, place an improvised pallette of straw, sacks or other soft material below the window and lower it out on to this. Where possible, get help, for windows may prove heavier than they look.

First, remove the screws fixing the windows to the window frame. It is easier to remove screws on the actual frame once it is taken out of the surrounds.

Before attempting to take out screws, remove all paint from the screw slots, so that the screwdriver gets a good purchase and does not break out the screw head. Clearing a paint-clogged screw head is best done with a spiked tool such as a sharpened nail.

If screws prove stubborn, first try to tighten them slightly since this will help

to loosen the threads. You can also give the end of the screwdriver a few sharp but careful taps with the hammer as this often frees a stubborn screw.

Penetrating oil can be left to soak in on rusted screws. If all else fails, you may have to drill out the screws.

Sash windows
Sash windows are correctly called double-hung sashes or box windows and operate with cords, pulleys and weights; these counter-balance both the inner and outer sash, while sliding up and down. One end of the cord is nailed to a groove in the side of the sash, while the other attaches to a weight, in a hidden shaft within the frame.

The pulley wheels attach to pulley stiles–the upright sides of the frame which hide the weights. Part of each pulley stile consists of a removable section of timber known as a 'pocket', which fits flush with the stiles and provides an access hatch to the weights. These pockets are usually screwed into place.

Remove the fixing bead round the inside edge of the window frame carefully. Start in the middle of a long bead by gently prising it away from the main frame by around 25mm. Use an old chisel. Now tap the bead smartly back into place. The pins securing it should pop up through the surface of the wood and can then be removed with pliers.

If this does not prove effective, you can drive a wedge in the middle and use a chisel to lever progressively towards the ends of the bead. Next, remove the parting bead between the sashes, using the chisel to ease it out of its groove.

The lower sash can be taken out and rested on the window sill. Before removing it, mark in pencil on the front of the sash the place where the ends of the sash cords come, and make a corresponding mark on the frame.

Remove the nails with a pair of pincers, while holding the sash cords. This prevents the weights at the other end from falling behind the stile boards. The inner sash can be removed next and stood aside. Repeat the marking procedure.

Finally, unscrew or lever out the pocket covers. Take out the weights by pulling them through the pocket openings.

Once the frames are removed, old glass can be taken out, following the techniques in the chapter on window glazing. All window and door furniture, such as catches, should also be removed.

On tenon joints, remove the wedges in the middle of the joints by drilling a hole in the middle and prise these out with a slim chisel. With dowelled joints, remove the dowels, using a drill of the same diameter as the dowels.

Once the window is taken apart it may appear to be something of a jigsaw. Mark, on each side of each joint, a letter or a number in sequence to make it easy to identify the correct piece when you reassemble the sections.

The joints can be taken apart by holding a piece of timber against the frame and tapping with a mallet. Take care to avoid damaging them. Once apart, use the chisel or a scraper to remove old glue, or brush the joint with boiling water to soften the glue. Finally, clean the joint with fine wire wool.

New tenons

Often, a tenon is broken or damaged and needs replacing. This is best cut off and replaced with a new tongue. A hardwood fillet provides the new tenon, half of which is inset into the horizontal member of the window sash, the rail.

To make this, cut a piece of hardwood to the same depth and thickness of the old tongue but twice the length, and add 6mm. The extra length allows the new tongue to project through the mortise so it can be sawn almost flush and planed smooth.

The new tenon slots into the rail, and may be drilled and pinned with dowels. First, cut off the old tenon flush with the end of the rail. Put the rail in a vice, mark out with a try-square the distance of the tongue back along the rail. Cut a slot for the section of hardwood to fit into, using a coping saw.

Next, drill three pilot holes in the form of a triangle through the rail so that the hardwood is just marked and remove the piece of hardwood. Make a mark with a nail punch at a distance of 1mm on the outside of these three points and then drill 10mm holes. These off-line holes pull the joint tight when it is later dowel fixed.

Drill 10mm holes through the rail and assemble the rail and hardwood fillet. Coat the concealed part of the fillet with glue, slightly point three 10mm dowel pieces, cut slightly over-size for trimming. Coat these with an exterior grade glue and tap home; allow the joint to set.

The joint can then be planed smooth. Finally, the tongues can be haunched back to fit the mortise slots.

Reassembly

After new tongues have been fitted, reassemble the sashes. Coat the tenons with adhesive and slide these into the mortises. Sashes must be quite square; check this by placing the inside of a try-square on the outside corners of the frame; these should be square at all points. Another way is to measure the diagonals; if these are equal in length, the frame is true.

Once the sashes are assembled, you need to drive in hardwood wedges to consolidate the mortise-and-tenon joints. These are the same thickness as the tenon and should be glued with an exterior grade of adhesive, then driven in from the outside at the edges, using a mallet or rubber-headed hammer.

Cramping

It is important to hold the work steady while doing this as the frame may go out of square or the tongues of the tenons might become stressed and damaged. It is best to use sash cramps; if you do not possess these, they may be hired.

An improvised wedge can be made up by nailing blocks of wood to a surface, and supporting the frame between these. In this method, the blocks are set at a distance slightly greater than the length of the frame. The frame is tightened between the blocks by driving in four small wedges between the block and the frame at one end.

Another way is to make up a tourniquet of rope, tightened with a piece of wood, to cramp tightly round the outside edges of the assembled sash.

Before the adhesive dries check carefully that the frame is true and wipe off any excess glue.

Sash cords

On sash windows, if attention is needed to repair the frames, it is probable that sash cords may also need replacing. You can obtain pre-stressed wax cords, or allow for stretching in use.

The lead mouse

You also need a length of string and a small, flat piece of lead called a 'mouse'. This is used to weight the new sash cord and is later removed.

The mouse is rolled round the end of a 150mm or 180mm length of string. It is about the thickness and half the length of a cigarette. The mouse should be bent slightly in the middle and fed over the groove of the outer pulley wheel until it falls down behind the stile.

Next, tie the new sash cord to the other end of the string, and pull this over the wheel and out through the pocket opening. The mouse can now be removed.

Tie the sash cords to the top of the weights. Use either a flat-finish knot, or bind the loose end of cord so that no knot or lump can interfere with the action of the window opening.

Pull the weights up about 50mm from the bottom and partly nail through each cord into the pulley stile. This is to hold the weights temporarily in position. Next, cut each cord level with the pencil marks made earlier on the stile.

The outer sash should be positioned so that you can fit a cord into its groove. Line up the end of the cord with the pencil mark on the edge of the sash, fixing it with four or five clout nails, starting at this mark.

Once both cords have been fastened, the temporary nails can be taken out of the cords and stiles and the sash can be lifted into place. Test the sash operation by sliding it vertically.

The weights for the inner (lower) sash are similarly fitted – except that these should be pulled up almost to the pulleys.

Finally, replace the pockets, spring back the parting bead, and lift back the inner sash. To ensure that the sash slides smoothly, put candle wax in the two channels and on the edges of both staff and parting beads.

Another problem is tightness of sashes. This may be caused by excess paint on the outer surfaces. Strip any build-up of paint and prepare and repaint the surface.

Reglazing

Reglazing of sashes follows the techniques of glazing casement windows. However, beware of old or weathered glass. This may be brittle and break easily. You may wish to contemplate replacement with a decorative, patterned glass. Similarly, casement or sash windows of various types may be removed and replaced with proprietary, aluminium-framed louvres.

You may also wish to extend and reinforce frames, so that you can fit one of the forms of double glazing.

Stages in the repair of window tenons

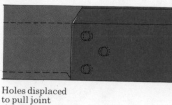

Detail of new tenon

Holes displaced to pull joint tightly together

Punch marks   Pilot holes

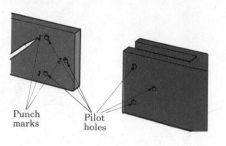

Improvised sash cramp

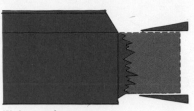

Wedges used to consolidate joints

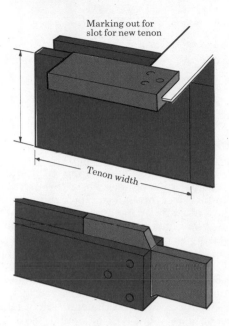

Marking out for slot for new tenon

Tenon width

Double glazing: an extra layer of comfort

Double glazing is one of the ways of preventing heat loss through the fabric of a building. It has been estimated that up to 20 per cent of heat waste through the fabric is lost through windows and around gaps in badly fitting frames.

It is important to look at double glazing as part of whole-house insulation. Potentially, out of money spent on heating an uninsulated house, 75 per cent is wasted. Loss occurs through walls, roofs, doors and windows, floors and flues.

Opinion varies on the question of how much money is saved by double glazing. Basically, it increases the comfort level but does not usually greatly cut heating costs.

A single sheet of glass is a poor insulator. If used in an exposed condition it can have as high a 'U' value as 5·67w/m² °C or 6·24.

The area around a window is a cold 'zone'; the nearer you get to the window the colder you find it. When expanding warm air reaches this cold surface, it cools and contracts, causing turbulence which creates a draught. A vacuum, a 'sandwich' of air or inert gas entrapped between two sheets of glass, raises the face temperature of the inner pane, so that warm air is no longer dramatically cooled.

Though double glazing a window area can save up to 80 per cent of the heat lost through the glass, as this usually represents only a small area of the total house fabric, the actual saving, in heat terms, may be as little as 10 per cent.

The amount of thermal insulation provided by double glazing depends on the gap between the two sheets of glass. Basically, the greater the gap, the greater the degree of insulation. A double-glazed unit with a gap of 5mm would have a 'U' value of 3·40, while a 13mm gap would improve the value to 2·96.

Before fixing double glazing, it is important to check that heat is not escaping through badly fitting window frames. It is pointless to fit double glazing if heat is escaping and you are prey to draughts from outside.

There are various methods of dealing with the problem. If the frame is badly distorted and the wood rotted or warped it may be better to repair or replace the entire frame.

A variety of window draught excluders are available, ranging from sprung-metal stripping, to go around door and window frames, adhesive-backed foam-rubber strip to a type in a tube which is squeezed out along the opening and allowed to dry. Before applying an adhesive-backed or plastic extruder, first make sure that surfaces are free from grease and dry.

As an aid to sound insulation, double-glazed units do not have very high sound-insulation properties. Domestic glazing units have a gap varying between 5mm and 13mm, but to provide an effective sound barrier this gap needs to be 100mm or more.

A unit like this could not be fitted easily to most domestic windows and would need specially modified window fittings.

Factory-made units

The pre-sealed, factory-made unit consists of a double sheet of glass, vacuum sealed or filled with inert gas. This type presents the appearance of conventional glazing and requires no further attention once fitted. With such units problems of condensation on the inner surfaces of the glass are virtually eliminated.

Factory-made units are heavy and may implode if dropped, so get help in handling these. Careful, correct measurement is most important. A rebate at least 13mm deep will be required if the unit is to be glazed into an existing wood or metal frame.

This allows for a 5mm gap between the sheets of glass. Units are made with smaller gaps. Check that the frames are in good condition and adequate to carry the weight of a factory-sealed unit, as this weighs at least twice that of a single sheet of glass.

Double glazing is a comfort medium, and may, if the gap between the two panes of glass is deep enough, provide effective sound insulation. Fixed pre-made double-glazed panes can be used, or one of the many types of applied or coupled glazed sashes, which offer a choice of system suitable for use with any type of existing single glazing

When fixing pre-sealed units to existing window frames the most satisfactory method of fixing is to use beading, tacked and then painted to match the rest of the framework.

Alternatively, the unit can be glazed, in the conventional way, using a non-hardening glazing mastic.

Pre-sealed units have the added advantage of providing only two surfaces to clean and are neat in appearance.

There are no summer storage problems which apply to other types of glazing units and no ventilation problems. Most suppliers of double-glazed units will supply and fix, or measure for you and then supply for you to fix.

Sealed units are available in over 100 standard sizes but most firms will meet a 'one-off' order. As this may take some time, try to anticipate your needs in advance.

Applied and coupled sashes

Applied-sash or coupled-sash units are popular forms of double glazing. These come in a variety of kits or you can evolve your own system. An applied sash is fitted to the rebate of the window or other window surround, while the coupled sash is fitted to the window frame.

It is possible to have coupled sash sliding units. Sliding-sash units usually consist of a head track, side member and sill track. The fixing position of the head track decides the final position of the window.

In deciding the position of the track, make sure there is room for any projecting window furniture between the existing window and the track. Some kits include a sealing strip to stop draughts.

For sliding windows to slide easily it is essential to have a true frame. The lack of this does not preclude this form of double glazing.

Most firms supply packing pieces which can be used to ensure a 'true' frame, allowing windows to slide easily. As the distance between the sashes is normally 100mm, it provides some acoustical advantage.

Coupled sash

This is simple to install and involves the fixing of a removable glazed panel, to the existing window frame. In summer this panel can be taken down and stored.

When making up a coupled-sash unit, the frame of the glazing unit should normally be 19mm less than the dimensions of the window opening and the glass 8mm less than the dimensions of the frame.

Cut the main frame channel to size and fit the glazing strips round the glass. This should be first laid flat. The basic components of the majority of systems are usually four main channels and four corner hinges, locking nuts and screws and neoprene sealing strips.

To assemble, the four main channels and corner hinges are placed roughly in position. The locking nuts and screws are fixed loosely to the corners.

Cut the neoprene sealing strips to the correct length, mitre the corners (some kits include a mitre block) and then insert the strips into the channels. After fitting the corner hinges to the main frame, the glass is fitted into the frame.

Usually, a sliding foot is provided for the window stay. This is fitted into the groove of the bottom channel. The unit is then tightened and offered up to the window frame. Mark the position of the hinges and set these so that the frame hinges accurately into place.

In detail, coupled sash units may vary but this is the method used to fix most units. For further insulation, a neoprene strip can be fixed to seal the joint between the unit and the window frame.

Before positioning any made-up double-glazing unit, remember to clean both sheets of glass thoroughly on both sides. Condensation between the sheets may prove a problem.

There are two methods of combating this. One is to drill a series of small holes upwards in the base of the frame to provide ventilation. The other is to use silica-gell crystals. These are placed along the bottom of the unit where they act as blotting paper to absorb the moisture. These may become saturated in time and need to be removed and dried out. Coupled-sash glazing frames can also be applied externally to window frames.

Kits, consisting of plastic framing, into which you fit your own glass, are available. Some types consist of a coupled sash which unclips completely, while others have an adhesive-fixed plastic head, into which the glass is fitted when needed.

Applied sash lifts into place, is fixed by clips, and can be removed in summer

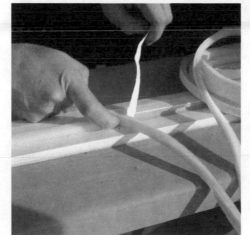

Foam draught excluder has sticky back — but clean surface before pressing down

Sprung metal excluder provides a close seal around the edges of an outside door

The frames for applied or coupled sash units can be made of plastic, wood or aluminium.

Moisture is drawn through the fibre of timbers, even when painted. A strip of aluminium foil – which is available in an adhesive-backed form – can be used to seal the reveal between the glass to keep out moisture.

When using applied or coupled-sash units, it is important to realize that provision should be made for adequate ventilation without draughts. A completely sealed atmosphere with no air changes is neither healthy nor desirable.

An adequate form of double glazing can be provided by using double-sided tape and acetate sheeting. The double-sided tape is placed round the window surround to hold the acetate sheeting in place.

Thermal insulation: making your room cosy

Heating the home is a relatively costly matter, so it is important not to waste heat through poorly insulated structures. Up to 75 per cent of the heat produced can be lost through roofs, walls, floors and window areas in poorly insulated homes. This article tells you how to keep down costs by using correct insulation materials.

Thermal insulation

To achieve comfort in the home and keep heating costs down, warmth must be retained for as long as possible. Good insulation helps to keep the home warm in winter and cool in summer. In many homes, huge heat losses occur as a result of poor thermal insulation.

In homes that are empty all day, then heated when the family returns home, internal linings with good thermal-insulaation qualities reduce the time taken for the temperature to reach an acceptable level. The fabric of the home will also more readily retain heat.

Of all money spent on heating, up to 75 per cent is lost through the fabric of the house, largely through chinks, gaps and poor insulation. Heat is lost in two ways—by conduction via the exterior structure and ventilation through air changes.

The major points where heat is lost are through the walls (25 per cent), roofs, windows, flues and doors (all 20 per cent) and through floors (10 per cent).

The thermal efficiency of a material is expressed by what is known as its 'U' value, or thermal transmittance co-efficient. This is the amount of heat lost from one side of a structure to the other, per m^2 per hour and per degree difference on each side.

This is usually expressed by the formula: 'U'w/m^2°C. This means transmittance of heat in watts at °Celcius per m^2. A high 'U' value means a high heat loss and poor insulation. The lower the value, the better the insulant qualities of the structure.

For example, a roof with simply tiles on battens has a 'U' value as high as 3·17, while tiles laid on felt and with ceiling insulation consisting of 25mm quilt or 50mm of loose fill, has a low 'U' value of 0·85.

Walls

Wall structure may be one of three types: solid walls of brick or stone; cavity walls with one brick wall and an inner leaf, either of brick, building or aggregate block; or an outer brick leaf with an inner 'dry' plasterboard or similar lining. This latter type of construction is often found in frame houses.

The method of insulating a solid wall is by fixing the insulant materials to the inner skin. Heat loss will be cut and cold surfaces on which condensation forms will be warmer.

Materials

Polystyrene This resembles wallpaper, is barely 2mm thick and is hung with a special adhesive. Quite fragile, it dents easily but insulates the wall and raises the surface 'touch' temperature.

Aluminium foil-back paper can be used in the same way. These materials are applied in a similar manner to ordinary wallpaper–cut with scissors or a trimming knife and the rolls butt-jointed and fixed with an adhesive.

Polystyrene tiles can also be used but they are more commonly fixed to ceilings. Polystyrene tiles should never be painted with gloss paint as thus treated they represent a fire hazard.

They are best painted with an emulsion or fire-retardant paint. Many of these tiles are now of the self-extinguishing, fire-resistant type. Special adhesives are made for fixing polystyrene tiles. It should be applied evenly over the backs to inhibit the spread of flame.

Insulating boards These consist of polyurethane or polystyrene sandwiched between a variety of materials and may be backed with aluminium foil.

Wood cladding This is a natural insulator, makes not only a good insulant surface but also provides an attractive decorative appearance. The method of fixing is to nail the board to battens screwed to the wall. Added protection would be provided by a layer of **mineral-wool quilting** fixed behind the battens.

Fitted units, particularly in bedrooms, provide good insulation but if these are on the inside of exposed walls it is sensible to line the backs with expanded polystyrene sheets or slabs which also help to reduce condensation. These cupboards should be ventilated by drilling holes at the top and bottom of the doors.

Cavity filling Cavity walls can be filled with 'liquid' insulating material. This may be mineral wool, urea-formaldehyde, polyurethane or other insulating products. The material is injected into the wall, under high pressure, using special machines.

Holes are first drilled at intervals in the structure, to remove a core from the brick. The nozzle of a high-pressure pumping machine is inserted into the hole and the material forced into the cavity.

Once the nozzle is removed the brick plug is replaced and remortared to blend in with the original surface.

This work is carried out by specialist firms. This method is increased in its effectiveness if the inner wall is of cellular building blocks which have high thermal properties.

A 75mm thick cellular building block has the same insulating value as a 325mm thickness of ordinary bricks.

Thermal plaster also adds to the heat-retaining qualities of a wall.

Floors

Floors are of two types: suspended floors, timber-boarded floors laid on joists, or solid concrete laid on to a waterproof membrane. In some very old properties the floor may be laid directly on to subsoil.

A suspended floor has a 'U' value as high as 2·71 and can be a considerable area of heat loss. There must, of course, be underfloor ventilation to combat timber decay, but draughts blow up through badly fitting floorboards and gaps between the skirting and floorboards.

If you have to lift floorboards to fit central-heating pipe runs or electrical wiring, a quilt of 13mm insulating material or aluminium foil-backed paper can be laid across the joists to provide an insulant layer.

The entire floor may be covered with hardboard if floorboards are unlikely to be

Micafil vermiculite is raked to depth of 50mm–75mm, using home made gauge

Glass-fibre wrap is unrolled between joists. Wear protective gloves to handle

A hot-water cylinder should be lagged. This jacket has glass-fibre filling

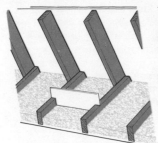

Loose fill Loose-fill material, polystyrene, cork, vermiculite or Rockwool are ideal for infilling between joists with irregular centres. Pour material to a depth of 50mm–75mm, levelling and raking it. **Value** 0·567–0·852

Blanket Blanket material of glass, mineral or Rockwool material laid between joists. Material from 25mm–100mm thick. **Values:** 25mm 0·908 100mm 0·454.

Blanket Glass, mineral, slag or Rockwool or eel-grass quilt, a 25mm thick blanket laid loosely across the joists. Lap by about 25mm and tuck down carefully at eaves. Does away with need to insulate pipes separately beneath blanket. **Value:** 0·795.

External brick walls (cavity or solid) An unventilated cavity wall, with an inner brick leaf, plastered, has a **'u' value** of 1·476-1·703 w/m2°C. A block inner skim of 100mm decreases the **'u' value** to 0·956 w/m2°C, varying with the density of the block. A solid, 225mm wall, with internal plastering, has a **'u' value** of 2·089 w/m2°C.

Insulation fixed to the wall Rigid insulation board or polystyrene can be fixed either directly to wall surfaces and plastered over or to sound plaster. Skim-coated polystyrene, of 25mm–50mm, has a **'u' value** of 1·079. Fixed to a 225mm wall, the **'u' value** is 1·306. Fibreboard, 25mm–50mm thick, has a **'u' value** of 1·192.

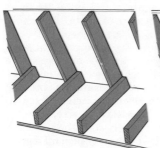

Ceiling tile or sheet Plasterboard, acoustic tile, insulated board, polystyrene, urethane, cork or asbestos, in tile or sheet form. Decorative or finished surface can be glued or pinned to existing roof. Useful on flat roofs or where loft is difficult to insulate.

Reflective foil Flat/corrugated sheets, 25mm–50mm, in rolls, laid over joists. Allow an overlap and staple foil to joists. Secure at eaves. Where laid, allow slight droop. **Value:** 1·192.

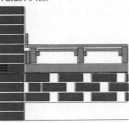

Board materials Insulating boards, 25mm, capable of supporting floor loads, can be laid over joists. This involves re-fixing skirtings, doors, fitted furniture. A better method is to cut the board to fit between joists, supported on treated battens. **Value:** 0·965-1·079.

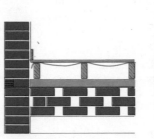

Floor insulation A simple method of underfloor insulation. Ideally should be used with tongued-and-grooved floorboards as foil is rendered ineffective by dust. **Values:** Paper-reinforced foil, double sided: 1·420. Combined corrugated and plain foil: 0·852-1·249.

Boards fixed to battens Insulating board fixed to 25mm × 50mm battens give a cavity of still air which is a good insulator. The **'u' value** of foil-backed plasterboard, 6mm thick, unskimmed, is 1·079. Fibreboard, skim coated and 25mm-50mm thick, has a **'u' value** of 0·965.

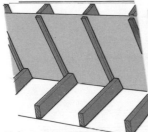

Reflective aluminium foil Reinforced foil used to insulate whole roof space. Should be pinned or stapled. **Value:** 1·306. Value can be reduced to 1·022 by fixing plasterboards on battens over foil.

Board Whole roof-space insulation achieved by fixing insulation board, cork, foil-backed plasterboard, asbestos, urethane, polystyrene to rafters. Example: 25mm polystyrene gives a **value** of 0·908.

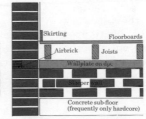

Floor insulation Blanket insulation should be draped over joists. Adjacent lengths should be butted. Nail down floorboards to compress material over joists. Board may need chamfering to fit under skirtings or doors. **Value:** 0·852-1·022, dependent on blanket thickness.

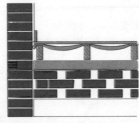

Solid floors A solid-concrete ground floor in contact with the earth or subfloor has a **'u' value** of 1·13. A wood-block surface decreases this to 0·85. Ventilated wood floor. The traditional timber floor on sleeper walls has a **'u' value** of between 2·71 and 1·42. Do not block up ventilation grilles or air bricks

Semi-rigid boards Resin-bonded, wool-type materials, formed into semi-rigid insulation slabs. Varying thicknesses are laid between 25mm × 50mm treated battens. The slabs are then covered with plasterboard. Slab 25mm thick has a **'u' value** of 0·795.

Insulation blankets Insulation or wool blankets fixed over wall battens 25mm × 50mm thick. A second layer of 25mm × 50mm battens are fixed for application of the plasterboard. 75mm-100mm blanket has a **value** of 0·738; 225mm wall and reinforced foil: 0·852.

Cavity-insulation foam Granulated Rockwool or urea-formaldehyde foam, injected under pressure through holes drilled in external walls. Improved **'u' value** about 0·567.

---

lifted frequently. This not only excludes draughts but provides the necessary first base needed for many floor coverings.

Any gap between skirting and floorboards may be filled with a piece of quadrant fixed firmly to the floor—not to the skirting board as there may be floor movement.

Large gaps between boards can be filled with thin pieces of wood or with a proprietary cellulose filler mixed with a little PVA adhesive. This can be rubbed down when dry and stained to match the boards.

Even folded pieces of newspaper pushed between gaps in floorboards will cut draughts and improve insulation.

Solid floors have a lower 'U' value– 0·20. Additional comfort can be gained by careful choice of carpeting. Use the best-quality underlay and the thickest carpet you can afford or, possibly, one of the newer foam-backed vinyl floor coverings.

'U' values
These are the 'U' values of various types of floors:

- Wood floors on joists: 2·71 to 1·42
- Parquet or lino over floorboards on joists: 1·42
- Thermoplastic tiles on concrete: 1·13
- Wood blocks on concrete: 0·85

Roof space
There are two ways of insulating the loft space. You can either insulate between the joists on the floor of the roof space or between the rafters on the ceiling of the area.

Unless you wish to use the loft space as a work room or it is to be converted for extra living space, the easier method is to lay insulant material between the joists.

Polystyrene, slab or granulated, vermiculite fill, eel-grass, mineral wool, glass fibre, felted wool or vegetable fibre and cork, compressed in slab form or in particles can be used.

Glass fibre
Where joists run at even widths, glass-fibre matting can be laid between or over the joists. This can be cut with household scissors. Protective gloves should be worn as minute glass-fibre particles may irritate the skin.

Rolls of insulant matting are made in various lengths and, when laid, should be 25mm at least wider than the space between joists so that no part of the ceiling is left exposed.

When laying the matting over joists, use 1m wide matting and overlap the edges by at least 75mm. Drape the matting over the end of the joists to prevent draughts getting underneath.

Loose fill
Expanded polystyrene, mineral wool, vermiculite and cork are obtainable as loose-fill materials in particle or in pellet form.

These are poured between joists to a depth of about 50mm. As the material is poured, it should be raked level with a timber template cut to the depth and width of the joist space. Do not compress the material.

The ends of the joists can be sealed with building paper but do not block any air vents as this may cause condensation. Once laid, loose-fill material is quite stable.

Mineral wool
Mineral wool is available in semi-rigid slabs which can be laid between joists. The

depth of insulation depends on the type of home heating you have.

The more heat produced in the house, the more is lost through the roof space, and, therefore, the greater depth of insulation needed.

Foil-backed lining

The second method is to insulate the gaps between rafters. Attach foil-backed insulating felt or bitumen-backed paper between the rafters. Apart from cutting down on heat loss, this will help to keep the roof area clean. Slabs of expanded polystyrene can be placed between the rafters.

Lagging

It is important to realize that if you insulate the floor of the roof space you then create a much colder roof area. The warm air from the house is no longer rising to fill the space.

Therefore, it is important to lag all pipework and plumbing services located in the loft. Pipe coverings are made to fit standard pipe sizes.

They are either rigid, of glass fibre, cork, mineral wool or expanded plastic, or flexible, of synthetic rubber, expanded polystyrene or foamed polyurethane. These 'sleeves' fit round the pipework.

Each section should be overlapped, taking care that joints and entry points to the storage cistern are covered.

Such lagging materials can be cut with scissors and secured at intervals with tape or string.

Cisterns and hot-water cylinders should be insulated. Lagging sets consist of panels of expanded polystyrene, compressed insulant board or glass-fibre jackets.

Another method of insulating a cistern is to construct a case of chipboard, leaving a 50mm–70mm gap round the sides and at the top, filling the space with loose-fill insulant material.

Do not put insulant materials under the cold-water storage cistern. The trickle of heat from below will avoid freezing when the outside temperatures fall.

Any pipes positioned between the joists can be covered with loose-fill material or matting.

Draughts

Draughts can cause needless discomfort but can be greatly reduced. A completely air-tight home, though almost impossible to achieve, would be very uncomfortable. There have to be regular air changes to remove stale air.

Movement of air within a building is caused by outside wind pressure and warm air, which rises, filling the colder areas.

Doors and windows

The main sources of draught are from ill-fitting windows and doors and, in homes with open fires, the chimney. A fire must have air in order to burn but a great deal of heat can be saved by fitting a chimney throat restrictor.

It is very important to realize that insulation does not mean no ventilation, as all solid fuel and gas appliances need a balanced free flow of air. An electric fire should be placed in front of the chimney opening to prevent loss of heat up the chimney.

Draught excluders

The gap round a door through which heat is lost and draughts come in can be very large indeed. Under-door draughts can be cured by a draught excluder.

There are two basic types: the coupled draught excluder, which is fitted to the door, and the threshold type, fitted to the floor or door frame.

The coupled draught excluder works on a drop-bar principle, in which a bar of metal, wood felt or plastic adjusts to different floor levels, forming an effective seal when the door is closed. The bar rises as the door is opened, clearing the carpet.

An excluder made of felt rides more easily over uneven surfaces. Some draught excluders can be fitted into a groove made under the door but this is a longer job as the door must be removed first.

Threshold excluders are made of metal, wood or plastic. They are fixed with screws, panel pins or adhesive. This type of excluder is usually chamfered or shaped to prevent the hazard of tripping.

Coupled excluders suitable for either internal or external doors are available. For external doors a metal extruder with a water bar should be used.

Metal stripping

Another method of insulating the door surround is to use sprung metal strips, made of either aluminium or bronze. These are fixed around the door frame and then 'sprung' outwards so that the metal strip presses against the door when it closes to form a seal. A metal threshold seal on the door sill is also needed.

It is possible to fit 'sprung' metal strip windows, but it can be an expensive business. Some cheaper and effective methods of stopping draughts include foam rubber or plastic which is fixed to the frame usually with adhesive.

Some foam rubber strip has self-adhesive backing; you merely peel off a strip of protective paper and press the foam rubber into place. The surface must be grease-free and dry to ensure good adhesion.

Type and description	Use
Expanded polystyrene Thicknesses vary from 6mm to 75mm or more. Normally supplied in slab form and is a spongy, plastic material. Breaks or damages easily; needs handling with care. Usually flame resistant. Available in sheet or tile form; supplied also in thin form in rolls.	Lagging cold-water cisterns; insulating ceilings; as underlay for wallpaper (thin version).
Mineral wool and glass fibre Available in several forms: loose-fill, in bags; in matting, semi-rigid slabs, and as quilting. Can cause irritation to skin; is rot-proof. In slab form, fibres are held together with bonding agent.	Insulating attic floors (loose fill and mat); fixing to joists before putting up cladding (quilt); lagging cisterns (semi-rigid). Used for hot-water cylinder jackets.
Fibre building board In rigid sections and normally made from felted wool or other vegetable fibre. Can be nailed, screwed or glued and may be painted.	Fixing to joists, rafters and battens.
Felting Supplied in rolls; impervious to fungicidal attack, although jute felt is susceptible under damp conditions; generally combustible.	Nailing to battens before fixing cladding; fixing to rafters and joists.
Compressed straw A natural insulator; susceptible to fungus in damp; may be treated to give flame resistance; easy to cut; can be pinned or nailed.	Lagging cold-water cisterns; fixing to battens and rafters.
Cork Available in loose fill or in slab form; can be plastered or painted and used between two sheets of plywood or plasterboard.	Insulating attic floors (granulated); slab form is suitable for insulating walls or attics.
Gypsum Intended for inside use; can be painted or plastered. Obtainable in loose-fill form; possesses only moderately good insulation properties.	Used for insulating roof slope, ceilings and so on; loose-fill suitable for attic floors.

A good basis to start from

The surface quality of a finished floor is only as good as that of the sub-floor beneath. There are various types of floor surface and a variety of ways to renew or merely reinforce these. Whether you renew worn areas or provide a base for a decorative surface, an even and properly prepared sub-floor is important.

NUFLOOR LIMITED BASILDON ESSEX ENGLAND

Sub-floors consist of two types:
Solid – concrete tiles or stone floor and
Suspended – timber boards or sheets fixed
to timber joists.

Solid floors

Solid floors provide an excellent base for
any type of wood flooring but must be dry
and level. Any problems of dampness must
be cured, at source, before a new floor is
laid. An uneven surface may need rescreeding.

Minor irregularities in level can be
rectified by using a proprietary self-
levelling compound.

Suspended floors

Suspended floors may present more problems than solid floors. Even a sound surface will tend to move, as wood expands
and contracts with the fluctuation of the
moisture content in the air. Normally,
this movement can be offset by laying a
covering floor skin, such as hardboard.

Chipboard

If the floorboards are in a poor state of
repair they may need completely renewing.
New tongued-and-grooved or square-edged
boards can be laid, but a flooring grade of
chipboard, 19mm thick, is worth con-
sidering. Chipboard consists of wood chips,
bonded and consolidated with resin, under
heat and pressure. The result is a hard-
wearing surface which is quick to lay and
can appear attractive when sealed with a
clear polyurethane varnish which provides a hard, durable finish.

First, remove old, worn floorboards.
Check the condition of joists and replace
damaged sections as necessary. Measure
the centres of the joists, as the width will
determine the size of chipboard sheet you
use. The edge of each chipboard section
must fit along the joist centres.

To fix down the ends, you may have to
insert cross pieces, or noggins, between
the joists. These are angle nailed through
the joists with 75mm wire nails. At the
end of a wall, the nails are driven in at an
angle through the noggins into the joists.

Careful measurement of a room is
needed to establish how many whole and
part sheets are needed to ensure the most
economical floor coverage.

Before laying chipboard, any projecting screw heads or brads should be removed or knocked down and the top of
the joists cleaned, so that the new board
will fit evenly. At the borders of rooms,
chip back plaster projections with a
bolster and a club hammer.

Chipboard is fixed with 50mm countersunk screws at 300mm intervals along the
board edges. At adjacent edges, stagger
the position of the screws to even stress.
Work round each section, partly driving
in each screw. Go round again and finally
screw down. This ensures that boards go
down evenly.

Flooring-grade chipboard can also be
laid over badly worn and uneven floorboards. Prepare the floorboards, using a
rotary sanding machine if necessary and
nail the chipboard to the flooring with
75mm wire nails.

Hardboard

Hardboard also provides a firm base over
worn floorboards. The boards must be
fixed securely and smoothed down to
remove any ridges or irregularities. Before
securing a hardboard surface to a floor,
ensure that wiring or pipe runs remain
accessible.

Flooring-grade hardboard 5mm–6mm
thick, should be used. Where floors are
subjected to humid or damp conditions,
oil-tempered hardboard should be used.
Standard hardboard can be tempered by
sponging or brushing the mesh side of the
surface with water to allow the boards to
expand to their fullest extent.

Place the sheets back to back, and
leave them for 48 hours before fixing.
Boards should be fixed with 13mm hardboard nails at 150mm centres.

If there is likely to be any movement on
the sub-floor, nail it down securely before
fixing the hardboard. Make sure the joints
between the hardboard sheets do not
coincide with those between underlying
floorboards.

Hardboard can be nailed down or
screwed. If it is to be screw fixed, pre-drill
for the screws but do not counter-sink.

Another method of fixing is to use a
suitable grade of flooring adhesive to
stick down the hardboard to the sub-floor
which must be clean and free from dust
or grease.

Before fixing hardboard to a concrete
screed, again ensure that the surface is
clean and free from dust and grease. Worn
areas can be built up with a self-levelling
compound or a filler consisting of a 1:3
cement: fine sand mix with one part of
PVA adhesive, diluted with three parts of
water. Trowel on the mixture and feather
off the edges.

Apply adhesive to the backs of the hardboard sheets, taking care to cover edges
and corners. It is not essential to cover
the back of the sheet entirely. Once in
position, the sheet should be weighted
down until adhesion is complete.

On new concrete screeds, hardboard
may be laid after allowing two to three
weeks for drying out. Ensure that the surface is free from dust, apply adhesive and
then position the hardboard.

Floorboards in good condition can be
rubbed down and treated with polyure-

thane varnish, to provide an attractive
floor finish. First, nail boards down securely and fill small gaps with papier
mâché filler.

Sanding machines

A large area can be smoothed down with
a hired sanding machine. The machine has
a bag to collect the dust and various
grades of sanding sheets are supplied
with it.

Preparation of the area before sanding
is important; check that all the floorboards are secure, and punch down any
nail heads and remove tacks or remnants
of floor covering.

A floor sander will remove varnish, old
paint, stains, grease and dirt from any
type of wood.

If, however, the floor has a very thick
paint covering, remove this with a proprietary stripper and scraper. Thick paint
will clog the sanding discs and be rubbed
back into the wood.

Using a coarse abrasive sheet on the
sanding drum, first work diagonally one
way across the room, and in both directions, if necessary. Change to a medium or
fine abrasive sheet and smooth the floor
in the direction of the floorboards.
Between each sanding operation, sweep
the floor clean.

Use an orbital sander, a drill attachment with a sanding disc or a hired edge
sander for awkward corners and near
skirtings. Rub down small difficult areas
with medium glass-paper wrapped over a
block of wood. Once the surface is completely stripped and dust free, apply clear
polyurethane varnish, stain or a sealant
to choice.

Sometimes it may be necessary to lay
a screed where a suspended floor has been
removed or where an old screed has been
hacked out. When laying a screed in place
of a suspended floor, ensure that there is
adequate underfloor ventilation for remaining rooms with suspended floors.

Damp-proof membranes

Before rescreeding, lay either a bituminous liquid or 500-gauge polythene
damp-proof membrane. In plastered rooms
chip away the bottom few millimetres to
expose the damp-course. The membrane

Self-levelling screed, such as Evode
levelling compound, used on solid floors

Floor sander enables uneven wood floors
to be smoothed. First use this diagonally

This is trowelled out to find its own
level. Surfaces should first be cleaned

The sander is next used down the centre
of floor boards; dust is collected in bag

An edge finisher can be used to smooth and to clean up the corners of a room

Royalboard floor-grade hardboard is put down in staggered formation

Apply self-adhesive tiles, such as Halstead on to a clean surface

To finish off in tight corners, an orbital sander can be used for light sanding

When laying tiles, work outwards from centre points from crossed diagonals

Overlap a tile on a tile and mark cut position with another tile when edging

must join or be cut into this.

A bituminous membrane is usually applied in two coats with a stiff broom. The first coat is diluted by some 25 per cent water, to make it easier to spread and ensure that the liquid flows in to all corners and crevices. Sweep the coating up the wall so that it finishes above the level of the DPC. Splashes can be wiped off plaster.

Allow the first coat to dry and apply a neat coat about 24 hours later and leave the floor for several days. Any traffic at this stage should be over temporary boards as the bitumen coat will lift if walked on.

Screeding

Prepare a 1:3 cement:sharp sand mix, using only a little water, until it is of the consistency of brown sugar. First, mix the sand and cement dry thoroughly, make a hole in the middle of the heap and add water sparingly.

You need some sections of straight timber, 1850mm long × 50mm × 25mm to provide screed rules. These are used to set out the screeding area in bays or sections, and are laid at intervals of about 1850mm. Place one rule along one wall, at your working height, or datum point; mark the height of this point, so that all levels are the same, around the room.

The rules should represent the height of the screed, so pack screed beneath the first to bring it to the correct height. Do the same with the second rule and check, with a spirit level, that this is level with the adjacent rule. If the level is short, rest this across a straight edge.

Next, fill up the bay with screed and, with a section of straight-edged timber, plane the screed smooth, using a to-and-fro action, with the timber rested on the rules. Work, section by section, towards a door

or window, so that you do not find yourself trapped at the wrong end of a newly screeded floor! Use a plank at least 1850mm wide, laid across the screed rules, to work from.

Work over short distances of about 1850mm. After finally checking levels, lift out each screed rule in turn and fill the holes left with screed.

Plane the screed surface overall with a wood float and finally polish smooth with a steel plasterer's or screeding trowel. Keep the blade damp to stop the surface from dragging, but take care not to make it too wet. The secret of a good finish is to keep the screed just damp.

Work across the room, returning to the starting wall for next and subsequent rows, completing the final section from outside a door or French window.

Allow at least a week before allowing light traffic. The surface may be dusted with sharp sand, which prevents the surface pulling up if it is walked on while still slightly tacky.

Choosing flooring

When choosing a vinyl or linoleum flooring, there are two considerations to keep in mind—the suitability of the flooring for the area to be covered, and the décor effect that will be achieved.

Suitability means that the flooring should be chosen with regard to the amount of wear to which it will be subjected. With so many qualities available, this is basically a matter of common sense. The greater the wear, the better the quality of product that should be used.

Soft floor furnishings, both sheet and tiles, come in various thicknesses, graded to give satisfactory wear in all areas of the home.

There are two basic types of smooth-surfaced flooring—**linoleum** and **vinyl**.

Linoleum

This is produced by blending together a number of natural products—cork, linseed oil, gum, resin, woodflour and colour pigments—which are rolled on to a compressed felt or canvas backing. The product is then left to mature.

The most basic material is felt base. The felt is saturated, treated, coated, printed and sealed. Felt base is economical to buy, but will not stand heavy wear.

A pattern that will not wear off is found in inlaid linoleum. Chips of linoleum are compressed into the material under great pressure. This flooring is very hard-wearing.

Another hard-wearing surface is pattern-inlaid linoleum. The pattern is made by cutting coloured linoleum shapes and placing them in various patterns on to the backing material. The design is then welded together, on to the backing material, with heated rollers. A three-dimensional textured effect can be imparted by embossing a basic inlaid linoleum.

Lino tiles

There are two types of lino tiles, both consisting of inlaid linoleum. Lino tiles can be used to create a variety of designs. The basic lino tile is loose laid; self-adhesive tiles have an adhesive bonded in to the backing and are stuck down after being dipped into hot water, to activate the adhesive, or peeling off a protective backing paper.

Vinyl

Vinyl is made of PVC (a resinous substance called polyvinyl-chloride) which is combined with a mixture of colour pigments, fillers and plasticizers.

This can be divided into two main types, according to method of manufacture. In one, the pattern is printed on to the vinyl and sealed by a layer of pure PVC. The second method is to inlay the pattern into the material.

An inexpensive vinyl floor covering is felt-backed vinyl. The pattern is printed on to the felt backing and covered with a coat of PVC. Patterned vinyl gives a strong, flexible floor covering. The pattern is printed on and covered with PVC. This is a hard-wearing surface for use in heavy traffic areas, such as kitchens and bathrooms.

Particles of contrasting vinyl, are pressed, under heavy rollers, into vinyl sheet to give the marbled effects of vinyl sheeting.

A resilient, vinyl flooring is produced by backing vinyl sheeting with a latex foam or thick wool-felt backing. This gives a comfortable, quiet and resilient floor covering.

Vinyl is also used in tile form. Flexible vinyl tiles, some of which can be cut with scissors, are made in a range of thicknesses and qualities.

Rigid vinyl tiles, also known as vinyl-asbestos tiles, are very tough, hard and durable. These are made of vinyl, reinforced with a mineral filler. They are suitable in areas subjected to very heavy wear.

How to beat damp
and condensation

Damp and condensation are twin spectres, which often go hand in hand to cause damage to fabric, furniture and fittings in the home. Much can be done to relieve the problems by abating the conditions causing condensation and eliminating structural and related problems which allow damp to penetrate the structure.

Rising damp
This often occurs in older structures without a damp-proof course (DPC), or where an existing DPC has broken down. Water rises from the ground and, through capillary action, is absorbed into porous brickwork and through the plaster. The result is a band of staining, usually at skirting level, paper peeling from the walls and effloresence – mineral salts drawn out on to the exterior brickwork surface.

Timber joists and floorboards adjacent to the failed dampcourse area may be affected by wet or dry rot.

Treatment
It is necessary either to renew, repair or insert a damp-proof course, or to use a suitable proofing alternative. DPCs should be some 150mm above exterior ground level. They can be inserted by the following methods:

Cutting out
By cutting out one section of brickwork at DPC level at a time. A chain saw is needed to cut through brickwork. Insert a layer of bituminous felt or slates encased between layers of waterproof concrete. The slates are overlapped in an under-and-over arrangement.

DPCs can be made of hard engineering bricks. Work around the building, cutting out a section at a time, mortaring the bricks in place and then making good. These bricks are impermeable and resist the passage of water. This is an involved and skilled job.

Silicone injection
Where cutting out is not a practical proposition an injected DPC can be used. Drill holes at intervals of 230mm, using 12mm or 25mm masonry drills, at an angle of 45°. Stagger the holes 100mm above floor level along the brickwork. This work can be done either internally or externally.

It may be necessary to hack back any wet plasterwork and remove skirting boards. The method of treatment varies slightly between systems. Silicone, water-resistant liquid can either be injected into the holes under pressure, a method usually carried out by specialist firms, or allowed to drip in to the wall, a method you can use yourself.

In this method, 570ml bottles, containing the silicone liquid, are inverted, placed in the holes and the liquid is allowed to permeate the wall interior. This solution will seep into the brickwork until saturation level is reached, when no more will flow from the bottle.

Bottles that empty quickly should be refilled as this indicates a natural internal cavity that must be filled.

Once a protective silicone layer is formed, the reverse of capillary action occurs. The surface tension created by the barrier forces rising dampness down.

Electro-osmosis
Where cutting out or drilling are not possible, such as with thick walls or along party walls, a process called electro-osmosis can be used. This is done by specialist companies.

Copper wiring or a ribbon of copper are inserted into the walls at DPC level. These are connected to copper earth rods set in the soil.

This method utilizes the fact that an electrical charge exists, associated with the moisture rise, between the wall and the earth. The copper ribboning and earth-rods, placed carefully, create a low-resistance circuit between the soil and building.

The electricity is discharged to earth. Damp cannot rise above this charge and the walls dry out as the moisture evaporates.

Damp-proof courses
Damp patches on the inner walls of cavity walls may appear because the DPC has been broken or bridged. Earth should not be piled up against external walls above the DPC level, as the DPC becomes ineffective and there is no barrier to prevent moisture from rising up the walls. This may need only removal of débris, piled higher than the DPC.

Problems such as a break in the DPC or a mortar-encrusted brick tie in a cavity wall require drastic treatment. Sections of brickwork in the area of damp will have to be cut out to insert a repair section of bitumen felt to a DPC or for access to a dirty brick tie.

Floors laid directly on to earth, without a damp-proof membrane, may give trouble. This can be temporarily remedied by covering the floor with a damp-inhibiting epoxy-pitch resin. If this fails, you will have to lift the old floor and lay a new floor over a bituminous, liquid membrane or a sheet of heavy-duty, 500-gauge polythene sheeting.

Whichever method is used, make sure the waterproof layer reaches at least 150mm, preferably cut into the horizontal DPC where this exists, up the walls to form an efficient seal.

Condensation
Air always contains a certain amount of water vapour, which is a true gas. Water vapour gets into the air as liquid water vaporizes. This occurs as air takes up heat by conduction, convection or radiation from its surroundings.

If, however, the heat is removed from the vapour, it condenses–that is, reverts to its liquid state.

Air can only retain a limited quantity of water vapour in its gaseous state, and this quantity depends on the temperature of the air–the warmer it gets, the more vapour it can hold. As soon as the maximum is reached, the excess water vapour turns back into liquid water, usually on cooler surfaces such as walls, windows and ceilings.

The air is said to be 'saturated' when it cannot hold any further water vapour, and the temperature at which this happens is the 'dew point'.

Condensation, therefore, results from a loss of heat by vapour, causing its temperature to fall below dew point. Its effect is simply to concentrate and make visible a quantity of dispersed and hitherto invisible water, present in the air in the form of a gas.

A simple example is the bedroom window which, on cold, damp, winter mornings, may be running with water. This happens because human breath emits a considerable quantity of moisture, so condensation forms on the window, a cold surface. This can only be cured by ventilation–opening a window or using an extractor fan.

The presence of condensation depends on three factors.

First, the amount of water vapour released into the air inside the home.

Second, the temperature of the air, of walls, ceilings and windows, because on these depends the amount of water vapour that can remain in the air.

Third, ventilation because it enables moisture-laden air to be carried away and replaced with drier air.

Many of the problems of excessive condensation are not the fault of the people in a building, but due to faulty planning and design.

Certain kinds of plaster and building materials cannot allow water vapour to pass through them, and create a build-up of vapour inside the home. The lack of effective wall or roof insulation keeps these surfaces cold, this cools the adjacent air, so condensation results. Adequate ventilation is essential to reduce the level of condensation.

Intermittent heating, as happens with some forms of thermostatically controlled central heating, can also cause condensation. Inside surfaces have no real chance to warm up, and moisture vapour, released in the warmed air, condenses on these cold surfaces.

The weather may also influence condensation. If there is a sudden rise in temperature, combined with dampness, streaming condensation on walls and windows may occur as they are slower to warm up than the surrounding air. Spasmodic or irregular heating may not warm a house fabric sufficiently, in cold conditions, to 'lift' wall surface temperatures.

Reducing condensation
Condensation can be avoided by supplying a constant level of heat, introducing ventilation and by carrying out a thorough programme of insulation in the home.

A combination of warm, inner surfaces including walls and ceilings and warm air should eradicate condensation as a persistent nuisance.

The intermittent, concentrated outbreaks that occur during activities such as cooking and running a bath, usually require some form of extra ventilation.

The easiest method is to open a window, but an extractor fan is more efficient and will quickly remove the saturated air without creating draught.

In an average-sized kitchen or bathroom, a 150mm domestic fan will probably be sufficient, but in a large room, two correctly positioned units, with the capacity to deal with the air changes required, may be more efficient.

All extractor fans should be installed as high as possible in a wall or window and as near sources of steam as possible.

Louvred windows, a series of adjustable glass slats, aid controlled ventilation. Operated similarly to Venetian blinds, they can be opened to the extent necessary to provide sufficient ventilation, while the slats can be angled to prevent cold draughts. A simple device that will often cope with 'minor' condensation problems is the plastic window grille, which is activated by air pressure.

Condensation can often be reduced by following a few basic rules:

When running a bath, or carrying out the weekly wash, keep the door closed so that steam does not disperse to other parts of the home.

Always try and minimize the 'escape' of any steam by enclosing hoses to washing machines. Trap the hose under the lid and always keep the lid in place while the machine is working.

To help prevent the formation of condensation when running a bath, first run a small amount of cold water before drawing off the hot.

To overcome condensation problems altogether, if practical to do so, fix a hose to the hot tap so that the water is fed under the layer of cold.

Surface damage
Condensation can, of course, cause both structural and surface damage, as well as being very unsightly. It often creates the conditions in which various damaging and unsightly moulds can grow.

It is possible to increase the resistance of the structure to heat loss, so that any heat generated is used effectively, fuel bills are reduced and temperatures within the home are kept steady. This greatly reduces the likelihood of condensation.

Holes are drilled at 45° angle at 200mm intervals for Wykamit DPC fluid treatment

Filled bottles are then inverted into the holes for wall to absorb DPC liquid

Exteriors of porous walls can be treated with silicone fluid applied with a spray

Electro-osmosis inverts capillary action of water through low-charged copper strip

Mortar-encrusted brick tie may form a bridge, causing inner-wall damp entry

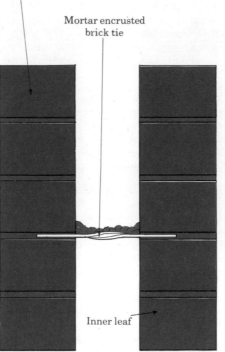

Outer leaf

Mortar encrusted brick tie

Inner leaf

A chain saw is used to cut a slot into brickwork to insert a DPC, such as slate

Strip is looped into holes in wall and electrode is earthed via a junction box

barrier, such as polythene sheeting, between the joists, before laying the insulating material.

Cavity walls

The walls form about 85 per cent of the external vertical surface of a house, while 15 per cent consists of windows and door openings. Walls are vulnerable heat-loss areas.

Modern homes are built with cavity walls, consisting of either two brick leaves or a brick outer and building-block inner leaf. The cavity prevents water from reaching the inner walls, but in doing so, the free-moving air, circulating in the cavity, carries away the heat.

A cavity wall is a poor insulator. The thermal qualities can be improved by filling the cavity with a material such as mineral wool or urea foam, which is injected under pressure. These treatments are carried out by specialist firms. This type of insulation raises the 'touch temperatures' of the inner wall and helps to reduce condensation.

Solid walls

In houses with solid walls, the problem of overcoming condensation or the mould growth, often apparent in damp conditions, is more difficult.

A simple preventative method is to line the walls, before papering or finish decorating, with a polystyrene wallpaper. This layer, about 2mm thick, is supplied in rolls. Also suitable for this type of lining is aluminium foil-backed paper. Both types raise the touch temperatures.

A more substantial inner skin consists of dry lining. This is in the form of cladding with insulating material such as preformed insulating board. This type of cladding is nailed on to battens fixed to the wall. To provide extra insulation, a layer of mineral wool quilting can be fixed behind the battens.

The board used should have its own built-in vapour barrier. This is necessary because condensation can occur in the middle of a 'cold' wall; and the water will then work its own way back to the warmer inner face and appear as a damp patch.

Wood cladding is a good natural insulant and provides a decorative surface. Its insulant properties can be further increased by using mineral quilting behind battens to fix this.

Insulation

Insulation here means the resistance to the passage of heat from the inside of the house to the outside atmosphere. The most common ways of achieving this are roof insulation, cavity-wall insulation, double-glazing and floor lining.

There are some vital points concerning roof insulation. Many people overlook the possibility that condensation may occur in the roof area after efficient roof insulation has been completed. Because of the decrease in air temperatures in an insulated loft, and the fact that water vapour will be moving up from the house into the loft area through ceilings, ventilation is neces-

sary in the loft area. This should equal one 900th of the roof area and should be in the form of cross ventilation.

While ventilation usually exists naturally, careful consideration should be given to this point. Sometimes, air outside the house is so heavily weighted with humidity that any additional water vapour entering the loft from outside will cause an acceptable level of humidity to be exceeded, resulting in condensation forming within the loft area.

There are two solutions: Either to fix the insulation material on to the rafters so that the loft area benefits from the heat from the house, or to fix a water-vapour

Floors

Floor insulation is most easily achieved by laying carpet with the appropriate underlay. However, where thermo-plastic floors are used, problems can occur since, in any room, the lowest temperature is at floor level. Therefore, if the floor itself is cold, condensation may result because a low temperature causes the water vapour in the air to condense on its surface.

The only solution may be to relay the floor, using a material, such as cork, or foam-backed sheet flooring, both of which have higher insulant properties. These will be warmer underfoot and raise the surface temperature.

Curing woodworm and dry rot

Wood under attack is always a cause for alarm. Wet and dry rot, and woodworm, may cause fundamental damage. The signs of attack, once spotted, should be dealt with immediately, eradicating affected areas, replacing, as necessary, with new wood and treating to prevent further unseen encroachment.

Woodworm

The term, woodworm, refers to the larvae of several species of wood-boring beetles which are able to digest the substance of wood. The adult beetle lays eggs on the rough surface of unpolished wood and the grubs which hatch out bore into the timber. These leave no sign of entry, and tunnel inside the wood, for as long as up to ten years.

When ready to pupate, the larvae make a pupal chamber just below the surface of the wood. The adult beetles then bite their way out, leaving tell-tale 'flight holes'.

Piles of white wood dust, or 'frass', on horizontal surfaces, will indicate where the grubs have been active above, and close examination will reveal the flight holes, which vary from 2mm to 4mm across.

Sapwood, which is used in a high proportion of modern building, is particularly susceptible to attacks, and because of their generally small dimensions, modern rafters and joists may not readily withstand severe attack.

Treatment

Treatment of structural timbers in a house can be carried out by one of the specialist firms, which guarantees work for 20 years and offers a free survey and estimate. If, however, you decide to treat an attack yourself, remember it is no use just treating the area where you see woodworm holes; other larvae may be active but unseen in the adjacent timbers.

Thoroughness is the keynote to success in all timber treatment. For woodworm attacks in rafters, joists and flooring, apply woodworm fluid with a coarse spray using 5 litres to 18·50m² of surface area.

Estimating

To estimate the area of timber to be treated in a roof where the rafters have been boarded in under the tiles, find the area of each slope of the roof. Add the sums together and to this amount add twice the depth of a rafter, multiplied by its length and by the number of rafters.

If, however, the roof is not boarded, simply add the thickness of a rafter to twice its depth, then multiply by the rafter's length and by the number of rafters.

Use a similar procedure for the joists and purlins. A close-boarded roof of a detached house may work out as in the following example:

	m²
Two slopes each 9·15m × 3·66m	33·49
Gable end or hip-roof triangle (half base × height) 3·05m × 3·66m	11·16
50 rafters each 100mm deep × 3·66m long	18·30
50 joists each 100mm deep × 4·57m long	22·85
Total =	85·80

Allow a little more, say 90m², for purlins and gable-end rafters. At a coverage rate of 18·50m² per 5 litres, a minimum of 38 litres of fluid is needed, but if the timber is very dry, it may soak up more fluid.

Treatment may be carried out at any time of year and modern woodworm fluids, such as Rentokil, will destroy all stages of the woodworm's life cycle and prevent future attack, provided all timber surfaces are treated.

Before commencing treatment, all timbers must be thoroughly cleaned down to allow penetration of the fluids, and water cisterns should be covered throughout the entire treatment process.

Cistern lagging and roof insulation should be removed or protected from the fluid, and any exposed rubber-covered wiring cables should either be covered or coated with a polyurethane varnish before you start spraying.

Make certain any electrical wiring in the area to be sprayed is sound and well insulated. Never smoke during spraying and wear a pair of old leather or rubber gloves.

Eyes should be protected with suitable goggles and a light fume mask should be worn, to avoid the inhaling of vapour which builds up in the confined roof space.

Let us spray

The selection of a sprayer is important but the majority of garden sprayers are suitable provided they will maintain good pressure. Ideally, the unit should hold at least 5 litres and have a fairly coarse nozzle

⌃ A fungal growth which shows the
presence of wood rot; early attention is
necessary

which will produce a 'fan' spray pattern.
Suitable sprays may also be hired.

Too coarse a nozzle may result in excess
fluid staining the ceiling area; on the other
hand, a very fine nozzle will tend to vapor-
ize the spray, making the work unpleasant
and reducing the amount of fluid penetration into the timber. A 610mm-long extension line will also be required to reach into
the roof apex, eaves and any other less-
accessible areas.

If you are treating a floor against woodworm, take up every fourth or fifth floorboard, so that you can treat the joists beneath and the undersides of the boards.
Replace the boards and then thoroughly
treat the upper surface.

It is then necessary to cover the floor
area with a large sheet of polythene if you
wish to re-lay floor coverings immediately.
Alternatively, you may wait seven to 14
days for the surface of the timber to dry
out.

After treatment, floorboards will take
at least six months to dry out completely,
if they have been fully impregnated, and an
impermeable floorcovering, such as vinyl
tiles or sheet material, will be spoiled if
laid directly on them. A temporary floor-
covering should be used wherever possible.

Finally, if by accident during treatment
you stain plaster with fluid, leave it for a
few weeks to dry and if it still remains,
apply aluminium primer and then redecorate.

Dry rot

Fungi are living plants, of which there are
thousands of species, and over a dozen are
known to cause deterioration of timber.
Wood-decaying fungi reduce the weight of
the wood, spoil its appearance and take
away its strength. True dry rot is the name
given to the decay of timber brought about
by one particular species of wood-rotting
fungi, *merulius lacrymans*.

The term 'dry' is descriptive of the dry
and friable conditions to which the rotten
wood is reduced. Dry rot is often a symptom
of neglected maintenance or the conse-
quence of faulty design or construction of
buildings, because the fungi thrives only
in conditions of dampness and poor ventilation.

Dry rot cannot develop in wood containing less than about 25 per cent moisture, and the optimum moisture content for
its growth is probably between 30 and 40
per cent.

The characteristic signs of the decay by
which the dry-rot fungus can be identified
are:

Rust-red dust caused by gathering spores
from a fruiting body indicate an advanced
attack of some duration. The spores only
accumulate in still, unventilated conditions.

The characteristic yellow fruiting body,
or sporophore, of *merulius lacrymans*

≫ The effects of dry rot; great damage may be caused if this is not treated early

A covering of matted fungal strands external to the timber occurs as thin sheets of silvery-grey or mouse-grey appearance, tinged here and there with lilac patches; bright yellow patches may also occur. This type of fungal *hyphae* is known as *mycelium*.

In damp, humid conditions the mycelium grows rapidly. It is snowy white, rather like cotton wool, but where the edge of such *mycelium* comes into contact with drier air or exposure to light, it becomes bright yellow.

The specific name, *lacrymans*, refers to the characteristic it shows in damp conditions when in active growth. Innumerable globules of water sparkle in the light of a torch like a large number of teardrops –*lacrymans* means 'weeping'. The generic name, *merulius*, refers to the bright-yellow colouration which occurs on the mycelium, similar in colour to the beak of a male blackbird (*Merula*).

Wood decayed by the mycelium shows deep transverse and longitudinal fissures and the wood breaks up into cubes, sometimes of large dimensions. Such cracking is seen on the surface of the wood.

The wood becomes very light in weight, owing to the extraction of the cellulose by the fungal hyphae.

The wood becomes darker in colour, usually brown; it is friable when rubbed between the fingers; and the wood loses its characteristic fresh, resinous smell.

The appearance of a sporophore or fruiting body, which is thin and pancake-like, white round the edges, with the centre thrown into corrugation. The colour of the spores makes it rusty-red. When in active growth, the sporophore and the mycelium have a strong mushroomy smell.

A very important characteristic of *merulius lacrymans* is the ability of the fungus to produce water-carrying strands or *rhizomorphs*. These strands are formed from

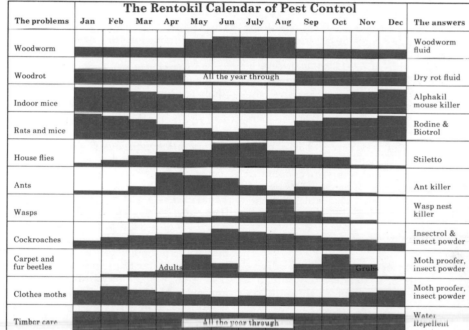

The problems	Jan	Feb	Mar	Apr	May	Jun	July	Aug	Sep	Oct	Nov	Dec	The answers
Woodworm					▓	▓	▓	▓					Woodworm fluid
Woodrot					All the year through								Dry rot fluid
Indoor mice	▓	▓	▓							▓	▓	▓	Alphakil mouse killer
Rats and mice	▓	▓				▓					▓	▓	Rodine & Biotrol
House flies					▓	▓	▓	▓	▓				Stiletto
Ants				▓	▓	▓				▓			Ant killer
Wasps						▓	▓	▓	▓				Wasp nest killer
Cockroaches						▓	▓	▓	▓				Insectrol & insect powder
Carpet and fur beetles				Adults						Grubs			Moth proofer, insect powder
Clothes moths			▓	▓	▓	▓	▓	▓	▓				Moth proofer, insect powder
Timber care					All the year through								Water Repellent

≫ This photograph, taken by x-ray, shows wood-boring larvae in action in timber

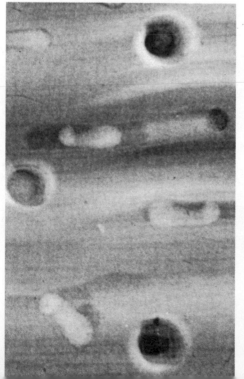

≫ Though apparently outwardly sound, the body of this timber has been eaten away

The woodworm grub feeds on the timber and leaves a pile of 'frass' behind it

hyphae and modified to form vein-like structures. They may be as large in diameter as a lead pencil.

The importance of the rhizomorph is that it conveys the water from wood, which has decayed to dry wood, elsewhere, the strands passing over brickwork, stone or metal.

It is in the hyphae constituting the rhizomorphs that food reserves are stored, so that even if the affected wood is taken away, the rhizomorph is still capable of further growth and infecting new wood. The rhizomorphs are also able to penetrate soft brickwork and mortar.

Wet rot
Outbreaks of wet rot, known generally as cellar fungus, or *coniophora cerebella*, are almost twice as frequent as those of dry rot, but are seldom as difficult to treat. Wet rot requires moister conditions than does dry rot, and the optimum water content for growth is between 50 and 60 per cent—hence its name. It is, therefore, sensitive to drying and all activity ceases when the source of moisture is removed.

The special characteristics by which cellar fungus, and the decay caused by it, can be identified are:

The fungal strands are never so thick as those of dry rot, seldom exceeding the diameter of thin string or twine. These strands are brownish or black, but when freshly produced, are yellowish-brown. The fungal strands, when growing on the surface of the wood or over damp plaster, often develop a dark fern-like shape. They are vein-like in appearance and are said to be similar to the blood-vessels of the cerebellum (part of the brain); hence the specific name. They do not penetrate into brickwork.

White mycelium is never produced by this species, either in the cottonwool or in the sheet form. The sporophore is rarely found in buildings, although it may be common out of doors. It consists of a thin plate, olive-brown in colour, of indefinite shape, covered with small tubercules.

The spores are rarely found indoors in any accumulation, but are so light that they are present almost everywhere in the air, consequently any timber in buildings with a sufficiently high moisture content is likely to be attacked by this species.

Other species of fungus also causing wet rot in buildings are the white pore fungus or mine fungus, *poria voillantii*, and *paxillus panuoides*, both of which attack only softwood.

Treatments
Dry rot
Any outbreak of dry rot needs prompt, thorough treatment. Defective plumbing, faulty damp-proof courses and blocked air bricks or similar faults must first be rectified. Also, replace any broken air bricks and clear blocked ones. If the house has been flooded, or burst pipes have soaked timbers, check that the wood has dried out thoroughly.

Even if the location of any outbreak may seem obvious, make a systematic inspection inside the house. Look for signs of surface buckling of the timber and test with a sharp knife or tool.

Inspect beneath the floorboards for the signs of decay listed earlier. If evidence of an attack is found, consider that point as being the centre of a sphere, having a radius of about 1m, and make an extremely close examination in every direction within this area.

Whenever continued evidence of decay is found, extend the 'sphere' principle of investigation until the limits of the attack have been found and the causes traced.

All timber in the affected area and 1m beyond the last visible evidence of decay must be cut away, provided this does not weaken the structure. If there is such a risk, seek expert advice. Any plasterwork or rendering coats which have been penetrated by the fungal strands should be removed.

The whole area of attack should be opened up, thoroughly cleaned down with a wire brush and the decayed material removed from the building by the shortest possible route.

All affected timber should be burned immediately and any plaster sprayed with a fungicide such as Rentokil Dry Rot Fluid. These measures are vital to avoid further infection spreading to other areas of the building.

If masonry is affected, drill a series of holes covering the contaminated parts at staggered centres to allow dry-rot fluid to saturate the affected area. It will then reach all possible mycelium within the masonry. Working from the highest level downwards, apply a good proprietary fungicidal fluid to all brick, block concrete and earth surfaces until they are saturated; 5 litres of fluid to 4·64m, for surface treatment, is normally adequate when applied with a coarse spray.

If the fungal strands have penetrated the brickwork or masonry, then both sides of the wall should be treated by the hole-drilling process.

All replacement timbers must be thoroughly treated with a fungicidal wood preservative, and the sawn ends steeped in the fluid for at least five minutes before installation. Any joist ends are best protected with fungicide, plus a coat of bituminous paint, before setting these into a wall.

Apply two liberal coats of fungicidal fluid to all timber surfaces adjacent to the area of cutting away, to a distance of 1·52m from the furthest extent of the cut-away timber. Allow the first coat to be absorbed before applying the second. Five litres per 18·58m² should be applied.

Allow any brickwork or masonry to dry out completely before redecoration or rerendering. It is advisable to apply a 6mm thick coat of zinc-oxychloride plaster over the rendering coat before applying the finishing coat of plaster.

This zinc-oxychloride coat should extend 300mm beyond the limits of the attack to inhibit fungal growth. Any areas not to be replastered, can also be treated with two coats of zinc-oxychloride paint.

Wet rot
The treatment of wet rot is less drastic than that required for dry rot, and as long as the cause of dampness is removed and the timber allowed to dry out, no further growth of the fungus will occur.

Test all the timbers in the area of fungal attack with a strong, pointed instrument to determine the extent of sub-surface breakdown. Cut out and burn all timber which has suffered surface or sub-surface breakdown due to fungal attack, together with any dust, dirt and general débris.

Select thoroughly dry, well-seasoned timber for replacement. Cut it to size and apply two liberal coats of dry-rot fluid on all the surfaces and also over the adjacent existing timbers, and on brick, block and concrete areas before replacement timbers are fitted. This pre-treatment of new timber is a vital part of any remedial work and must be carried out after the timbers have been cut to size.

If an extensive outbreak of rot is suspected—especially with dry rot—it is wise to consult a reliable specialist timber preservation company, which will conduct a free survey, submit an estimate and report without obligation, and issue a 20-year guarantee on completion of any work.

First aid for brick walls

Brightening the brickwork can give a new lease of life to the appearance of the home. It is, however, also important to be able to patch up or to replace damaged bricks, cure flaws and deterioration to bricks, joints and surfaces and to recognize the problems of settlement, as well as the lesser one of shrinkage.

Old pointing

Brickwork may occasionally need smartening up. This may mean no more than cleaning it down with a stiff broom and clean water. Mould or lichen can be removed with a mixture of one part of household bleach to four parts of clean water. Do not use detergent, as this may affect the face work of the brick. Difficult patches of dirt can be brushed down with a wire brush. Avoid rubbing too hard, however, as this may again damage the brick face.

Dull and faded brickwork can be brightened by one of the brick dyes. These lighten after a time and need renewing periodically.

Efflorescence

Efflorescence is a discolouration of white powder or feathery crystals, similar to damp salt, on the face of new brickwork or freshly plastered walls.

It forms because rainwater or water used in building a house soaks the brickwork and dissolves any soluble salts in it. The water evaporates, drawing the salt to the surface.

This does not damage brickwork but is unattractive. The walls can be brushed off periodically with a stiff-bristled broom. If you use a wire brush, avoid damaging bricks and pointing.

A neutralizing liquid can be applied to remove efflorescence. Using a 100mm brush, two or three coats of a proprietary preparation should be used, allowing about 15 minutes between applications.

Redecorating on interior walls can usually take place about a day after treatment.

A club hammer and cold chisel are the basic tools used to remove old mortar

You should not wash off efflorescence with tap water, since this usually contains chemicals which accelerate reappearance of salts.

Vegetable staining

Surrounding vegetation may also stain brickwork. First find the cause and remedy it, and then clean the brickwork with a stiff broom. It is wise to apply a coat of colourless fungicide. The wall should be treated in dry weather, so that the solution is not washed away by rain.

Rust

Rust is another discolouration which may appear on brickwork joints or around ironwork embedded in brickwork. Brickwork can flake and crack as a result of rust, so mortar around ironwork should be raked out. Clean the metal thoroughly and prime it. You may need to use a rust-neutralizing agent on the metal.

Rust in brick jointing occurs as a result of ironstone in the sand. The mortar will have to be raked out and repointed.

Replacing bricks

Brick is porous and takes in moisture in wet weather which evaporates when the weather is dry. On very porous bricks, water may accumulate inside and freeze. Ice expands and may cause the brick to crumble or 'spall' at the edges. The brick then ceases to offer resistance to the weather and should be replaced.

Use a club hammer and bolster to remove damaged bricks, but protect your eyes by wearing safety glasses. Cut back till you reach solid brick. Remove loose material with a wire brush and then cut back the mortar joints with a narrow cold chisel.

A matching half brick can be used to replace the damaged portion. This is called a queen closer–that is a brick cut in half along its length. You can cut a queen closer with a bolster and club hammer, working steadily around the brick until it comes apart into two halves.

Either cut the queen closer slightly undersize, or cut back to slightly more than half a brick. This allows a sufficient bed of mortar for the brick to fit flush with the existing bricks. Apply a bond of PVA adhesive to both faces, and mortar in place using a 1:3 mortar mix, plus a little PVA additive. Point finally once bricks have set.

Sometimes you may have to remove entire bricks. This is done by removing the pointing around the brick and using a narrow cold chisel to dislodge the brick.

You may also have to break out an old

Keyed pointing

The pointing tool enables a wide range of keyed finishes to be used on joints

Weathered pointing
Draw trowel down edge of brick on right

Press mortar into horizontal joints; use straight edge and trowel to trim

brick in sections in order to remove other bricks more easily.

Damaged brick at ground level or below should be removed after first being exposed by raking the soil clear.

Water repellent

It is also worthwhile treating a wall with a water repellent. This will ensure, in the case of porous bricks, that frost does not damage the brickwork again.

Once you have made good any damage, form a thin 'apron' of rendering about 150mm high along the front of the wall. Add a waterproofing liquid or powder to the mortar or a water repellent to the rendering mix.

Jointing

Before repointing badly deteriorated joints, lay a sheet of polythene down to collect mortar droppings. A plugging chisel and a club hammer are used to clear out old mortar from about 1m² of wall at a time. First clear vertical joints and then horizontal ones. Clear them to a depth of about 15mm, for any deeper may damage the wall.

Brush down the joints to remove dust and old mortar, and soak the brickwork, so that it does not absorb moisture from the new mortar.

Only mix up enough mortar for about two hours' work. Use a hawk, and first practise picking up mortar with a smooth upward sweep on the back of the trowel from the mix.

Make sure that new joints match the old. Weather-struck joints give maximum protection from damp and are advisable on chimneys and house walls.

With rough-textured bricks, recessed joints are attractive, but flush or rubbed joints look better with smooth-surfaced bricks.

With the weather-struck joint, a sloped surface allows rain to run off. The horizontal joint is recessed beneath the top brick and overhangs slightly the lower.

Push mortar into the joints, first into the uprights and then the horizontals, the top and then the bottom.

Form the slope on weather-struck joints as you go. With other joints, leave the mortar flush with the bricks. Weather-struck joints are trimmed at the horizontal joints with a pointing trowel.

Slope vertical joints to one side, matching the horizontal with the trowel. Use a small trowel or a 'Frenchman', a tool to cut off excess mortar at the bottom of the horizontal joints, in conjunction with a straight edge.

The straight edge acts as a guide while you run the Frenchman along with the angled tip pointing downwards. Once the mortar has set, brush off the area you have been working on. Repeat the process over the next square metre of working area.

To form a flush joint, let the mortar become semi-stiff and rub a piece of sacking along the joint in one direction to flush this with the brickwork. Brush off when dry.

A recessed joint is formed with a piece of metal with a pointed curved end. This can be made from a piece of metal bucket handle, using the inside bend to strike the joint. Use the pointing tool to scrape mortar from both vertical and horizontal joints to a depth of around 6mm. Rub down the joint gently with a piece of wood so that the surface is smooth and water-resistant.

In repointing you can add a vegetable dye or proprietary colourant to produce a matching or decorative effect. The colour will, however, be mutated by the texture of ordinary sand, so white sand should be used.

Settlement

This is a problem which may have been caused by imperfect foundations or movement of ground beneath the home. Common reasons are land on an unstable surface, such as an old rubbish tip, or building on clay subsoil, which moves in accordance with the amount of ground moisture.

Other reasons are rotted or decayed timber, which loses volume and causes subsidence, and tree roots affecting foundations. The roots of a tree roughly cover the spread of the branches. Roots may crack foundations or take moisture from the ground and cause soil to subside.

Subsidence is usually indicated by running cracks through brickwork joints. Gaps around door tops and window frames may be other indications, though these can be caused by natural shrinkage of timber.

There are two simple ways to check whether subsidence has ceased. Fix a piece of glass across a crack, using an epoxy-resin adhesive. Since glass has low tensile strength, any slight new movement will cause it to crack. You can bridge the gap with plaster of Paris. This will also crack if there is further subsidence.

All new structures settle and shrink and plaster cracks are not in themselves indication of subsidence.

Subsidence caused by building on clay may be apparent because cracks in inside walls may open and close with the weather. Serious settlement involves a costly and expert job of underpinning, in which hydraulic jacks may have to be employed.

Shrinkage

Shrinkage may appear as stepped cracks in the brickwork joints, and sometimes even through the bricks. These can be repaired by raking out joints and repointing, or replacing cracked bricks.

Repairs

Repairs should be carried out during dry weather, so that brickwork is dry, using a 1:2:9 mix of well-graded soft sand.

If it is difficult to point cracks you can feed a mortar grout into the fissures. Grout is a thinned mortar mixture.

The cracks should be masked with a plastic modelling or soft clay, or other impervious masking. The grout is poured into the fissure using a funnel and a piece of plastic tube. Allow the grout to dry out partially, and neatly point the cracked surface.

Bricks can be repaired with mortar containing a pigment or a matching mortar made up with powdered brick of the same type.

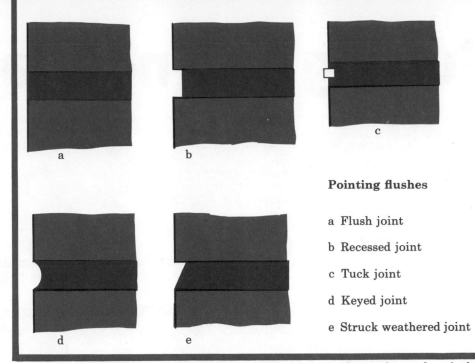

Pointing flushes

a Flush joint

b Recessed joint

c Tuck joint

d Keyed joint

e Struck weathered joint

A routing attachment in an electric drill can also be used to clean joints

Keyed pointing
Apply mortar proud of joint; rub with sacking when nearly dry, then wire brush

Putting on a new face:1

An external facelift gives a new lease of life to any home. Whether you are merely repainting woodwork or applying a decorative and protective wall surface, it is important to choose the right time of year and the correct weather conditions for working. There are numerous modern surface finishes which will add colour and texture to any home.

Exterior decorating is best carried out during spring or early autumn. External decorating work, as a rule, starts at the top and proceeds downwards. Conditions need to be dry, but not too hot.

For a complete façade facelift, start on the soffits (the boarding under the eaves), bargeboards (under the roof or gables) and fascia boards.

Next, deal with guttering and any wall cladding at the upper level that needs treatment. Whole-façade rendering should be completed, where possible, in one operation. Paint downpipes, masking the wall area behind, then tackle window frames and doors.

Where an entire façade is to be painted or rendered, particularly when using one of the highly adhesive mortar mixes, mask wood before starting.

As exterior paintwork does not usually require the fine finish of interior work, medium-quality brushes can be used. Always use a paint kettle and dispense only a workable amount of paint at a time, so that paint is not wasted through evaporation. A paint kettle is also easier to carry or attach to a ladder than a tin.

The 'colour' most often used on rendered surfaces is white. This can look most attractive, particularly in clean-air areas or near the sea, but, with a little thought, other colours can be used to great advantage. The colours used on a house can help to emphasize good features and disguise those less attractive.

Basically, house exterior decoration is a matter of taste, and care must be taken to make the best of attractive features, while minimizing the least pleasing facets. Very violent colour schemes may be exciting but rarely blend in with the surrounding area.

Each house has a particular character of its own, and this should be complemented by the external decoration.

Colour
The house is part of the environment and the colour chosen should complement the surrounding area. While your home can be painted any colour you choose, except in areas of particular natural beauty or historical interest, it is better to decorate in a way that will enhance rather than detract from the general appearance of the surrounding houses.

Not only should the house match the locality and blend harmoniously with it, but the colours should also blend with the other textures and colours used in the building, particularly roof tiles and brickwork.

The use of white is necessary to add brightness to any house colour scheme. It may be used liberally, or just to highlight particular features.

When choosing a colour for rendered walls, try to see what effect a large area of the colour will give. A small sample on a colour card may present quite a different appearance over a large area.

Houses in areas that are not always bathed in sunlight can be decorated in such conservative colours as grey, cream and beige. It is possible to branch out and use less-orthodox, darker colours, or warm shades of orange and yellow. In areas that have clear, bright natural light, pastel shades or white look most attractive.

Different areas of a house may be painted in a variety of colours. Usually, all the walls of a house are painted in the same colour but this may not be necessary on a terraced house, where the front may conform with a road scheme, while the back can be painted to complement the garden colours.

Woodwork and pipes can be made to blend in with the background by painting them in the same colour as the rendering. To make a feature of the woodwork, either use white, white framing or a tint of the background colour.

With a light paint scheme, it may be

better to paint pipes in a darker colour, as light pipe-work tends to attract dirt, particularly in heavily polluted areas.

An unattractive entrance area, if proportionately wrong for the house, can be disguised by painting the door to match the lower part of the house. A door that has unattractive proportions should be painted in a shade of the surrounding brickwork colour or rendering. Large doors, such as garage doors, might also be painted to blend with the colour used on the lower section of a house.

'Adding' width
A narrow house can be made to look wider by painting a wide band in a light colour across the front of the house. A band of decorative moulding may be suitable for this treatment. A sense of height can be suggested by painting vertical features, door architraves and window surrounds in a contrasting colour.

Features, such as porchways, decorative mouldings, and window sills may be painted white or in contrast colours, to break up the wall surfaces and add interest to the façade.

Cladding
Many modern building developments lack individuality and can be improved with the careful use of decorative external finishes. The house may lend itself to being divided into two distinct sections. The top half may be faced with white plastic or timber cladding.

Plastic cladding can be fixed vertically or horizontally to complement the proportions of the house. It requires no maintenance, other than an occasional wash down. The insulation properties of plastic cladding are good and can be further improved by laying insulant matting behind the fixing battens.

Wood cladding – matching board or shiplap – can be fixed horizontally or vertically. Wood has good insulant properties. Timber, however, requires regular maintenance. New timber needs priming, undercoating and two top coats of a suitable semi- or hard-gloss paint and will need repainting regularly, particularly if the area is white. Coloured finish coats can be used and, perhaps, picked up in window frames, door or garage colour finishes.

Natural wood cladding, such as cedar or pine, can be either treated with a protective wood preservative, which allows the natural colour and grain of the wood to show through, or a clear polyurethane varnish.

Front and side dormer areas might be clad with cedar – to match timbered panels under ground-floor windows and, perhaps, wood-finish garage doors.

Façades
Façade areas may be part pebble-dashed or treated with a textured masonry finish. Natural stone can be used to face feature areas – such as a half section of a house, a wall set at an angle to the main house area, or a chimney.

Care must be taken in adding additional decorative features, for unless the existing

tile and brick colours are considered, additions may not blend in with the old.

Another way of giving a facelift to an ordinary façade might be to alter doors or windows. Again, in keeping with the character of the house, wooded doors may be replaced with glass, or a complete glass entrance area.

Windows may be enlarged, sills lowered and, possibly, picture windows fitted to replace fussy window frames with thick surrounds. A glass porch, framed in painted or preserved natural wood, may make an attractive feature, also giving an added bonus of extra storage area.

A porch should be an integrated feature of a façade and not resemble a box, stuck on without thought as to the overall effect.

Timber treatment and maintenance
External woodwork is vulnerable to weather and atmospheric pollution. The natural colour of wood is destroyed by 'leaching' – bleaching by the sun – and by the effect of pollution. Moisture and dryness also cause timber to expand and contract, loosening the surface fibres and allowing a mould to form.

These cumulative effects can be remedied by using timber preservatives, varnishes or water-repellent preparations.

Before treating the timber, first prepare the surface. Most should be brushed down to remove dirt and grit. Preparations are applied with a brush, rag or under vacuum pressure, a commercial treatment. Timber may also be dipped in preservative. Avoid using a spray, unless recommended by the manufacturer.

Preservatives

Preservatives fall into three basic types—water-borne; coal tar; and organic solvents. Some of these are poisonous, so wear protective goggles when applying and immediately wash any splashes off the skin.

Coal tar oils, such as creosote, are used for fences and sheds. It is brushed into the timber.

Water-borne preservatives, which are colourless, are normally applied commercially. Timber so treated has a high degree of protection and can be stained, painted or varnished once dry.

On a decorative timber surface, organic solvent preservatives, coloured or clear, are suitable. They can be painted over when dry.

Water repellents, which may contain preservatives, help to preserve the natural appearance of timber cladding. Dipped or applied with a brush, they can be clear or stained. To prevent moisture penetration, water repellents containing oil and wax are best but cannot be painted over.

Natural oils

Sometimes, natural oils are used on ex-terior woodwork. To give maximum penetration, dependent on the porosity of the wood, a mixture of boiled linseed oil and white spirit gives the best results.

However, oils do not give the effective protection of good water-repellent preservatives. The advantage of oils is that the grain and natural colour of the wood show through, but the surface, according to climatic conditions, may need treatment twice a year.

Before applying an oil-based preservative, the area should be brushed with a stiff brush and rubbed down with medium glasspaper.

Clear varnish

Exterior clear varnish gives an attractive finish and allows the natural timber to show through. Varnish is composed of alkyd, copal or phenolic resins, combined with drying oils. Four coats are needed on new timber. The first coat should be thinned.

This treatment should be renewed at the first sign of any breakdown in the surface. Remove the varnish with a solvent. Clean off with white spirit, to remove any remaining wax in the solvent and then apply two coats of varnish. On a sound but dirty surface, wash down with soapy water and finally wash again with clean water.

Use a wet-or-dry abrasive paper to rub down. Fill any holes or cracks with hard stopping, which should be coloured to match the surrounding area. Stain any bleached areas and then apply two coats of varnish. Varnish should only be applied on completely dry wood, as moisture may cause it to peel off.

Polyurethane varnish can be used externally. Again, a minimum of four coats should be applied, ideally at four-hourly intervals. Choose a dry, warm day, with a temperature of 15–25°C, and ensure that the surface is completely dry.

Polyurethane varnish tends to be brittle and peel away at the edges, and a coat of alkyd varnish may help to prevent this. If the surface has broken down, the gloss must be completely removed, the surface cleaned and new varnish applied.

If the surface colour of the wood has faded, it can be re-coloured with a stain. These are of two types. The first, in a water-repellent or organic solvent preservative, is applied initially and fades as the coat wears. These can be washed off.

The second type darkens the wood and should be used with care. This is used on timber which was originally treated with a clear water-repellent preservative, but has lost its natural colour.

External timber surfaces that might need treatment include cladding, timber window and door frames, external doors, garage doors, sills, thresholds, greenhouses, sheds, gates and fences.

Painting timber

On timber cladding to be painted, use an alkyd-resin paint in the colour of your choice. On new wood first use a suitable primer. Highly resinous woods, such as cedar and some pines, are better sealed with an aluminium primer. Use one under-

Rendering a wall: mix mortar on a dampened spot board. Turn over well with a trowel

For external angles, line up a rule, fixed some 6mm proud of the corner

The rendering coat is laid on, using upward strokes of the steel trowel

Key the floating coat, using only horizontal strokes of the comb scratcher

Use the wooden float to flatten out the burrs on the surface of floating coat

Apply the butter coat, which provides a base for the shingle, using steel float

coat and two top gloss coats for maximum protection.

When repainting, if the surface is sound, it may not be necessary to strip back and reprime. Wash down the surface, allow to dry and then rub down with abrasive paper. Wet-abrasive rubbing is easier and prevents too much dust from flying about.

Any blemishes or blisters in the paint should be rubbed down and re-primed. Knots or resinous patches should be treated with patent knotting. Holes, cracks, or joints should be filled with hard-stopping, where necessary, and rubbed down.

Badly blistered or cracked surfaces must be stripped or burnt off and the area treated as new timber. An outdoor grade of emulsion, with an appropriate primer or primer-sealer, may be used on cladding.

Aluminium cladding may be painted with an undercoat and two top coats of alkyd-resin paint. Before painting, clean the surface with white spirit and touch in any worn areas with zinc chromate primer.

Asbestos treatment

Asbestos cement can be used externally for roofing, cladding, gutters and down pipes.

It can be painted successfully, but as the material has slightly absorbent properties, paint may blister. The degree of absorbency over the surface varies and this can give a patchy finish. Another problem may be paint flaking, stickiness, discolouration

and yellow staining. This is caused by alkalis in the asbestos attacking the paint.

New sheets of asbestos should be left to dry thoroughly before painting. If the asbestos is to be used in humid conditions, it is wise to paint the back of the material with bitumen paint. Take care not to allow the paint to get on to the face of material as bitumen paint 'bleeds' through the decorative coat.

To minimize the risk of attack by alkalis, new asbestos should be allowed to weather for at least four weeks.

To prepare the surface for painting, brush off dust and any loose material. If any mould or lichen has developed, wash down with a fungicidal solution, allow to dry and then brush off the growth.

Asbestos can be painted with exterior-grade emulsion paint, oil paint, distemper, cement paint or lime wash. Before using emulsion, oil-based paint or distemper, roughen the glazed patches of asbestos which exist where the surface is more absorbent.

Apply an alkali-resistant pigmented primer before applying the top coat. Lime wash or cement paints do not need a primer but the surface should be wetted before the first coat is applied.

Alkali attack

Some paints are highly resistant to alkali attack. When using a paint that is not highly resistant, use two coats of primer to prevent the alkalis seeping through to attack the top coat.

Primer sealers can be used before

painting to counteract uneven suction but will not prevent alkali attack. When impermeable paints are used on the surface, paint, where possible, the backs of the asbestos. When not possible, use a porous alkali-resistant paint for the surface which allows the asbestos to 'breathe'.

Sheeting or soffits should be either painted with porous, alkali-resistant paint or with an impermeable paint where the sheet has previously been 'back painted'.

Down pipes and the insides of gutters should be painted with bitumen paint. Allow this to dry thoroughly before painting the outside. Applying bitumen to the insides of pipes is difficult and is usually done during production.

Roofs

Asbestos roofs are not normally painted as the cost of maintenance is high. To help asbestos roofing to blend in with surrounding roofs, the sheets can be darkened with ferrous sulphate, mixed in the proportion of 455 grammes of sulphate to five litres of water. This will give a durable brown colour, but the coverage will often be uneven.

When treating a roof, use a cat ladder, as asbestos is not safe to walk on. Flaked paintwork on asbestos should be removed with a wire brush or proprietary paint remover and washed down. Never use a paraffin or gas blow torch as the heat will crack the surface which may explode dangerously.

Do not let paint remover sink into the asbestos surface as this will crumble it.

Key the surface well with a scratcher. Make 90-degree cross diagonal strokes

'Work to rule' to ensure accurate surfaces. Brickwork is often irregular

Next, apply the floating coat, again working carefully to the timber rule

Flick the shingle systematically from a bowl or plastic bucket; avoid 'bunching'

Before the work sets hard, pat the shingle down with wood float to 'firm' surface

Keep the float dry with a piece of cloth so that cement does not coat the shingle

Putting on a new face:2

Even the most drab home exterior can be quickly transformed, using one of the many available decorative wall finishes. Materials which can be used to give your home a 'face lift' vary from simple exterior paints to more elaborate surface finishes, providing a wide choice of both colour and texture.

Masonry and stone paints

Rendered surfaces can be improved by the application of a paint coat. The most satisfactory type is masonry paint. This is waterproof and so is protective as well as decorative.

Some types dry to a smooth surface which facilitates easy cleaning. Before using a masonry paint, brush the surface down thoroughly with a wire brush and apply a masonry paint sealer.

Among many types of masonry paints are those reinforced with minute, short nylon fibres, which fill minor imperfections, or paints which incorporate minute particles of crushed rock. One type has a vinyl-resin base and is available in a range of colours or a two-tone mix.

Some paints are applied by brush, and others with a steel trowel.

With such surface coatings, large imperfections in external rendering must be hacked back and filled with a mix of the same consistency as the surrounding area, otherwise stress will occur between the two surfaces.

Emulsion

Exterior-grade emulsion can be used to decorate external walls. Available in a wide range of attractive colours, it provides solely a decorative finish and has no waterproofing properties.

Applied rendering

Some types of applied rendering, such as shingle dash, snowflake and Tyrolean finishes do not need painting, unless you wish to change the colour. Normally, their

Roughcast is prepared to a sloppy consistency, then flicked over the wall surface

A trowelled finish coat can be used as a basis for cement-fining or Ashlar surface

Using a wood float and slurry to prepare the surface for a cement-fining finish

Similarly, measure and mark out horizontals, again ensuring line is level

Carefully rule in the lines, using a piece of filed metal or a cut nail as scriber

Gently rub the edges of the score lines with the sponge to remove any slight burrs

attraction lies in a two-tone colour or textured effect. Rough-textured surfaces may be difficult to cover, as the paint has to adhere to the stone and crevices of a cement mixture.

Roughcast
Roughcast, which incorporates shingle in a mortar mix, does need a decorative finish, either a waterproof paint or emulsion. If using emulsion, a colourless water-repellent sealer can be applied before the emulsion coat.

Preparation
Before starting work, mask surrounding paintwork, window frames, pipes and secondary roofs. Also, remember to protect paths as spilt paint may be difficult to remove.

A large brush or roller can be used to apply a decorative coat to rendering, other than on a roughened cement finish. Cement finishes should be applied with an expendable brush as, once used, it is impossible to clean off the hardened cement.

A stiff nylon brush must be used on a very rough textured finish to push the paint into the crevices.

External wall treatments
Cement finishes
A good way to improve the external appearance of house walls is to apply a decorative cement finish. This is not a difficult task but needs care. Cement rendering can be applied to bare brickwork, cement, stippled or shingle dash surfaces. Additional care must be taken if the surface is painted.

Three coats of sand and cement are applied to external walls. Often called rendering coats, the three layers have distinct functions.

The first coat is the rendering coat. This is 'keyed' (scratched for adhesion) and covered by the floating coat, which straightens out the surface before the application of the finish coat.

On external plastering the system used in the final coat depends on the finish to be used.

Cement fining is the coat most commonly used. This is finished with a wooden float or sponge.

Shingle dash is another finish, in which fine shingle is embedded in a fatty 'butter' coat.

Different masonry finishes, such as roughcast, Tyrolean finish, and so on, are examples of finish coats.

Tools
Laying-on trowel
It is important to buy as good a trowel as you can afford. The blade should be of thin, well-tempered steel. A banana handle will give a good grip. A full-sized trowel blade is 280mm × 115mm.

Hawk
A hawk is a flat piece of wood or metal about 300mm², with a grip fixed in the centre. A quite adequate hawk can be made from a piece of marine plywood, with a short piece of broom handle, fixed in the centre, as a grip.

Skimming float
The skimming float is usually made of white pine. The blade should be 305mm × 115mm. A wooden float produces a slightly matt surface. A steel float can be used to give a smoother surface finish.

Water brush
A water brush is essential for damping down wall areas. A 100mm or 125mm brush is suitable.

Spot board
A spot board is used for mixing up the mortar. It should be made of marine ply or strengthened plywood. The board should be 610mm × 760mm and, if made of plywood, strengthened with battens.

The spot board should be used in conjunction with a stand or an old box to keep the board off the ground. A satisfactory working height is around 810mm.

Spirit level
A builder's spirit level, which indicates both vertical and horizontal levels is necessary.

Floating rule
A floating rule is a piece of straight-edged timber about 1830mm long and 100mm to 150mm wide. It is used to level off the

Cement fining: Lightly sponge to produce sandy texture resembling natural stone

A trowelled finish coat is ruled for Ashlar; this resembles stone blockwork

Use a builder's level to ensure that the line is vertical and make working marks

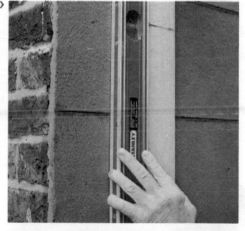

Vermiculation is a tooled finish, which looks effective with Ashlar blockwork

Tyrolean finish is applied from a machine. The 'spatter-dash' finish is attractive

Spar dash is another type of textured finish. Spar is flicked on to 'butter' coat

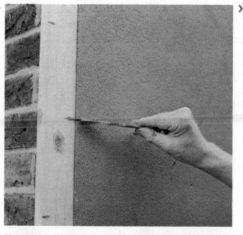

surface of a plaster or mortar coat, so that the surface is level with the screeds.

Feather-edged rule
A feather-edged rule is a piece of straight, tapered-edged timber, about 1m long. Where straight angles are needed, some pieces of straight-edged, planed timber 50mm × 20mm are required.

Scoop
A scoop-shaped shovel can be useful if applying a shingle-dash coat. This facilitates scooping up the gravel.

Devil float (and wood float)
This is frequently a wood float with nails partially knocked through the float face. These can be pushed through to enable the work surface to be keyed; they can then be pushed back to achieve smooth work.

Scratching to achieve a keyed surface may be also done with a commercially produced comb or one can be made by knocking some nails into a piece of wood. The comb is used to scratch diagonal criss-cross lines on the rendering coat and straight horizontal lines on the floating coat in preparation for the final coat. You can key the surface with a small trowel.

A bolster and club hammer will also be needed, for hacking back, prior to repair work. Two buckets, one to carry materials and one for water, are required.

If any material is loose it should be removed with a stiff wire brush or hacked out and the bare patches made up to the surface level with a 1:4:$\frac{1}{2}$ (cement: sand: lime) mixture. To give a good key, scratch the surface diagonally with criss-cross lines. Treat the base surface with a PVA primer to assist adhesion.

Brick surfaces should be brushed down

to clean off dust and dirt. Then soak the surface, allow it to dry slightly, and apply a PVA bonding coat with a brush. On a slightly doubtful surface, apply a bonding coat consisting of 25 per cent PVA bonding agent, one part of Portland cement and one part of building sand.

Mix in water until the slurry is the consistency of thickened custard. Then brush this solution well into the surface and allow to dry for 24 hours.

Ruling out
Large areas of wall surface to be plastered should be divided into sections to make for systematic working. Use 10mm battens to divide the wall area into 1·52m sections.

Fix, with masonry nails, the first batten at a corner, ensuring a true vertical by checking with the builder's level. The spaced battens will give working bays.

Start work at the bottom of the first bay. The mortar should be pushed on to the wall and spread, working upwards. Fill in each section and then level off the surface with a straight edge. Allow the mortar to set; this takes at least four hours. Then criss-cross keying marks, diagonally across the coat.

Cement paints or painted roughcast and shingle may be a little more difficult to work. If any material is loose, it should be removed, hacked out, and the bare patches made up to the level of the surface, with a 1:4:$\frac{1}{2}$ lime mix. Next, to give a good key, scratch the surface.

Smooth-surfaced stucco or cement work should be brushed down well with a wire brush and roughened to provide a key. A PVA slurry, consisting of one part PVA to one part sand and one part cement should be used.

A mortar plasticizer will help to spread

A colourful 'sunshine' face lift can brighten up the outside of many homes

the mixture. Lime added to the mix will facilitate the spreading power but increase suction. Suction is the rate at which the base coat absorbs water from the top coat. A high suction rate is required for some finish coats, while others need low suction.

Next apply two backing coats. The rendering coat consists of a 1:6:1 lime mix and is applied with a steel trowel. Mix these materials dry, turning well with a shovel. Make a hole in the middle of the materials and pour in water, push the inner part of the ring into the water and then add water again. Turn, until the mixture is well wetted, then mix thoroughly. If needed, a dry colourizer can be added at this stage.

Apply the mix with upward strokes, using the full length of the blade to 'lay off'. The coat should be smoothed out evenly with a floating rule and then roughened to provide a key. Comb the surface with diagonal strokes in two directions. This coat should be allowed to dry for 12 hours. The rendering coat should be 6mm thick.

The second coat, known as the floating coat, is applied to give a level surface. Lay a 275mm border round the area to be covered. This coat should be 12mm thick and is often best laid in two 6mm coats. Work each area systematically, a strip at a time, filling in the rendering as necessary and ruling off until there is an even covering. Ruling off reduces the thickness of the coat to 10mm.

The coat is then smoothed off with a wooden float. It depends on the finish coat whether or not the surface is roughened to give a key. If a roughened surface is required, use a comb to scratch horizontal lines across the surface.

Cement fining
A simple sandy-textured look with the appearance of natural stone is known as cement-fining.

Portland cement fining. This is applied to a surface with a low suction rate, so use only a little lime in the floating coat. Fining is applied to a keyed surface. The sand used should be sifted or even washed to

Looking the worse for wear, a fascia much in need of repair and redecoration

A nylon-based exterior paint is easy to apply, using a fairly stiff brush

Removed flaked surfaces and make good; apply a stabilizing solution if needed

The finished effect. The results, with correct preparation, are long lasting

remove any clay, which can cause the finish surface to craze or crack. Sand is mixed in proportion of two parts to one part of Portland cement. The cement can be white or grey, or coloured for decorative effect.

Mix the sand and cement to a firm consistency and apply on to a 6mm floating coat, which should be 'ironed' into the base coat and then rubbed over with a wood float. If there are hollows they can be filled in at this stage. Use a sponge to finish off, with light, delicate circular movements.

Blockwork

The same finish is used when a stone block, or **Ashlar** effect, is required. Decide on the size of block needed and then draw a master line, using a spirit level, to make sure the work lines up.

Mark out the rest of the horizontal lines, working from the master line, then mark in the vertical lines. If any of the edges are not quite accurate or have become slightly blurred, they can be smoothed off with a sponge.

An Ashlar surface, well executed, looks like a surface of stone blocks. It can be white, grey or coloured with a colourizer.

A variation of Ashlar is known as **vermiculation**. This is textured effect to give variety to an Ashlar surface. It is quite a lengthy process and for this reason a random effect is suggested.

Using a sharp steel object, cut out irregular shapes in the block while it is still wet. Leave a border of at least 13mm round the block and 6mm runs between each cut away area of the design.

Shingle dash

A shingle dash or roughcast finish coat can be achieved by flicking small stones or shingle on to a 'butter' coat.

The basic rendering coat should be scratched diagonally and the floating coat should be combed in horizontal lines. Smooth off any rough projections with a wooden float.

The floating coat should comprise one part cement to three parts of soft sand. A small quantity of plasticizer should be used in the mix, unless working in hot weather. In this case, a liquid water proofer should be added instead of the plasticizer.

The proportions are 25 per cent of waterproofer to 50kg of cement. After scratching in the horizontal lines, leave to dry for 24 hours.

The third coat is known as a 'butter' coat. The proportions are three parts sand to half part of cement and one part of lime. Working over a small area at a time, about 500mm², 'iron' on the coat to a depth of about 6mm.

Using clean, well-washed shingle and a laying-on trowel, flick the shingle on to the butter coat. The secret is to get the shingle applied evenly. One trowel load will cover an area one third greater than the area of the trowel.

Do not pick up too much at one time as it will be difficult to flick the wrist to apply the shingle, resulting in an uneven surface. Place a dust sheet below the work to catch shingle that does not adhere so that this can be used later. Work to within 50mm of the area being treated.

Next apply a butter coat to the next 500mm² area and apply shingle to this. When an area of about 2m² has been covered, use the wooden float to tap the shingle gently into the butter coat. The float should be used dry and wiped clean frequently.

Rough cast

Roughcasting is applied to a keyed floating coat. The mixture is made up of half a part of cement to one part of lime, to provide suction, and two parts of shingle. Pea gravel, a rounded gravel, provides a good roughcast surface. The mixture is applied directly to the surface, again using the flicking action.

The consistency should be sloppy and can be applied directly from a bucket. Many find this an easier technique than shingle dash. Gravel applied too thickly will slide down the surface.

Stipple

A variation of cement fining is a stipple finish. Lay a coat about 6mm thick on to a well-keyed float coat. Smooth down any uneven areas with a wood float and then, using a stipple brush, stipple carefully over the surface.

Another finish which offers a variation of texture is based on the same technique as cement fining. Apply a 6mm finished surface and then use a hard wire brush to make horizontal streaks on the surface. As the surface begins to harden, trowel lightly over the surface. When finished, a veining effect will be achieved.

A finish called **Granosit** consists of a dried material, mixed with water, and allowed to stand for 30 minutes. The float coat should be well keyed. Apply the mixture with a steel trowel to a depth of 10mm. As the surface starts to harden, using a wooden float, finish the surface with horizontal sweeps. This surface, which is water repellent, is obtainable in white and coloured finishes.

Tyrolean

This is a closely textured finish, and is applied with a special machine. A proprietary mix of Portland cement and aggregate is applied dry mixed. One bag of the mix, stirred into half a bucket of water, will give the correct consistency.

Before starting work, mask the surrounding area. Pour the mixture, a small amount at a time, into the machine. Turn the machine to the wall area and crank a handle; this will cause small blobs to be flicked on to the surface. The size of blob can be adjusted by a gauge on the side of the machine. Keep the machine moving to avoid an uneven build-up in one particular area. When working at angles, such as the corners of a building, continue to crank the machine and apply the mixture round the corners.

When re-rendering external surfaces, it is important to achieve a straight, clean edge at the outer corners of the building. The render coat can be applied, working from either side of the angled edge, with a trowel. For the floating and finish coat it is necessary to work to a wooden batten that will help to give a perfect edge.

Nail a length of a straight-edged board, using 50mm cut nails, into the brick joints. The wood should allow about 10mm thickness on one side. Fill in the lime-cement and sand floating coat, bringing this flush with the board. Use a rule made of another piece of board about 1m long. Scratch in the horizontal key lines and, when set, remove the wood and repeat the process for the other side of the angle.

Reveals

The reveals round doors and windows are treated in the following way. Fix the straight edge board to the reveals and apply the floating coat on to the main surface. When this surface is dry, remove the wood and fix to the main wall faces. Fill in the float coat in the reveals, working out towards the corner. Immediately wash off any cement splashed on to the window or door frames.

When applying a top coat of shingle or pebble-dash, use the same technique for making a good angle as the floating coat. This time, only one board is needed. Fix this, leaving it 10mm proud of the surface, and apply the finish to this board. Allow the surface to set hard and then carefully remove the board. The second side of the angle can be completed by applying the finish up the straight line already set.

Clearing blocked drains and gullies

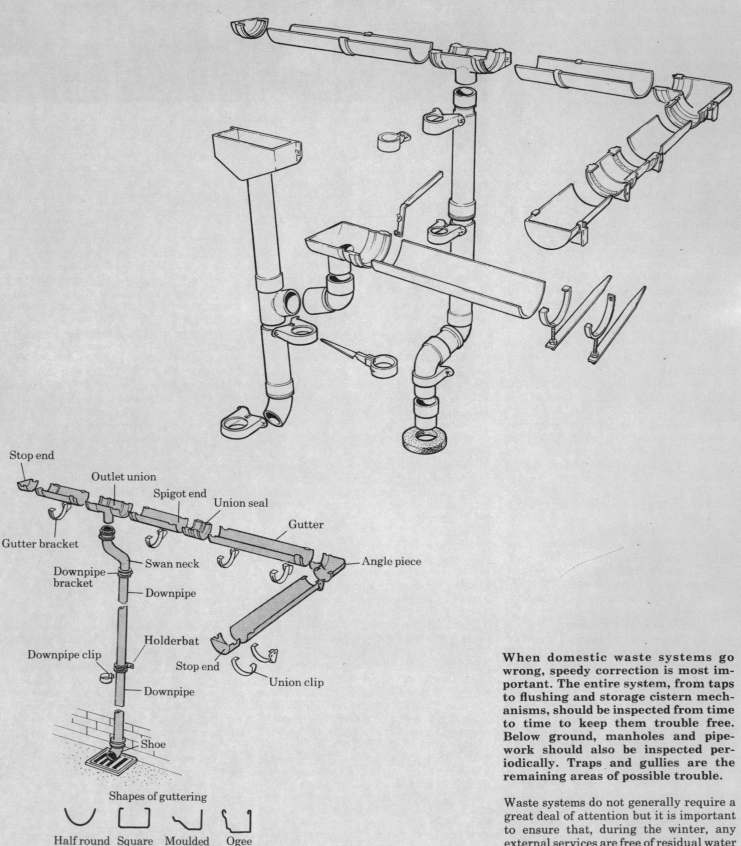

Stop end
Outlet union
Spigot end
Union seal
Gutter
Gutter bracket
Swan neck
Angle piece
Downpipe bracket
Downpipe
Holderbat
Downpipe clip
Stop end
Downpipe
Union clip
Shoe

Shapes of guttering

Half round   Square   Moulded   Ogee

When domestic waste systems go wrong, speedy correction is most important. The entire system, from taps to flushing and storage cistern mechanisms, should be inspected from time to time to keep them trouble free. Below ground, manholes and pipework should also be inspected periodically. Traps and gullies are the remaining areas of possible trouble.

Waste systems do not generally require a great deal of attention but it is important to ensure that, during the winter, any external services are free of residual water –such as may happen in runs of horizontal pipe-work or if a waste pipe should sag.

Types of drainage pipe-joint

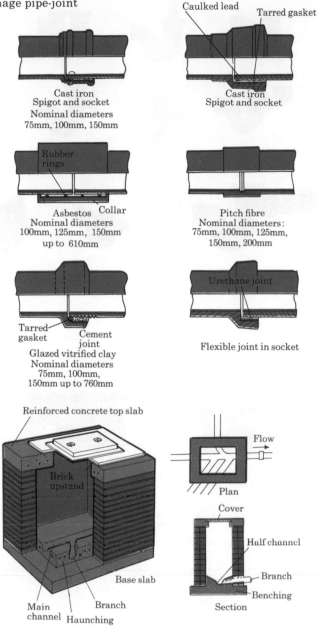

Caulked lead   Tarred gasket

Cast iron
Spigot and socket
Nominal diameters
75mm, 100mm, 150mm

Cast iron
Spigot and socket

Rubber rings

Asbestos   Collar
Nominal diameters
100mm, 125mm, 150mm
up to 610mm

Pitch fibre
Nominal diameters:
75mm, 100mm, 125mm,
150mm, 200mm

Tarred gasket   Cement joint
Glazed vitrified clay
Nominal diameters
75mm, 100mm,
150mm up to 760mm

Urethane joint

Flexible joint in socket

Reinforced concrete top slab

Brick upstand

Base slab

Main channel   Branch
Haunching

Flow

Plan

Cover

Half channel

Branch

Benching

Section

Drainage inspection chamber

One way of helping to prevent large blockages is the routine inspection and clearing of waste traps, gullies and manholes. A blocked waste trap can usually be cleared with a rubber plunger cup.

When using this, half fill the sink or basin with water. Block, temporarily, any overflows and then work the plunger up and down over the drain exit, with a vigorous, jabbing motion.

Waste traps
If the blockage persists, this will necessitate access to the trap which provides the water seal. This entails removing a plug in the side or bottom of the trap. First, place a container of sufficient size beneath to collect débris and water when the plug is unscrewed.

Traps may be made of copper, lead or plastic. Do not impose excess strain on the trap or you may fracture it. Support it while you are undoing the plug and then hook out any débris with a piece of wire.

WC pans
A blocked WC pan may respond to treatment with a plunger but this should be used with great care to avoid stress on the pan which may cause it to break. It is, however, unusual for blockages to occur or persist in the soil system.

Manholes
Blockages may occur in manhole inspection chambers at point of entry or outflow for a variety of reasons. The main causes are roughened surfaces or fractures, permitting débris to adhere, or benching which is inadequate–perhaps too low, allowing an obstruction to build up.

Fractures or other damage should be speedily rectified, since these would represent a public-health infringement and health danger. Flaws in benching should also be corrected; the benching should be smooth, and gently sloped on either side of the outflow pipe.

Drain rods
Sometimes, a blockage may occur through no fault of the system. Normally, this can be cleared easily by prodding free with a stick. In other cases, you may need a set of drainage rods, together with fittings, to deal with a variety of circumstances.

Rods screw together and are each about 1m long. These provide reasonable flexibility, allowing them to be fed along a blocked pipe from within the manhole or along the pipe from outside, in the case of shallow manholes.

The main attachments, which screw on to the head, are a rubber plunger, corkscrew head, hook, scraper and brush head. The brush set resembles those used by chimney sweeps. The corkscrew is intended for lifting plugs in manholes but can also be used to clear blockages. Rods can be bought or hired.

To find a blockage, start at the house and open up each inspection chamber in turn. When you locate an empty one, this indicates that the blockage is between this and the previous one.

Place a temporary barrier over the mouth of the outflow in the empty chamber. A piece of chicken wire rolled into a ball is suitable and allows water to pass but stops solid matter. Take care, however, that the wire does not enter the pipe and further block it.

Next, attach the rubber plunger and insert this at the blocked-up chamber. Turn the rods in a clockwise direction as you insert them as this ensures that they do not unscrew. You should, in most cases, be able to push the obstruction clear. If this fails, you will have to try the hook. Use the scraper to remove débris adhering to surfaces.

Once the blockage is dislodged, remove it, or break it down, and finally flush with water to disperse. Then use a hose to flush out the length of drain. Use the brush to clean off any encaked débris as this may cause a blockage to recur, then sprinkle disinfectant.

Once the blockage is cleared, check the cause as a flaw or deterioration may need to be remedied. Inspect carefully before replacing the inspection cover on the manhole.

Manhole covers
Where a manhole cover is broken and needs replacing it is generally necessary to buy a new rim as well as the lid, since these are made as a matched pair to ensure a good fit.

Although a matched rim and lid should fit together tightly, they will not provide a totally airtight seal. It is necessary to apply manhole grease liberally to the rim before putting on the lid.

Where the lid is removed for inspection, it is advisable to remove all old grease and repack the seal, which also prevents dirt and foreign matter from getting into the manhole and, possibly, causing a blockage.

Rims are usually set in concrete surrounds, so are relatively simply to replace. To take out an old rim, chip away the surrounding concrete, using a club hammer and small cold chisel. Any deterioration in mortar and brickwork should also be made good.

Care should be taken not to damage brickwork below the rim. Bed this rim or cover frame in a 1:3 cement: sand mix over the entire area to ensure an even bearing for the frame.

Place the lid in position to avoid twisting the frame; make sure that the cover is evenly in place and will not rock. Check that alignment is accurate with a spirit level.

Benching should be shaped so that it slopes from the channel in the centre to the sides of the manhole at a gradient of about 25mm:152mm.

It should be made of a mixture of 1:4 cement: sharp sand and finished with a steel trowel. It must be kept clean, and if any cracks appear, these should be at once repaired.

When remaking benching, take care not to allow mortar to fall into the gulley — if any does, remove before putting the drain back into commission.

When repairing cracks, a PVA adhesive should be used to bond new mortar. The existing surface should first be cleaned thoroughly with a wire brush.

Brickwork should also be inspected at fairly regular intervals, and if any rendering or faulty pointing is noted, this should be repaired.

Testing manholes

If a manhole defect leads to a loss of water, the fault should be traced, rectified and the manhole loaded and tested continually for an hour, during which there should be no significant water loss.

A fall of more than 25mm in this time would be excessive and not accounted for by absorption within the chamber walls or by dissipation.

The section of drain adjacent to the suspect manhole should first be isolated and charged with water. This is done by means of drain plugs, which have rubber walls, expanded by means of a screw on the centre of the plug body, to fit into the entry point of the channel.

By unscrewing a centre nut, the section can be drained slowly. Always reduce the pressure of water by first releasing this nut, as the pressure of water might drag the plug into the pipe and be difficult to extricate.

Types of manhole

If you have to carry out a substantial repair of an inspection chamber, it might be as well to consider replacement with one of the newer prefabricated units — plastic, concrete or pitch-fibre.

Channels in the base of a manhole can be pre-cast, half-round self-glazed or of pitch-fibre pipe, or formed in a concrete base with a smooth object, such as a tin. These must consist of a 1:4 cement: sharp sand composition.

Sharp angles should be avoided in channels as this could lead to blockages.

Manhole sides must be constructed of dense and non-porous bricks, such as engineering bricks, which are able to withstand constant conditions of damp. These should be laid using an English bond.

Where conventional bricks are used, these should be 'parged' or rendered to provide the same protection as engineer-

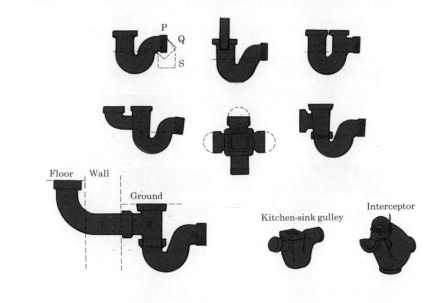

Types of trap

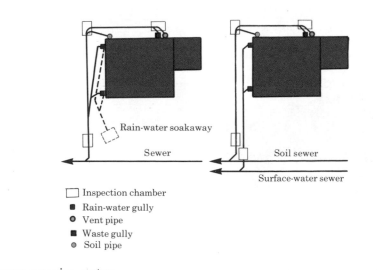

Left: new one-pipe system
Right: older two-pipe system

ing bricks. Not all local authorities will permit the use of ordinary bricks.

Burst pipes

The burst pipe, of which the first indication is usually the ominous drip of water following a thaw, is becoming a thing of the past. This is partly because of new, versatile materials, which are less prone to burst, and higher standards of lagging and loft insulation.

Before the onset of cold weather, check all lagging. Bursts are more likely to occur in lead pipe than copper, stainless steel or plastic.

Burst pipes are caused by the formation of ice, which expands, distends, and then bursts the pipe. Sections of most modern pipes are often connected using compression-type fittings and the effect of ice formation in the pipe will usually be to push the fitting off the pipe.

Provided this is noticed before the thaw, it is easily rectified by reconnecting the joint, saving yourself from possible flooding.

If a burst is detected, first shut off the water supply. Using a blow torch, gently

heat the area of the burst — keeping a receptacle handy to take the thawed water. It is simple to cut out a damaged or distended section and place a new piece of pipework in position, joining this with a capillary or compression connector.

If the pipe is in leadwork, cut out the damaged section and replace it with a piece of of copper or stainless-steel pipe. The jointing technique is the same as that for connecting a stopcock on lead supply pipe — the only difference being that you will finish up with a pair of joints.

Alternatively, you can hammer the split closed, clean and prepare the pipe and wipe plumber's metal around it to repair it.

The same procedures apply if a hole is knocked in a pipe.

Lagging

Prevention is better than cure and periodic inspection of vulnerable pipes should take place during cold weather. Exposed pipes should be carefully lagged with bandage, polystyrene or foam lagging. Pipes above loft insulation should also be lagged.

Avoiding trouble from the top

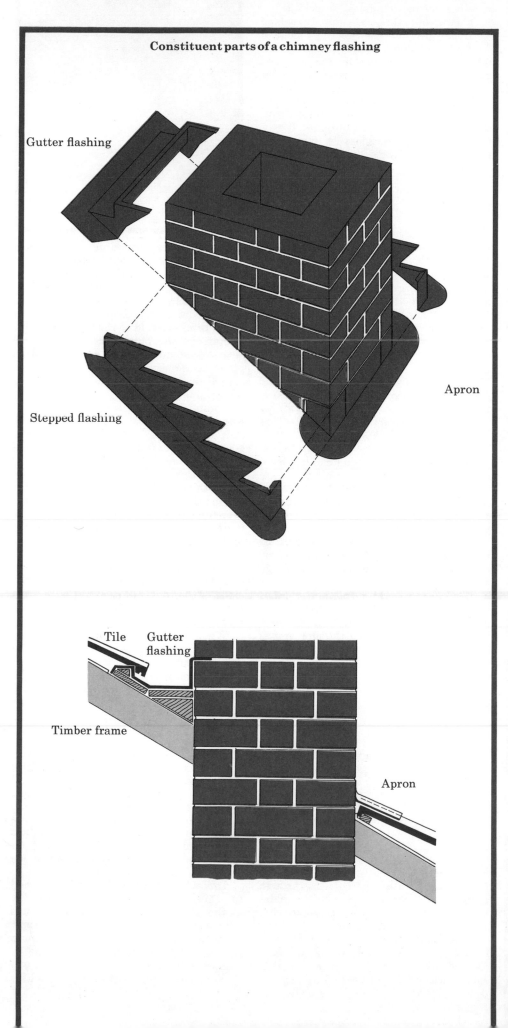

Constituent parts of a chimney flashing

Gutter flashing

Stepped flashing

Apron

Tile

Gutter flashing

Timber frame

Apron

Moisture seems to have a capacity to get in almost anywhere, and keeping out damp can prove quite a problem in older homes in particular. However, both traditional and modern methods can often be allied to keep the home dry and free from water damage.

Flashings consist of various types of water-tight joint outside homes. These are used where chimney stacks come through roofs, where a roof abuts a wall, or around roof lights and dormer windows.

The traditional flashing materials are lead, zinc and copper. However, lead-beating is a skilled job calling for special tools. Though this is not necessarily beyond the skill of a handyman, other materials are easier to work and can usually be used. Both lead and zinc may deteriorate in time and need replacement.

Aluminium-based flashing, such as Evode Flashband, and mastics, can often be used for repair and replacement. Mastic glazing tapes and cords can also be used to effect repairs to deteriorated flashing.

Another type of flashing material is a pliable bituminous sheeting which can be softened with heat and manipulated to replace damaged areas.

The intrusion of damp into areas such as chimney breasts, the loft or an attic ceiling or bedroom is an indication that all is not well. The best time to detect the source of the trouble is during heavy rain.

In some cases, porosity of brickwork may be the cause, or a joint in zinc or other metal sheet may have lifted. Mastic or cold asphalt may be used to effect a repair.

Chimneys

A roof ladder is needed to carry out repairs to chimneys. A form of flashing around chimney pots is the sloped mortar fillet called flaunching.

This may have cracked and broken away as a result of normal expansion and contraction of the fabric of the home. While these are natural conditions in any structure, they are more intensified near sources of heat, such as chimneys.

Careful inspection may show that slight damage can be repaired with a mastic, or damage patched up with new mortar. Where patching up of damaged or deteriorated flaunching using mortar still does not solve the problem, you may have to remove and replace the entire flashing.

In older homes, the flashing around the base of a chimney may be a mortar fillet or haunching. Modern flashings consist of stepped, side flashings, with a gutter flashing at the chimney top and an apron flashing at the bottom of the chimney. The stepped flashing is cut into steps and inserted into mortar joints down the side of the chimney.

Lead is a malleable metal and made in various weights. 1·81kg lead is needed for roof purposes. The brick joints should be raked out and the new flashing cut with

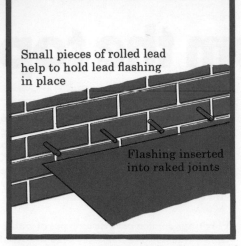

Small pieces of rolled lead help to hold lead flashing in place

Flashing inserted into raked joints

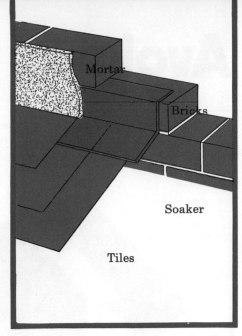

Mortar

Bricks

Soaker

Tiles

metal shears and inserted. Small pieces of rolled lead should be inserted to fix the flashing into position and the joint re-mortared with a 1:3 mortar mix.

When repairing mortar fillets use a little adhesive to bond new mortar to old. Make sure that you brush off any algae.

Cracks, however, may open up again, and some bituminous mastic or a flexible compound should be used. This can be applied with a special 'gun', so that the joint is effectively penetrated and sealed. These mastics may also be applied by trowel from a tin.

When removing old mortar from a chimney, rake out a single section of the stack at a time to a depth of 15mm–20mm. Before repointing, dampen the joints and form a weather-struck joint.

Damaged flaunching should be chipped away and replaced. Use a club hammer and chisel and work carefully, avoiding cascading large chunks of mortar down the roof. Keep a bucket handy and place the broken mortar pieces in this.

Chimney pots

It may be necessary to replace or refix the chimney pot. If you do have to remove this, seal up the fireplaces below so that dirt, dust and soot do not damage furnishings and fabrics.

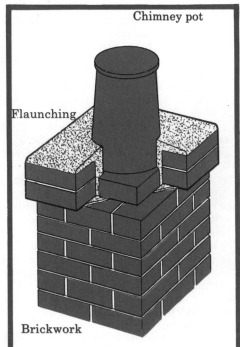

Chimney pot

Flaunching

Brickwork

Once you have removed the old flaunching, locate the chimney pot back into position, dampen the surround and apply a 1:3 mortar mix with a high-alumina cement and a little PVA adhesive to assist bonding, for new chimney flaunching.

This might be the opportunity to replace a chimney pot with a terminal if a modern heating appliance is employed, or to cap off a chimney if the fire is no longer in use. Modern terminals are usually made of a light weight material and easy to handle.

Chimney pots are usually heavier than they seem, so you may need help, if you have to lower it to the ground. If one crashes down, considerable structural damage may be caused, and someone could be injured.

Secure the pot with a stout rope, fixed round the stack. It is advisable to organize help so that you can lower the old pot to the ground.

You may have to fit pieces of slate or tile around a new pot to make it vertical. Use a spirit level to check this. Make sure that the new mortar fillet fills the gaps between the base of the pot and brickwork, and take care that mortar does not go down the flue. You can also fit a cowl to an existing chimney.

Junctions

Mortar, which seals the weatherproof junctions between a wall and chimney, frequently cannot absorb the natural movement in a structure and cracks. This is often met in older homes.

It may, however, be necessary to replace an ancient fillet. You can use lead, zinc, or felt, or remake in mortar.

Zinc is cheaper than lead and is 'dressed' similarly. You need a dresser, which is a special tool made of boxwood or hornbeam.

Any adjacent gutter outlet should be temporarily blocked off so that old mortar does not block up the stormwater drainage system.

If you are remaking the mortar fillet, apply a 1:4 mortar mixture, with a PVA additive, using a wooden float. Make a fairly stiff mix and when the mortar has dried, cross-hatch the surface with a trowel or scratcher, to provide a scratch coat for a finish coat.

Allow the mortar to go off for about a day and then apply a finish coat of about 15mm thick, with the wood float. Finally, polish this to a fine finish with a steel float.

Make sure that you maintain an even slope so that rainwater cannot collect and percolate through any point into the home.

Soakers are a flashing which go under tiles and are often covered with a sloped mortar fillet. Both the mortar and the material, frequently zinc, may have deteriorated.

Again, an aluminium bituminous-backed strip may assist to put right the trouble, but if water is percolating through surrounding roofing, usually–in older property–slates, you may have to chip away the fillet and replace the soakers.

Sometimes soakers may be in long strips, which are cut into the wall and located beneath slates and tiles, or just in small sections. A damaged section can be lifted up, once surrounding tiles or slates are removed and cut out with metal shears. A new piece can be inserted and lapped over the old by some 150mm.

Zinc must first be dressed to replace worn or damaged soakers. The joints between bricks should be raked out to about a depth of 25mm. Zinc, 305mm wide, should be cut laid on a board and dressed to provide a 20mm strip at right angles. This angled section fits into the mortar gap of the original flashing.

Establish the angle of slope, using a woodworking, adjustable bevel. Turn the strip of zinc over and lay it on a thicker board. Hammer it down, working progressively outwards from the centre, until it matches the angle of the bevel; constantly check this.

Once it is moulded to shape, dash water into the gap between brickwork to assist mortar adhesion and insert the new soaker or flashing. Provide a 150mm overlap at joints.

Fold in small wedges of zinc at each end and then gently adjust the flashing to the slope of the roof. Fill the joint with a 1:4 mortar mix with a little PVA added. Trim off surplus mortar with a small trowel.

When working on sloping roofs always work from a crawling board and scaffolding. A scaffolding tower can be used in most cases for primary access.

Damaged slates or tiles may have to be replaced and surrounding brickwork repointed where necessary.

Self-adhesive flashing

Self-adhesive, aluminium-faced sealing can be used without the need of special tools, saving a great deal of time and effort. Width must be sufficient to overlap adjoining surfaces by at least 25mm, while making sure that the sealing is 'snug' into angles and corners. On overlapping glass and other surfaces, avoid forming air pockets in the angle.

In cold weather, it should be warmed to achieve maximum initial tack. Priming of the surfaces to be sealed also assists adhesion and grows stronger with time.

At the top of a glazing bar leave enough flashing to tuck around the bar end to complete the seal.

Very rough-textured surfaces such as

Bitumen primer is applied to the area to be covered by aluminium flashing strip

The flashing is dressed down on to the primed surface. It can be cut and trimmed

Leaks on many types of roofs can be cured by applying a brush-on bitumen

pebbledash and rustic brick require an additional seal at the leading edge – such as a knifing grade of bituminous mastic.

A major product of this type is Evostik Flashband, made in 9·75m lengths and in widths of from 50mm to 610mm. A primer is available in various quantities.

Application

All surfaces must first be cleaned. Other than for smooth, non-porous surfaces, such as glass and metal, apply the primer, after removal of dust, rust and old putty. The primer dries quickly and the surface can then be treated.

The material is simply cut to length with a pair of scissors. A release paper on the back peels off and the material can be pressed and contoured into place. Warming improves the application properties.

Finishing can be with a cloth pad, roller or square-section piece of wood, first pressuring the strip firmly into any angles of the area to be waterproofed.

Brushing on

Brush-on roofing treatments for flat or pitched roofs, include Evo-Stik Supaproof, a rich bitumen-content emulsion, which can be used on roofs of concrete, asphalt, asbestos, cement, corrugated iron, zinc felt, slate or tiles. This is made in four colours – black, tile-red, slate-grey or green.

The technique of use is to brush thoroughly to remove dirt, dust and moss from all cracks.

Fill all large cracks and depressions with a filler paste, made from clean sand mixed to a trowelling consistency, using the emulsion. If reinforcement is needed to bridge the gaps in the roof, to provide a continuous surface, a sandwich of jute, hessian, linen or canvas can be laid between two coats of the product.

It should be applied when weather conditions are suitable for rapid drying.

Weatherproof tapes can be used to seal glazing bars, which must be clean and dry

Mastic sealing is a popular method of joint sealing. This can be tube applied

Do not use in frosty or damp weather or when rain appears imminent.

Apply, with a hand brush or soft broom, a good generous coat. A similar second coat should be applied when the first has dried thoroughly. A coloured finish may be used as the second coat after a first coat of black.

Brushes and brooms should be washed out immediately after use with water. Do not use paraffin or white spirit for cleaning or mixing with the emulsion.

Weatherproof tape

Weatherproof tapes are another way of sealing. The surface must be clean and dry and wiped with a cloth moistened with paraffin or petrol. All traces of the solvent should be allowed to evaporate before applying the tape.

This is pressed firmly on the surface, smoothing down the centre first, and then working outward along the length of tape, ensuring that the edges are firmly bonded and all air is excluded. On sloping surfaces, start at the top and work downwards.

Unroll as you proceed and take care not to stretch the tape, which should be pressed well down into angles, and should overlap joining surfaces by at least 6mm.

Joints are made by placing one piece over another and smoothing down. On sloping surfaces, the upper piece should always be placed over the lower.

This type of sealing does not normally need painting, but paints may be used, provided care is taken to allow the paint to flow on with the minimum of brushing. Avoid painting immediately after or during hot weather.

The compound on the tape can be cleaned from surrounding areas with a rag moistened with paraffin, white spirit or petrol. Avoid splashing the tape with solvent.

In cold weather application is improved by storing in a warm place before use.

When time on the tiles is well spent

The weather, and water in particular, has a habit of getting in where it is not wanted, more often than not through leaks in roof surfaces. Regular inspection of the roof is essential if you are to keep out the elements as an unwelcome visitor. Loose slates and tiles are not difficult to replace and flaws should be rectified quickly before damage has a chance to strike and spread.

Slates

Roof slates are laid, working upwards from the eaves. Each row, or course, overlaps the one below it, and as the vertical joints between slates are staggered in adjacent rows, any slate partly covers the two below it.

The design and slope of the roof and position of battens, to which slates are nailed, determines the size of the main slates. However, there are several sizes of slate used in slate roofing. Those on eaves are the same width as the main roof slate but are shorter. Another slate is half as wide again as the main slates; this is used at the end of alternate rows.

A narrow slate, or creasing or verge slate, is often used at the end of each course on a gable end. This type of slate is laid underneath main slates and tilts the roof edge upwards, to prevent rain from running off the roof edge and down the wall.

Since slates vary in size, shape and thickness, establish that replacements correspond with existing ones, otherwise the roof may let in water. If you cannot match a slate exactly in size, obtain the next largest size of the same thickness. The slates can then be cut to fit.

Slates can be cut to any size or shape. The tile is marked with a nail or a trowel and then laid over a board and chopped with that part of the trowel nearest the handle. Chop half way and then turn the slate round and chop from the other end.

To make holes in new slates, establish the method of fixing and position each slate, bevelled edge downwards, on a flat board and drill the holes with a brace and bit or use a hammer and nail. A good way of making sure that holes are correctly positioned is to lay an old slate over a new one and make the new holes through the holes in the old slate.

Slates are made in different colours so that you can match the roof. New slates can be bought singly or in bulk. Demolition sites are another source of supply, but check carefully that slates are in good condition. These cost only about two-thirds of the price of new slates.

One firm makes concrete tiles which resemble slates. Since these are a good deal heavier than slates you should check that the roof battens are equal to the load.

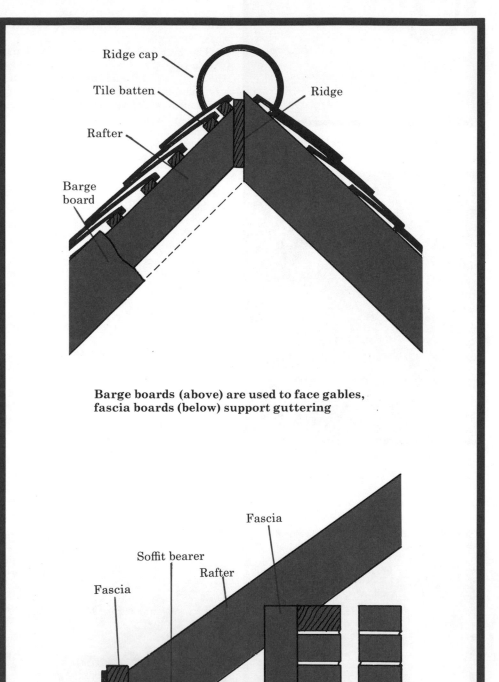

Barge boards (above) are used to face gables, fascia boards (below) support guttering

As slates age, they may flake and powder, particularly near nail holes. Hairline cracks, often difficult to see, develop along the grain. If slates have deteriorated at the edges, provided these are oversized, they can be cut down.

Slates are often referred to as bests, seconds and thirds. This has nothing to do with quality but refers to thickness and texture.

Take care when handling slates, since these are very brittle and break easily if roughly handled. Hold a slate along the longer side and tip it when lifting. Never try to lift slates from a pile, and if you are carrying several, wear canvas gloves and hold the slates on edge under an arm. Carried flat in a pile, they are likely to break or crack. Slates taken up to a roof should be stacked on edge, in a canvas or a plastic bag.

Before starting work, check the condition of the battens. If these are damaged or have deteriorated, they should be replaced. New battens should be nailed against the edges of the old ones with 50mm copper or zinc nails. Damaged timber should be cut out.

Main slates may be fixed by two edge nails or at the centre. The top and eaves courses of slates are always held along the top edge by two nails. In repairing a slate roof, always fix the new slates in the same way as the original ones.

For the first course above the eaves, short slates are used; these are covered completely by the second row. To stagger joins, nail slates either along their top edge or at centres. These are staggered in adjacent rows to make the roof watertight. For the courses at the ridge, short slates are used. These partly cover the course below, providing double thickness for weatherproofing.

Roof slates may crack or break or nails securing them may corrode. This can be caused by ageing of a house, causing movement in the roof structure, or through high winds, making the slates shear.

A tool for removing slates is called a ripper. These are not expensive to buy but can be hired. The ripper is slid under the slate directly above the one which has to be replaced. The head of the ripper is designed to hook the curved edges around the nails holding the broken slate. This 'rips' them away. It may take a little effort to remove the nails, but this must be done before the slate can be replaced.

Once the slate has been worked loose, a batten or slat will be visible and the new slate attaches to this. Slates are secured by 25mm galvanized nails. Before the nail is driven home, a length of lead 25mm × 230mm or a piece of thin copper wire, 230mm long, should be fixed to the nail. Drive the nail through the lead; wind copper wire round it before the nail is finally driven home. Line up the bottom edge of the slate with adjoining slates and bend up the end of the lead clip to secure it firmly in place.

To refit a section of slates, start work at the eaves by sliding a short slate under an adjacent, full-length slate, up to the batten centre line. As the first slate is partly covered, fix it with one nail. The others along the row are fixed with two nails.

Carefully check that each slate is on the

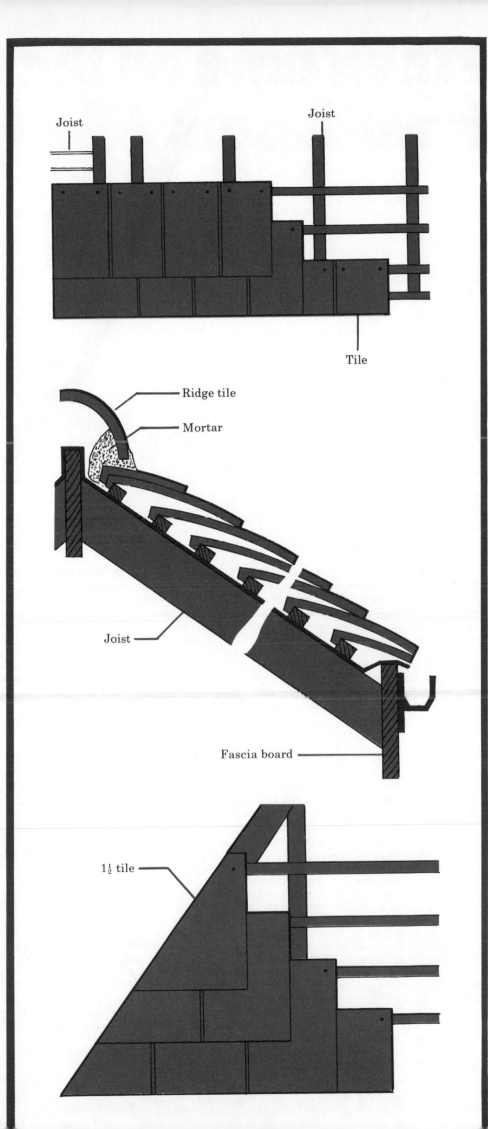

Joist

Joist

Tile

Ridge tile

Mortar

Joist

Fascia board

$1\frac{1}{2}$ tile

centre line, in order to allow the second row to be fixed to the same batten. Next, lift the slate in the row above and slide the first new full-length slate beneath it, making sure that the new slate aligns with the centre of the batten. Fix this with a single nail.

Lay remaining slates in the same row, so that these cover the vertical joins in the rows beneath. Carry on working up the roof and cover previous joins and securing nails with each fresh slate.

Since the nail holes are covered by the rows above, it may not be possible to nail the last few slates. Cut 25mm × 230mm lead clips to hold these slates. Fix the clips between nails securing adjacent slates. Again, fit these slates so that the bottom edges are flush with the remaining slates in the row and bend up the clips. Alternatively, you can make clips from thin copper wire.

Mortar between the ridge slates on top of the roof may fall out with age. Loose ridge slates should be lifted free and taken to the ground. Chip away old mortar from inside the slate with a trowel edge. Use care since you may crack the slate. With a club hammer and bolster, or cold chisel, remove old mortar from the roof. Apply a 1:3 cement and builder's sand mix along the ridge, roughening the surface with a trowel.

Locate the cleaned ridge slate on the mortar and tap it gently until it lines up with the height of the adjacent slates. Trowel mortar into the joints on each side and along the bottom, then smooth. Take care not to dislodge the slate before it sets.

Tiles

Laying or replacing tiles involves a similar operation, though these are heavier than slates. Tiles are again laid in courses, working from the eaves up to the roof ridge. Each course overlaps the one below, and vertical joins are staggered in adjacent rows, so that a tile partly covers two in the row beneath.

A slate ripper is helpful but not essential on tile repairs.

There are six basic types of tile: plain, pantiles, double pantiles, interlocking tiles and Roman and Spanish tiles. Unlike slate, tiles cannot be cut to size. The most common is the plain tile, measuring 265mm × 165mm × 13mm. These are slightly curved to ensure that tail ends bed evenly on the tiles below and to prevent water from creeping up, by capillary action, under the eaves.

There are three sizes of tiles – a standard tile for the main area; a tile half as wide again, called a tile and a half, at the end of alternate rows; and a shortened version of the tile and a half for the course along the eaves and along the ridge.

Tiles may be nailed to roof battens at intervals with 30mm galvanized nails; usually at every fourth course. Some have small projections called nibs, which fit over the battens. When replacing the odd tile, it is not normally necessary to use fixing nails. Nibbed tiles may be nailed, but unnibbed ones must always be nailed.

Try to match your tiles but if this is not possible, remove tiles from an inconspicuous area, using these to replace tiles in the

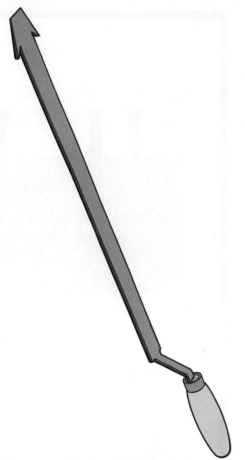

Ripper – used primarily for removing slates; can also be used for tiles

visible area, and use the new ones in the less noticeable place.

If several tiles in an area are broken, it is a good idea to strip out the entire area and retile, with new ones in one patch. Broken tiles near a verge, ridge or hip are more difficult to replace. Verges, ridges and hips are usually bedded in mortar. This bedding must be picked out with a cold chisel and tiles removed until the replacement can be effected. When reinstating the bedding do not use too strong or sloppy a mortar mix. Use a 1:3 cement/mortar mix sufficient for a solid, watertight job.

To take out a broken tile you just push it back slightly, lift it and withdraw it. Slipping the trowel beneath an adjacent tile, and lifting this slightly, will assist the operation.

If tiles are nibbed, prise the sound ones up with a trowel and lift the damaged ones over the batten. Nailed tiles should be rocked gently from side to side to loosen them. Use a ripper, if necessary, to remove the nails. You can also use a tiler's hammer which has a head designed for knocking in tile nails and shaped on the other side for lifting tiles.

Alternatively, you can remove the two tiles above, which will expose the nails, pull out the nails and then the tile, substitute a sound one and slide the other back, over the batten then down until the nibs engage.

If the new tile is too large, nibble off an edge with pincers, a little at a time, until it is the right size. You can rub the edge smooth with a coarse carborundum stone. Allow a 12mm gap between tiles.

Tile from the eaves upwards, and to fit

the last tiles, wedge up one of the tiles and lift the others and slide in the new tiles.

The under-eaves tiles measure 165mm × 150mm, and comprise the first and lowest course. These tiles are sometimes called half tiles and may be used to form the last course beneath the ridge. Verge tiles, which measure 230mm × 255mm, are used at edges and also for cutting to the mitre angle of hips and valleys. If any of these are broken or missing, water can get behind the fascia board. This course is completely covered by the second row of tiles.

Valley junctions are shaped tiles which interlock with each other to form tiled gutters.

Tiles are usually fixed to sawn deal battens, though you may encounter feather-edged board.

On some roofs, narrower tiles, called creasing tiles, may be used at gable ends. These are laid beneath the end to tilt the edge of the roof slightly, so that rainwater does not run down the gable wall.

Pantiles, sectionally shaped like a flattened letter 's', also interlock or lap over each other. These are pointed along the verge and may have nibs or hooks and are also nailed. First, chip away pointing where necessary, lever this slightly to loosen the bed and then push and twist sideways to remove the tile. If these are nailed, a ripper may be used to remove them.

Ridge and hip tiles may deteriorate through stresses or inherent weakness, or flake and spall through combined water and frost action. This may expose the ridge timbers. A broken ridge can also slip down a roof and do a lot of damage.

Ridges are generally right-angled or semi-circular, with a 230mm diameter. The edges formed by two sloping surfaces, called hips, have semi-circular or bonnet-shaped tiles.

Chip out the old ridge and remove all bedding material. Clean the adjacent edges of ridges and try the new ones for fit. If the tile is too long, allowing a 6mm overlap on each side, mark a line, then nibble off with the pincers.

You can cut a section by bedding the ridge solidly in damp sand and chipping a groove all round with a sharp cold chisel. Concrete ridge tiles are more difficult to cut than clay ones.

A new ridge must be bedded solidly along the edges. The joints should be firm and when the cement has slightly dried, the joints should be trowelled smooth. On the end ridge, the 'open' section must be filled in with mortar and tile slips. These are small pieces of tile to reinforce the mortar.

Pieces of tile must be used to reinforce the mortar of the ridge tiles and in the tiles on the verge.

Sarking (bitumenized) felt is laid on modern roofs, primarily to keep out dust. This felt tears easily. Always fit new felt if the existing cover is torn.

Felt should be overlapped by 150mm at both horizontal and vertical joints. The bottom run of felting on a roof should be overlapped at the front to provide a drip into the gutter, while the top should always overlap the ridgeboard to form a watertight seal.

The right way– with the right tools

The choice of hand tools today is very wide and it seems a daunting and bewildering task to choose those which are strictly essential. Why are there several types of plane and various patterns of screwdriver; what about all those other work aids and gadgets? Obviously, all have their specific or specialist applications. Proficiency and experience will provide the occasions for use of more specialized or sophisticated tools.

For home-maintenance and improvement jobs, a few basic tools should suffice. If, however, you make things or carry out more ambitious jobs around the home, you will steadily require more tools, including specialist tools or gadgets, some of which you can make.

The rule when choosing tools is to buy the best you can afford. A few good tools are better than a host of inferior ones, for these will probably not only give you poorer and discouraging results but break or wear out very quickly. Once you have bought a basic set of tools, you can always add more later.

Some people buy a tool a week or a month. Budget-plan buying such as this is a good idea and you will be surprised at how quickly your tool kit grows. A good rule is to avoid lending tools. There are more tool borrowers than buyers, and since tool borrowers may have little idea of use and maintenance, your tools can come back possibly the worse for wear.

Coupled with this is the inconvenience of not having to hand the tool you want. Tool borrowers may also be reluctant in returning tools; or in turn lend them to someone else!

The twelve basic types of tool suggested take into account the need for a number of types of chisel, screwdriver or drill bits. There is no need to invest in a full range of chisels, for example, at once. Choose only those you need for immediate use.

Cutting

A saw is the most-used tool in woodwork. A panel saw and a tenon, or back saw, are both useful acquisitions. You may buy these both together or one at a time. You will, however, need to invest in both at an early stage.

The tenon saw is essential for fine work. It has a stiffened backing to ensure a straight cut. A good choice is one about 305mm long with 14 points (teeth) to every 25mm.

The panel saw is designed for finished work but can be used for ripping (down the grain) or cross cutting (across the grain). Choose one about 550mm long with ten points to 25mm. Teflon-coated saws cut well through resinous or damp timber.

Drilling

A small hand drill, an assortment of twist drills and a masonry drill should cover most contingencies. The Stanley 'Yankee' Handyman push drill is a useful and easy-to-use drill, which comes with a variety of drill points. Later you will need to buy a hand or bit brace and a range of centre bits and augers.

Smoothing

A medium-sized smoothing plane about 250mm long with a 51mm cutting edge, will enable you to tackle a wide range of jobs from smoothing timber on the bench to easing doors and windows. Plan ing files can be similarly used though they are not really in tended for fine woodwork treat ment.

Holding

The vice is an essential part of wood-working and is the basic holding tool. While there are many cases in which you will later need clamps to hold timber, a portable vice is a good initial investment as it can be clamped on to many surfaces and can double as a clamp while glued and assembled work is setting. With a bench, a larger permanent vice is best.

Measuring and marking

A marking gauge is essential for any marking out of timber. This marks or scribes a line parallel with the edge of a board, by means of a small metal spike set on a wooden shaft with an adjustable crosspiece which slides up and down it. Later you will need other types of gauge, including a mortise gauge.

There are various types of measure. The retractable steel measure, in its own compact case, is a handy tool and enables you to measure longer lengths of timber than a wood or metal rule. These are very accurate, since the gradations of measurement are very fine.

However, a metal rule 610mm long is a more useful immediate acquisition for the serious woodworker and can be used to provide a straight edge. An alternative is the folding boxwood rule.

A try-square with a fixed blade is also necessary for ensuring accurate right angles – an essential in work of even limited precision. A size of 203mm or 228mm is suitable. It may be a good idea to invest in a combination try-square which enables you to mark other angles as well as right angles.

A slim marking knife is important. This marks with greater precision than a pencil. You could also use a trimming knife, which comes with a variety of blades for cutting various materials and also for cutting angles.

Sharpening

Chisels and plane irons need regular sharpening if they are to do the job for which they were made. If these become badly worn, they will need regrinding on a carborundum wheel and then sharpening and honing. To keep such tools in first-class order you will need a combination oilstone. These tools should be regularly inspected for sharpness, for poor or damaged work may otherwise result.

Joining

The two basic tools you need are the hammer and the screwdriver. Initially, you need only one hammer; the best one to choose is the claw hammer. The weight of hammer determines the work you can satisfactorily tackle. For general purposes, a 453-gramme claw hammer is suitable. You may shortly need to invest in the smaller Warrington-pattern hammer for a wider range of woodworking uses. You will also need a nail punch.

A good general screwdriver is about 254mm long. There are two basic types of screw head – the slotted and the cross-headed or 'sunburst' screw. You will need two or three general-purpose screwdrivers – a medium one and a cabinet screwdriver for screws with slotted heads.

The 'sunburst' head, usually under the trade name of 'Pozidriv', consists of a series of radial slots in the screw head. A range of four screwdrivers covers all possible types of Pozidriv head. This type of head prevents the screwdriver slipping in the slot and 'camming out'.

Wood shaping

The chisel is the basic wood-shaping tool and is made in various types to serve a variety of applications. Initially, a set of bevel-edged chisels – a 25mm, a 13mm and a 6mm chisel – should meet most or all requirements.

Optional extra

A useful additional tool which many people may want to regard as an early acquisition is the spirit level. This enables you to true up work and to make accurate fixings. A metal level is very durable and can also be used as a straight edge.

Using tools
Marking

Always mark the best-looking side of a piece of timber with a looped letter 'l' and the best edge with a small 'x'. These are carpenter's marks to show which side and edge will be exposed. These surfaces are known as the 'face side' and the 'face edge'.

Marking gauge

Hold the workpiece with three fingers and the gauge with one finger and thumb so that the stock is against the face edge of the work. Drag and not push the pin as this provides a firm, clean line for planing. Continue the line right round the work, always marking from the face edge.

To set the gauge, adjust the cross-piece with a rule to the required distance from the spike. Slide the tool up to the edge of the piece of timber to be marked.

The crosspiece maintains the spike at a constant distance from the edge, while the spike scribes a straight line.

Always work against the grain. This prevents grain from leading the point of the gauge into a non-waste section of the wood. Always mark away from the poorer edge of the timber.

When using the gauge to mark the thickness of joints, set it to half the timber thickness, minus a fraction of around 0·4mm, and gauge the setting. This should be tested by marking from both sides of the wood, which should leave just a tiny 0·8mm gap in the middle.

Marking knife

This scores more accurately than a pencil. By severing the fibres on the surface of the wood it helps to ensure a clean cut with saw or chisel. A knife with a replaceable blade will serve both as a marking knife and can be used for other jobs. The blade must remain sharp; otherwise it can slip and deface the work or provide an impositive working line. A knife with a replaceable blade ensures that you always have a sharp marking edge.

Try-square

Hold the stock of the try-square firmly on the face edge of the work with three fingers and the thumb. This forms a clamp and ensures that the work is steadily held as you mark with knife or pencil.

Sawing

Always saw on the waste side of the timber. As you near the end of the cut, support the timber so that it does not break off and splinter at the ends.

Panel saw

Steady the work by using three fingers and the thumb as a clamp on the saw handle. The feet should be comfortable and apart, in a boxer-like stance, and the body generally relaxed. Also, the body should not obstruct the work, as this may throw the saw off line. The arm should be free to move with a piston action, not catching the body in any way.

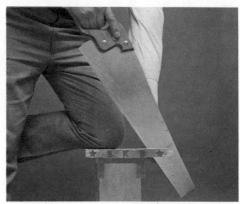

Start sawing at the front of the work, using the thumb as a guide and make a small backward movement of about 45° with the saw, first allowing the saw to drop on to the work across the marked cut line.

The blade should be kept vertical during sawing and the position should be such that the eye is able to sight down the cut line without contorting the body.

Maintain the saw blade vertically, gradually allowing this to drop until the handle end is on the guide line. Use an even, easy-flowing movement. Avoid short, jerky strokes which will cause the saw to move off line. Allow the saw to cut with its own weight and avoid great extra pressure.

Tenon saw

Hold this with its teeth almost parallel with the work surface. Again, use your left thumb to guide the blade for your starting cut. Draw the saw backwards, two or three times. Use as much length of saw as possible for each stroke.

Maintain your line of vision over the saw to help you to keep the line straight. When you reach the bottom of the cut, use three or four extra strokes to make sure that you do not leave a protruding fringe of fibres.

The first rule of carpentry is 'measure twice and cut once'. In using a folding rule or other measuring stick, the rule should be stood on edge on the piece of timber

being marked so that the marking graduations on the rule are actually in contact with the timber. This will avoid a marking

error, as the rule will be in contact with the timber at the points where you want to mark it.

Hammers

Drive the hammer, with a short upward swing and a full follow through. To lessen the risk of hammer 'bruises' on the surface, keep the hammer parallel for the last few strokes.

Bench hooks

These are used to hold timber firm when using a tenon saw. The hook consists of a batten or lip at top and bottom of a base board, running about two thirds of the way across. When the hook is placed against the edge of a bench or working surface, the batten beneath prevents the hook from slipping.

The bench hook is simple to make. Materials required are a base board measuring about 300mm × 250mm × 25mm thick and two pieces of batten for the lips, 51mm × 25mm and 200mm long. These dimensions are not critical, but it is important to make sure that the timber is not warped in any way, or the hook will rock when used and make cutting difficult.

You will need six 31mm panel pins and some woodworking adhesive.

First, drive two pins just through a batten at each end and then spread woodworking adhesive on to the bottom of the batten. Align the batten accurately with the top edge of the base panel and nail the battens home. The other batten is fixed at the corresponding position on the left, below the board, so that the hook can be used either way up.

Fixing: giving every means of support

No visible means of support

Before making a hole in any surface, first establish that it is safe to do so. Find out if there are any buried pipes, cables or other obstructions, and if you meet anything, stop and relocate the position of the hole.

With few exceptions, all fixings to hard surfaces must be made by first drilling a hole to insert a fixing device. It is important to see that the drill point is sharp and in good condition. Metals and synthetic materials are, as a rule, best drilled with an ordinary engineer's twist bit, used in a hand or power drill.

There are several basic types of fixing: masonry nails, plugs and screws (or bolts in the case of very heavy objects) are used for fixing into solid walls; and cavity-fixing devices for hollow surfaces, such as panelled walls or ceilings.

Screws and screwdrivers are main essentials in fixing. The length of screw, and its type, depends on the nature of the fixing and the load it has to carry. The intervals at which fixings are made and the load-bearing qualities of the surface have to be taken into account. If in doubt, use a larger fixing. Common sizes suitable for general use are No. 8 and No. 12 gauge screws of between 25mm, 31mm, 51mm and 64mm length.

The screwdriver is gauged or sized to the head of the screw you are turning. The best general type of screwdriver for many applications is a cabinetmaker's.

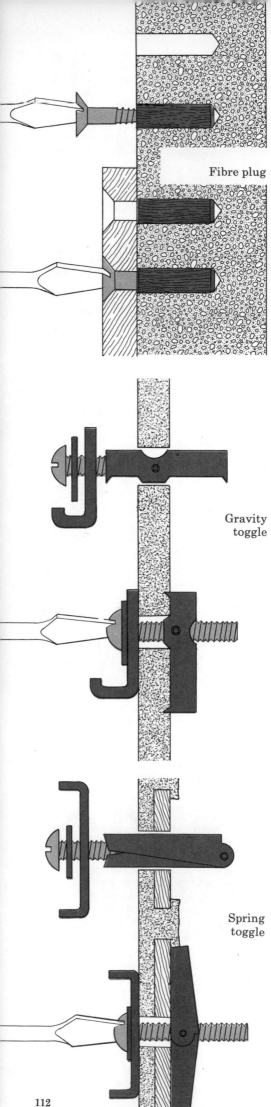

Fibre plug

Gravity
toggle

Spring
toggle

Types of surface

Solid walls are usually made of brick, concrete aggregate or lightweight cellular blocks. There are no special problems in attaching objects to brick or concrete materials. Care must be taken in making fixings in aggregate materials, since these break up more easily and have poorer load-bearing qualities than some other materials.

With very hard materials, such as solid concrete and hard brick, it may be necessary to use a percussive device—such as a percussion power drill or a 'jumper' and a heavy hammer.

Interior linings and finishings differ considerably in construction, thickness and strength. Plaster board, lath and plaster, fibre board, synthetic-resin compound panels are those most frequently used. Linings are generally fixed to a timber framework called studding. The distances separating the members of the framework are called centres. Where possible fixings should be made into these members, consisting usually of 75mm × 75mm timber, rather than into the actual lining material.

It is necessary to locate these centres, often at regular intervals of about 380mm. The best way to do this is to make small test holes through the lining until you locate the timber supports.

Where the framing cannot be used for direct fixing, only the lightest loads should be fixed to the lining. Expanding or anchor bolts can be used, but it is best to spread the load by screwing stout 'backing' boards to the timber supports and making fixings directly to the board.

Types of fixing
Wood plugs

Though largely superseded by more modern methods, the traditional hand-shaped wood plug can be useful where nail fixings have to be made. If the plugs are left proud of the brickwork they can be cut to any desired length where the brickwork is being lined or clad. Plugs should be cut with a gentle taper so that they have a tendency to twist and grip. Sharp tapers do not fill the recess and, as wood tends to shrink, become loose. Plugs should be a tight fit in the hole.

Plugs into external walls or in situations where dampness is likely should be treated with a preservative before being driven in.

If screw fixings are to be made, hardwood plugs should be used and, once inserted, a pilot hole, of slightly smaller diameter than the screw, should be drilled. Brass or bronze screws should be greased with wax or tallow before being driven home.

Preformed plugs

These are made in various materials, ranging from fibre, soft metal and synthetic resin. They require only a neat, round hole, matched to the size of the plug and a little larger than the screw to be used.

It is important that hole, plug and screws should match in size. The holding power of the plug depends upon the frictional grip obtained when the screw expands the plug.

If a small screw is used in too large a plug, the expansion will be insufficient to obtain a reliable fixing. A large screw in a small plug will be difficult to turn and may jam.

The composition of fibre and soft metal grips the hole and provides a firm fixing. Nylon plugs have teeth or ridges which grip the surrounding surface and stop the plug from turning.

Fibre plug sizes for any screw should be of the same length or slightly longer than the length of the thread, excluding the screw shank, which should never enter the plug. Fibre plug sizes are numbered to correspond with the size of screw and the drill or hole-making device used.

Plastic compounds

Sometimes, particularly in mortar or soft brickwork, a hole may become larger than desired—or a previous hole may be too large for the screw to be used. Plastic compounds, based on asbestos-fibre and cement, provide an effective and reliable fixing. However, avoid making any extra-large holes; reposition the fixing in that case. The compound is wetted with clean water, formed into a plug of the required size, and rammed into the hole; usually a tool is provided for this.

If the sides are parallel, the fixing should be secure. If the hole is wider at the face than at the back, the plug may draw out. It is then better to enlarge the hole at the back to produce a 'dovetail' shape. The tool supplied with plastic compounds is pointed at one end to form a pilot hole in the soft compound to start the screw.

The screw should be tightened into the moist filler, but where a large mass of compound is used, the final tightening should be left until the plug has hardened. These compounds should not be used in conditions where dampness exists.

Toggles

Toggles are used for fixing in hollow walls.
Gravity toggles: These have a swivel toggle which drops vertically when inserted through a pre-made hole in a hollow wall; used with bolts for heavier fixing.
Spring toggles: These have two spring-loaded gripping arms which expand after the toggle is pushed through a hole; used with bolts for heavier fixing.
Nylon toggles: Fasteners with a slotted collar which slips over a nylon strip attached to the toggle; used for screw fixing.

A selection of twist bits

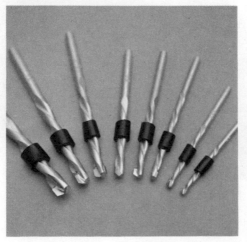

Collapsible anchors: These remain in place if the screw is removed. Insertion of the screw draws metal gripping shoulders against the inner wall of the fitting.

Rubber-sleeved anchors: Used for fixing plastic or metal sheet. These can be used in solid walls. The bolt compresses a rubber sleeve against the surface of the wall.

Nylon or plastic anchors: The action of tightening the screw draws the anchor to the wall.

Nuts and bolts

Machine bolts are used for certain fixing jobs, such as wooden framing for workbenches or light construction. These usually have square or hexagon-shaped heads.

Coach bolts are used for a variety of light or heavy applications. These have rounded heads with square collar locks to prevent the nut from turning while being tightened.

Machine screws are used for small woodworking projects or metalwork. These have countersunk round, pan or cheese heads.

Rag bolts or foundation bolts are used for general construction where framework is built on to concrete foundations. The ragged ends hold firmly in concrete, leaving the shank and thread exposed.

Masonry or anchor bolts are used for fixing to breeze or aggregate blocks, brickwork or concrete. With these a plastic anchor expands to grip the sides of holes in solid walls.

Masonry nails

These are used for jobs such as fixing shelving, battens, picture rails, skirting boards and studs for wall panelling. They are tempered to avoid bending and can be nailed straight in with a heavy hammer.

Masonry nails are in two types—one with a straight and the other a twisted shank. The latter improves penetration into hard materials.

These nails grip by compacting finely crushed material around themselves as they penetrate. This builds up a strong friction which exerts a tight grip on the nail.

The nails are made in three grades—standard, a medium and a heavy-duty pin. Standard pins are from 28mm to 70mm and will fix battens, shelving brackets and pegboard to ordinary brick or low-density concrete, aggregate or similar walls. Medium pins range in size from 22mm to 86mm and

Fixings illustrated on this page

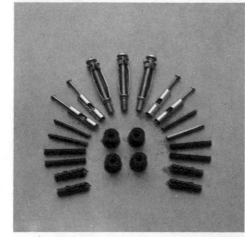

are used for fixing into harder surfaces. Heavy-duty pins are sized from 38mm to 89mm and have spirally twisted shanks.

Fixing

Masonry pins must always penetrate a surface at right angles. A heavy hammer, such as an engineer's pattern, is needed, and firm, well-placed blows should be used.

The nail should be long enough to penetrate at least 19mm into the main surface and not less than 13mm, or it may backlash or break in the wall.

Boring and fixing tools

A hand boring tool, or 'jumper', and a heavy hammer should be turned slightly with each blow in a clockwise direction. The weight of the blow should be gauged in accordance with the hardness of the material. Light, sharp blows and frequent turning will achieve results more rapidly. A too-heavy hammer used on a tool of small diameter may cause it to snap or jam.

As a guide, the weight of the hammer should be about 340 grammes for No. 6 or No. 8 screw gauges and about 677 grammes for No. 12 gauge or heavier. If there is a danger of flying particles, wear protective goggles.

Piston-and-cylinder fixing tools

Piston-and-cylinder fixing tools take a variety of fixing pins, which are muzzle loaded into the mouth of the cylinder. The tool is then held flat to the surface and struck with hammer blows on the piston, which recoils after each strike in preparation for the next blow.

These tools can also be used for driving in masonry nails made with threaded heads to take a variety of domed or hexagon nuts.

For many jobs around the home, the ordinary tipped masonry bit, up to about 8mm diameter, can be used in hand or in power tools.

A rotary drill bit, unless diamond tipped, may jam between particles. Standard domestic electric drills can be fitted with rotary percussion attachments, and some makes of drill are dual purpose both rotary percussion and standard.

Care must be taken to use a suitable speed when boring into brickwork or masonry, the most common surface materials.

These are the suggested speeds using standard twist bits:

Speed rpm	Cutting diameter
750–1,500	6mm, 8mm, 10mm
500–1,000	11mm, 13mm, 14mm, 16mm
300–600	22mm, 25mm, 27mm, 31mm, 35mm
400–800	19mm

To bore holes from 13mm to 38mm diameter, heavier core or trepanning bits are suggested. These are basically tubes with hardened cutting teeth set around the circumference at one end.

Speed rpm	Cutting diameter
400	13mm, 16mm, 19mm
300	22mm, 25mm, 27mm
200	31mm, 35mm, 38mm

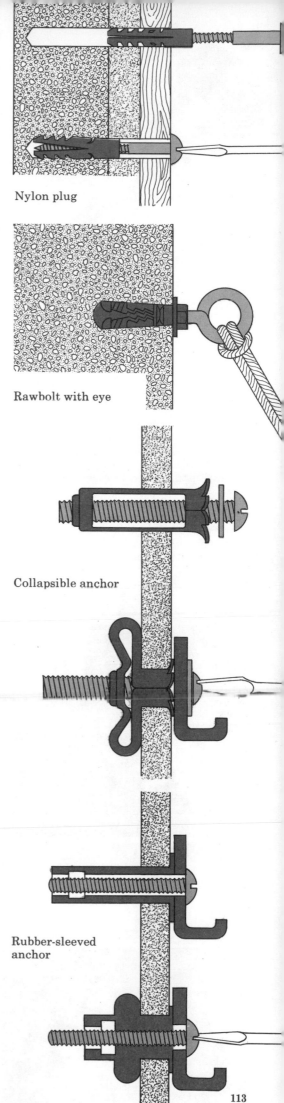

Nylon plug

Rawbolt with eye

Collapsible anchor

Rubber-sleeved anchor

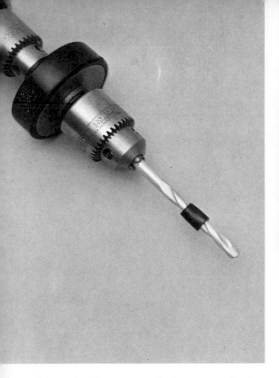

Cartridge hammers

Where you have a lot of fixing to do, such as extensive battening for putting up cladding, a cartridge hammer can be hired to speed up the work. The hammer is a type of gun which fires a hardened steel stud or pin into a surface, using a cartridge similar to that used in a ·22 rifle.

Many types of stud are made. Most have a plain flat head, like a nail, or have a threaded stem for removable fixings, the stud base remaining in position.

The penetration of the stud is governed by the material into which it is fired, the weight of the stud and the power of the cartridge.

A cartridge gun should never be used on brittle materials, such as aggregate, lath and plaster, fibre board and similar soft materials. Studs must not be driven within 50mm of the edge of brickwork, or this may break away.

Properly handled, a cartridge hammer is safe and efficient, but make sure that you are familiar with how it works; that you use the correct strength of cartridge (these are colour coded in order of power); and ensure that no one is in the line of fire.

As a rule, you should not fire a stud into a surface of less 'stopping power' than 230mm brickwork if there is a possibility of anyone beyond. Hold the gun firmly and squarely to the work to prevent ricochet.

A typical make of hammer is fired by a blow from an ordinary hand hammer on to a firing plunger on the base of the hammer. This fires the cartridge and propels the stud into the surface. With this type of hammer, firing through soft materials is virtually impossible.

A speed reducer attached to a standard drill

A shallow hole cutter can be used for larger holes. This consists of a tungsten-carbide tipped trepanning tool with a pilot drill for accurate centring which sinks holes of up to 89mm diameter to a depth of 50mm.

For drilling very deep holes, extension pieces are available which screw into certain types of drill bit.

When working with hand or power tools, ensure that the drill bit is sharp and

Marked adhesive tape prevents the drill wandering when drilling ceramic tiles

in good condition. Squeaking is a sign of bluntness, coupled with a drop in performance. Working with a blunt tip can overload the power drill.

If the bit tip turns blue, it means that excessive speed has been used and the temper of the steel will be ruined. Masonry bits can be resharpened at home, but this can be done professionally and many manufacturers provide for at least one free sharpening after purchase.

Two common fixing situations, a blind and a shelving system

Bench of all work

With constant use, a work bench top does, in time, become very worn—chipped and unsuitable to work on. An important feature of this bench is that the top can be turned over for further use and eventually replaced, simply by removing a few screws.

The bench is strong enough to hold a large-capacity vice, and the top is big enough for tackling among the largest of home-construction jobs.

The height is 800mm–suitable for most adults. If you are taller or shorter than average, you may vary the height to suit your requirements.

All the timber widths (80mm) are the same throughout, but the legs are slightly thicker (28mm) than the rails (22mm), for strength and for extra glueing surface.

The screws are countersunk, and all surfaces which come into contact with each other are glued. Surplus glue is wiped off with a damp cloth.

Construction is based on a top and a bottom tray. Start by cutting the six cross rails, required for the trays. These must be exactly the same length (575mm), and the ends must be square.

These are marked out using the try-square and marking knife. The marking knife and a marking gauge fulfil slightly different roles. The marking knife is used to mark wood across the grain; the marking gauge is used along timber and across the end grain.

A knife gives a more positive line than a pencil and acts as a guide to the saw when cutting.

Cut six pieces 15mm longer than required from lengths of planed softwood. Place the pieces together and cramp them with a 'G' cramp or a small bar cramp.

Using a try-square and marking knife, next square a cut line across all pieces, 5mm from one end. Measure 575mm from this line and square a cut line across at the other end.

Unfasten the cramp and square the lines right round the timber with the marking knife. Using a bench hook and tenon saw, carefully cut these pieces to length, sawing on the waste side of the line. Place these pieces to one side and cramp the four front and back rails, cut to 1·05m, in two cramps.

These pieces are a little more complicated to mark out, so extra care should be taken.

The end rails are both inset 40mm. The

115

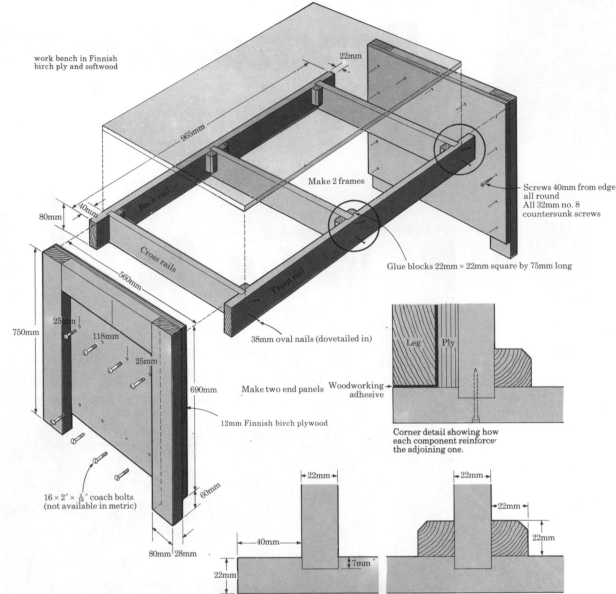

work bench in Finnish
birch ply and softwood

22mm

965mm

Back rail

Make 2 frames

80mm
40mm

Cross rails

Screws 40mm from edge
all round
All 32mm no. 8
countersunk screws

560mm

Front rail

Glue blocks 22mm × 22mm square by 75mm long

25mm

118mm

750mm

25mm

690mm

Make two end panels

Woodworking
adhesive

Leg   Ply

38mm oval nails (dovetailed in)

12mm Finnish birch plywood

Corner detail showing how
each component reinforce·
the adjoining one.

60mm

16 × 2″ × ⁵⁄₁₆″ coach bolts
(not available in metric)

80mm 28mm

22mm

40mm

7mm

22mm

22mm

22mm

22mm

22mm

cross rail is exactly centred. The top and bottom tray are made exactly the same. Housing joints are used to secure all tray rails.

A housing joint consists of a slot across a piece of timber, into which the end section of another piece fits tightly at right-angles.

Housings are measured and marked out with a try-square and a marking knife. Use one of the cross rails to provide a direct measurement, then square lines all round the timber.

Set the marking gauge to the depth of the housing joint and cut carefully to depth with the tenon saw.

Check that you cut accurately; it will assist if you keep the saw parallel as you near the end of the cut.

Remove waste with a 25mm bevel-edged chisel. First cut out waste on either side of the cut, holding the chisel at an angle of about 45°, with the bevel uppermost; do this on each side of the slot.

This will leave a 'hill' in the centre of the groove. With the chisel held flat, remove the centre waste and clean up the joint—first the corners, then the edge, and the bed.

Use one of the cross rails to mark out the width of the housing grooves by direct measurement, so that the housing is made to the exact width of the timber. Unfasten the cramps and square the lines across on

Turn bench upside down when drilling holes for the bottom bolts

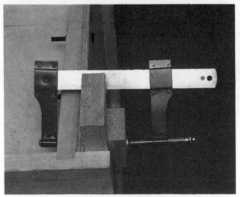

Use cramp with protective block of wood to hold frames together when drilling holes

the inside face of the rail and down the other edge.

Set the marking gauge to 7mm, and, between the pairs of lines now marked, gauge the depth of the housing. These housings may now be cut, taking care that cutting is to the waste side of the lines.

Saw one housing, remove the waste and test with a cross rail for tightness of fit. You should be able to knock the rail gently in with a hammer and a piece of scrap wood. If the joint is either loose or tight, make the necessary adjustments to your sawing when cutting the next housing.

Again, clean out the waste and test. Repeat this for all housings, making a tight but comfortable fit.

When all housings are cut, prepare the glue blocks required–eight for each 'tray', 22mm² × 70mm long. Spread glue in all housings and on the end of each rail. Assemble the frame, using 50mm oval nails, and secure each joint by dovetail nailing.

Spread glue in the corners of the frame and on each glue block. Put the blocks in place, using a 'rubbing' action, to squeeze out as much glue as possible. This action brings the surfaces close together. Secure each block with 38mm panel pins.

Try each frame for squareness by measuring the diagonals with a steel tape and checking that these measurements are identical. Any slight differences can

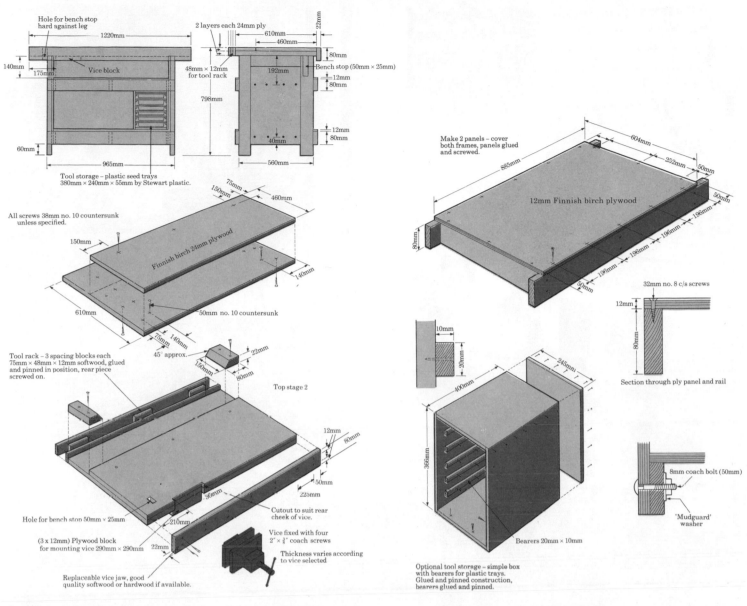

Hole for bench stop hard against leg

1220mm

140mm

175mm

Vice block

60mm

965mm

Tool storage – plastic seed trays
380mm × 240mm × 55mm by Stewart plastic.

2 layers each 24mm ply

610mm
460mm
22mm
80mm

Bench stop (50mm × 25mm)

48mm × 12mm
for tool rack

192mm

12mm
80mm

798mm

12mm
80mm

40mm

12mm
80mm

560mm

All screws 38mm no. 10 countersunk
unless specified.

75mm
150mm
460mm

150mm

Finnish birch 24mm plywood

610mm

140mm

50mm no. 10 countersunk

75mm
140mm
45° approx.

Tool rack – 3 spacing blocks each
75mm × 48mm × 12mm softwood, glued
and pinned in position, rear piece
screwed on.

150mm
22mm
80mm

Top stage 2

12mm
80mm

50mm

225mm

366mm

210mm

22mm

Hole for bench stop 50mm × 25mm

(3 x 12mm) Plywood block
for mounting vice 290mm × 290mm

Replaceable vice jaw, good
quality softwood or hardwood if available.

Cutout to suit rear
cheek of vice.

Vice fixed with four
2″ × ⅜″ coach screws

Thickness varies according
to vice selected

Make 2 panels – cover
both frames, panels glued
and screwed.

604mm
252mm
50mm

885mm

50mm

12mm Finnish birch plywood

80mm

196mm
196mm
196mm
196mm
196mm

50mm

32mm no. 8 c/s screws

12mm

80mm

Section through ply panel and rail

10mm

20mm

245mm

400mm

366mm

8mm coach bolt (50mm)

'Mudguard'
washer

Bearers 20mm × 10mm

Optional tool storage – simple box
with bearers for plastic trays.
Glued and pinned construction,
bearers glued and pinned.

be corrected by hand pressure. Leave the frames on a level surface to dry.

Check the overall length and width of these trays and cut panels of 12mm birch ply, 885mm × 604mm, to fit. It is important that the panels are an exact fit, so adjust the sizes slightly, to allow for any variations which may have occurred during construction.

All panels should be cut with a fine-toothed hand saw, to minimize splintering or breaking out on the underside of the panel. Trim the panels to an exact fit with a smoothing plane, mark out for the second countersunk screw holes and centrepunch the position of each.

Countersinking is the process by which a shallow depression is made in the timber, so that a screw head will finish flush with the surface. This may be done with a counter-sink or rose bit, held in a hand brace or in an electric drill.

Spread glue on the edge of the tray and on the underside of the panel. Place the panel in position and secure with four panel pins, placed on opposite sides. You may drill and countersink the holes in the conventional way, or use a tool such as the Stanley Screwmate, a small tool which drills and countersinks for matching steel screws.

The second tray is then prepared in exactly the same way. Both are set aside to dry thoroughly.

Cutting list – all mm sizes

Part	Qty.	Material	Length	Width	Thickness
Front and back rails	4	Softwood	965	80	22
Cross rails	6	Softwood	574	80	22
Legs	4	Softwood	750	80	28
Vice cheek (long)	1	Softwood	1220	80	22
Vice cheek (short)	1	Hardwood	305	100	25
Glue blocks	16	Hardwood	70	22	22
Well blocks	2	Hardwood	150	80	22
Tool racks	2	Hardwood	1220	48	12
Tool racks blocks	3	Hardwood	75	48	12
Leg panels	2	Finnish birch ply	690	560	12
Tray panels	2	Finnish birch ply	885	604	12
Top	1	Finnish birch ply	1220	610	24
Top	1	Finnish birch ply	1220	460	24
Mounting vice block	3	Finnish birch ply	290	290	12

50mm × 8mm Coach bolts   (16)
8mm Mudguard washers   (16)
50mm × 10mm Coach screws

32mm × No 8 steel c/s screws   (64)
38mm × No 10 steel c/s screws   (30)
50mm × No 10 steel c/s screws   (8)

Panel pins: few 32mm
50mm oval nails
Glue

Having completed the two 'trays' and ensured that they are rigid, check the measurements between the projections at the end of each. These should be identical, but if they are not, select the largest measurement and use this for marking out the two end (leg) panels. These should be 560mm wide and 690mm long. It is, however, more important to work to the framework dimensions, in case of variation.

Once these end panels have been prepared, plane them to an exact fit. These should go tightly into the space between the tray and the rails. Mark the panels and trays for ease of identification.

Cut the four legs to an exact length—marking these all out at the same time to a length of 750mm. Glue and screw these on to the end panels, using techniques similar to those in assembling the trays.

Once the legs have been secured, cut the top rail to fit exactly between the legs, glue and screw into position, and leave these assemblies to dry.

The top of the bench consists of double layers of 24mm Finnish birch plywood, providing a very solid and flat working surface.

Two panels cut from a standard 1220mm sheet of ply allows for a 'tool well' at the rear of the bench. Make one panel 610mm and the other 460mm wide.

These should be screwed together from beneath. There is no need, at this stage, to put in more than two screws. With the two pieces together, mark out, on the front edge, the cut out required to take the rear cheek of the vice.

All vices vary to some degree in their construction, and some are more difficult to fit than others. The vice used was from the Paramo range and was easily fitted. This vice requires a cut out 230mm long × 17mm deep. This is marked on to both

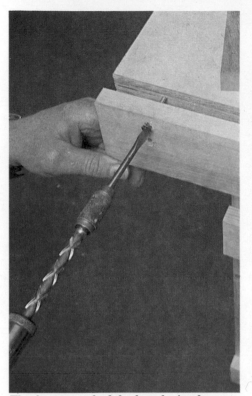

The front panel of the bench simply screws into place and is replaceable

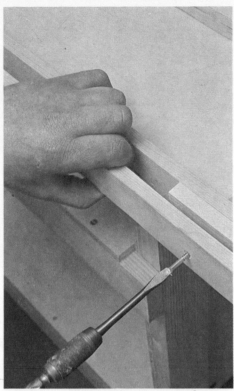

A handy rack for tool storage can be screwed on to the back of the workbench

Chopping out the slot in the bench top into which the bench stop is fitted

The serviceable vice is best fitted with coach screws; these provide a firm fixing

pieces of ply comprising the top and the cut out is gauged to depth.

Take out the screws and work on each piece individually. The cut out is best handled in the following way:

Cut down the lines marked to the gauge line. At 5mm intervals along the length of the cut, make a further series of saw cuts. This is waste material which has to be removed. Then, with a 25mm bevel-edged chisel, remove this waste.

Repeat this on the second panel and fix the vice block in position with glue and screws.

When the end panels are dry, mark out the lines of the bolt holes. These should be 40mm from the bottom and 192mm from the top of each end assembly. Mark out the bolt holes and bore, with a twist bit, holes for $\frac{5}{16}$ in. (8mm) bolts.

Clean up the end (leg) assemblies with medium glasspaper and then similarly clean up the two trays.

Check that the leg assemblies fit into their respective positions. If not, adjust by using a smoothing plane, finely set.

Cover all contact surfaces for the bottom tray with glue and bolt the legs into position, using mudguard washers on the inside. These are extra-large washers which help to spread the pressure when the nut is tightened.

Spread the glue and lower the top tray into position. Hold it in place with a pair of 'G' cramps on opposite corners. It will be easier to position this tray if the bench assembly so far is stood on end.

Once positioned, drill the holes and put the bolts into position. Put on the washers and tighten the nuts. Repeat this operation at the opposite ends, and check all nuts, making sure that all are really tight. Wipe off surplus glue with a damp cloth.

Rest the top on the bench assembly, with the vice block uppermost, and place the vice in position. Bore holes for the coach screws which hold the vice to the block. Use a 6mm bit in a hand brace to bore core holes for 50mm × 10mm Coach screws. Insert the screws and tighten up with a spanner.

Turn the top over and screw it into position with 50mm countersunk No. 10 screws. These screws go into the top rail of the leg assemblies and should be firmly tightened. If the top of the bench can remain a fixture, the contact surfaces may be spread with glue.

Place the top layer of ply in position and secure with screws.

A hole for the bench stop (50mm × 25mm) should be marked and cut. This hole must have its edge hard against the leg to ensure a 'frictional' fit.

Place a try-square on the front edge, with the blade protruding under the bench, to rest against the leg. Mark this position on to the front face and square this line across the front edge.

Square a line across the top surface of the bench and, from it, mark out the 25mm × 50mm rectangle of the bench stop.

Fix a piece of scrap wood with a 'G' cramp on to the leg under this position and 'chop' this hole right through, using a 25mm bevel-edged chisel.

Place the front 'cheek' of the bench in position and screw it but do not use glue. Ideally, this should be made of hardwood, but good-quality softwood will suffice.

This is the part of a bench which usually takes the most punishment and since it is easily replaceable, it can be readily renewed whenever it deteriorates too badly.

The rear tool rack is made from two pieces of 12mm softwood, 48mm wide. Cut these to length and prepare three blocks from the same timber, each 75mm long. These are the spacers.

Glue and pin the first piece in place on the rear of the bench. Position the three blocks, glue and pin, then glue and screw on the outside piece.

Make the end blocks of the trays from offcuts of the 80mm × 22mm rail material. Plane a 45° edge slope and fix these blocks with two screws each. The bevel allows dust and shavings to be swept out of the tray.

Rub down all surfaces with medium glasspaper and give the bench two coats of a clear polyurethane varnish. Similarly rub down the top, which is given a third coat of varnish. This final coat should have the gloss removed with a piece of fine steel wool, or use a matt polyurethane varnish finish.

Power tools: lending power to your elbow

Power tools are among the most valuable of handyman work aids. Saving time and allowing that 'professional' look to finished work, even the basic power drill, used with varied attachments, can provide great diversity in tackling a wide range of jobs around the home. When using power tools, always observe the limitations of the given piece of equipment.

Power tools of various types and suitable attachments can do much to take the hard work out of many jobs around the home, as well as often enabling them to be done more successfully.

Power tools are most popularly used for drilling, sawing and smoothing. There are two basic types of tool – the integrated tool, which is a purpose-designed unit for a given use, and the attachment, which fits to a power drill. There are also accessories, such as drill stands and sawing benches, which complement power tools.

Power saws may consist of either integrated units or attachments. Obviously, the integral saw is a better buy for major or continuous work. A variety of smoothing tools – orbital sanders, bench sanders and sanding discs – enable a range of smoothing operations to be carried out.

Jig saws are a more specialized form of power saw.

Other attachments include a paint stirrer, which ensures thorough mixing without using vast elbow power; a wire cup and discs, for removing rust from surfaces; a screwdriver attachment for repetition work, such as fixing down floor surfaces; and hedge trimmers and lawn mowers, which are either attachments or integrated tools. These use motors basically similar to those of a drill.

Devices for dowelling and mortise cutting are among the woodworking attachments which can be fitted to power tools. Special, but expensive, power planes are also made.

Extension cables, which can be wound on to reels for neat and easy stowage, are useful accessories. The maximum lengths of cable and thicknesses are related to the power of the motor and the length of the cable.

Drills

The basic power tool is the electric drill. In its simplest form it can accept a variety of attachments, to increase its versatility, but it may not always be designed for really hard work and difficult jobs. Too often, the drill is blamed because its limitations have not been observed.

It is wise to buy the best equipment you can afford and take advantage of the greater versatility and ability to tackle those jobs for which the better drill is designed.

All power drills basically consist of a compact electric motor in a shell – very

Sizing chart for extension cable

Cable length	Current (Consumption of drills in amps)				cable
	1–4	mm²	5–9	mm²	(mm²)
7·5m	6A	0·75	10A	1·0	All
15m	6A	0·75	15A	1·5	at 30°C
30m	6A	0·75	20A	2·5	ambient
42m	10A	1·0	20A	2·5	temperature

(Based on IEE recommendations).

Note: Keep cable on drum. Avoid intermediate connections in cable

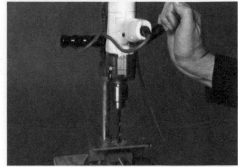

A bench stand with power tool enables accurate vertical holes to be drilled

often of high-impact plastic–with the electric motor double insulated for safety. Most drills operate on mains voltage and connect to a suitable power point with a three-pin plug.

At the 'business end' of the drill a chuck is mounted. This is opened and closed by a key, which should always be kept in a safe place or clipped to the cable of the drill. New keys can always be bought if you do lose one.

Chucks are made in a variety of sizes. The most usual are 6mm, 8mm, 10mm and 13mm. The larger, taking bigger attachments, are intended for the more powerful drills. Motors are up to ½hp (373W) in power and cooled with a fan.

The drill needs little maintenance beyond occasional replacement of motor brushes and the blowing out of any accumulated dust in the ventilation apertures at the rear. A drill with a 10mm chuck meets most domestic needs.

The less sophisticated drills run at a fixed speed–usually around 2,800 rpm. At these speeds, there is a limitation on the work the drill can do. For greater versatility invest in a twin or multi-speed drill.

Drill Speeds

Low (up to 1,000 rpm)	High (2,500–3,000 rpm)
drilling timber (over 10mm dia.)	drilling timber (under 10mm dia.)
drilling steel (over 6mm dia.)	drilling steel (under 6mm dia.)
Brick	sanding
Plaster	sawing
Mortar	grinding
Lime	hedge trimming
Cement	
Breeze, aggregate and cellular concrete	
glass	

Note: on hard surfaces, a hammer action is desirable; use special percussion bit. On glass, use a spear-point bit.

These run between speeds of around 900 rpm to 3,000 rpm. The slower speed is essential for drilling holes in hard surfaces. These two speeds cover most requirements. The speed is simply changed by a speed selector on the drill.

Rotary percussion

For drilling really hard surfaces, such as concrete, stone, hard brick and cement, a drill with a hammer action is needed. If you contemplate drilling hard surfaces frequently, you would be wise to buy such a drill, or obtain a percussion attachment for a standard drill. The hammer action

can be switched out and the drill then becomes an ordinary two-speed drill.

This percussive action is only used when hard masonry is being drilled. This hammer action is almost imperceptible in use; as the drill rotates it also percusses at high speed to penetrate the surface.

A special percussion bit should always be used and not an ordinary tipped drill bit, which is not designed for such work.

While a hammer attachment can be fitted to any standard power drill, if it runs at a high, fixed speed it is not suitable for drilling hard surfaces. You would need, in addition, a speed-reducing device if this is not part of the attachment.

Apart from variable-speed drills, speed reducers can turn a fixed-speed drill into a multi-speed one.

Another device which reduces speed is the right-angled speed reducer which fits into the chuck of the drill.

Using drills

A power drill should be operated with a steady, firm pressure. Excess pressure should never be applied to the work and the motor should not be under strain; it may seize up or burn out. Some motors have devices to declutch or lock out the motor when it is overstressed.

Before changing speed, make sure that the motor of the drill is stationary. Damage or wear may be caused to the gearing mechanism if you change speeds while the motor is running.

To fit attachments to some drills, the chuck has to be removed with a special spanner, supplied with the power tool. To remove the chuck, lock the spanner on the nut behind the chuck, and give the chuck a firm twist to the right. If it is tight, insert the chuck key and give this a sharp tap on the cross-bar end with a hammer.

The most common use for the power drill is to make holes. These can be made in almost any surface, provided the correct bit is used at the right speed.

When drilling in any surface, occasionally withdraw the bit from the hole to remove dust and débris which cause overheating. Masonry drills are prone to overheat, so allow the bit time to cool.

Most wood drilling can be carried out with bits similar to those used in hand drills. The only difference is that the power bit has a rounded shank.

Large holes are easier to drill if these are preceded by a small pilot hole which should be drilled very accurately.

For small drill bits (less than 5mm), use high speed; use a slow speed with larger bits if you are drilling metal. Always reduce pressure as the bit is about to break through.

If two pieces of wood are to be screwed

When hand held, the drill's vertical alignment can be checked with try-square

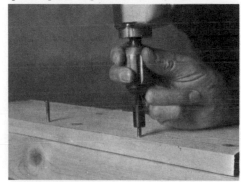

A screwdriver attachment in a drill can speed up the repetition fixing of screws

Hole-cutting saws and plug cutters can be used with drill on a variety of materials

Adjustable depth setting of a power saw should be slightly over depth of timber

Saw fence guide enables accurate lateral control of cut on a section of timber

Setting the depth carefully, a housing joint can be cut accurately with the saw

Mitres can also be produced, using the bench stand, with the saw set to an angle

Using the guide fence and protractor set to desired angle, mitres can be cut

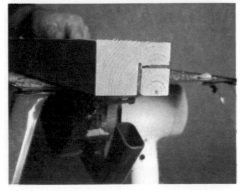

Rebates of various sizes can be cut on saw bench, using the fence as a guide

together three drilling operations are needed:

A pilot hole for the screw threads to bite into;

A clearance hole for the unthreaded screw shank;

A countersink for the screw head.

Special combination drill bits are made for drilling these three holes in one operation and are supplied with an adjustable depth stop which regulates the amount by which the head of the screw is set below the surface of the work. These combination bits are related to screw sizes.

Another bit which is available for drills is the plug cutter which produces small round plugs from the material you are using. These fit back exactly into the countersink holes to conceal the screw heads.

After use, rub down bits with steel wool and wipe with a thin oil. Any waste wood compacted into the grooves will cause the bits to clog, overheat or lose temper.

When drilling metals other than brass or cast iron, lubricate the drill bit. For steel, use a thin oil, for aluminium turpentine or paraffin, turpentine for glass and water for mirrors. The technique for drilling glass is described in the article on cutting glass.

Always mark the hole accurately and draw a cross to show the centre. To stop the drill point from slipping, either tap gently on glazed and smooth surfaces with a centre punch, just marking the glaze, to give a purchase point; or fix a piece of sticky tape on the surface and mark on it the drilling position.

Thin metal should be clamped to a piece of wood as this will reduce distortion and avoid jamming as the drill breaks through.

When drilling always carry the cable over the shoulder or clamp it in the hand. It can be dangerous if caught up in a powerful motor.

Always clamp workpieces firmly to stop them from revolving—a piece of spinning metal could be very dangerous. The drill must be at right angles to the working surface. You can use an upturned try square to check vertical alignment. However, a bench stand or a drill guide are more accurate means of ensuring accuracy.

The drill stand has many advantages, since it is adjustable for both height and radial swing. A variety of drills can be simply and quickly clamped into the stand.

Sanders

Sanders are of several types: belt, drum, orbital, finishing or disc sanders. Disc sanders are the most usual and have a rubber or flexible backing pad.

All types of these work by means of discs or belts of abrasive papers either revolving or vibrating over a surface. Abrasive papers are removable and replaceable.

The ordinary disc sander has limitations as it tends to leave swirl marks. If you are seeking finer work, it is best to use a backing bed with a knuckle joint which ensures that the pressure on the work is always even, reducing swirl marks, or the type which has a foam-rubber flexible backing.

The orbital sander consists of a vibratory attachment, or a purpose-made integrated unit capable of better work. These have a large surface pad to which an abrasive sheet can be attached.

This pad moves up and down and in small circles to impart a smoothing action to the surface.

A drum sander consists of a revolving drum of stiff foam rubber with an abrasive strip fixed around its edge.

Belt sanders consist, as the name suggests, of a continuous belt of abrasive material, enabling bigger jobs to be tackled and better results to be achieved.

Dependent on type, belts, discs and drum sanders are either tightened up on the power tool by means of screw and clamp washers or are stuck on to the abrading surfaces with a special glue or adhesive tape.

Discs, belts and sheets are made in coarse, medium and fine grades, in glasspaper or carborundum. The latter costs more but has an extended life. In addition, there are wet-and-dry and preparation papers for rubbing down paintwork.

The disc can also be used in conjunction with a lambswool pad for polishing purposes.

Bench sanders consist of a disc which is covered with an abrasive paper. It works in conjunction with a horizontal table and guide fences. The sander enables ends of timber to be sanded accurately. The guide fence can be set at 45° or 90° angles for mitreing.

A bench sander can be duplicated by a power drill, sanding-plate attachment, and a horizontal sanding stand.

Bench grinder

This enables blunted tools to be ground and honed. The best units provide a shaft on each end, with a coarse stone, for grinding, and a fine one, for honing.

Stands

Another useful attachment is the horizontal bench stand. This enables the drill to be locked into a position on a bench, and is ideal for jobs, such as sanding, polishing and grinding or wire brushing, using the appropriate attachments.

The bench stand can also be part of a lathe unit, which enables a wide range of wood-turning work to be produced. This is useful, not only as a hobby, but also for making mouldings to replace damaged ones not readily available commercially.

A drill stand permits highly accurate bench work. It can be adjusted for height and radial swing. The drill simply latches into a collar and is clamped firmly into place by a back screw. For repetition work, the drill stand enables accurate and quick location for each hole.

Attachments

Bench attachments should be screwed firmly to a stout bench, so that they do not vibrate or move during use.

The only other items of equipment you may need are a selection of 'G' cramps to hold, in some circumstances, the work.

Milling attachment with drill in stand to cut rebates. Scrap wood makes 'fence'

Combed joint can also be cut with saw attachment, here using a gauge plate

Power saw in saw bench can also be used to cut rebates by making two cut passes

Use a push stick to complete the cut on a saw bench; keep hands well clear

Kerfing—makes a series of close cuts two-thirds wood depth—to allow curve

Jig saw is first inserted at an angle when penetrating material is to be cut

A choice of blades enables a variety of materials to be cut with this unit

Removing old disc adhesive, with tip of old screwdriver, from grinding plate

Apply new adhesive to face of plate by pressing to surface with plate turning

Many handyman projects are made easier if a power saw is used. It is most important to buy the best equipment you can afford. There is a wide range of power attachments for such varied tasks as mitreing, planing and dowel-jointing. The best finish will only be achieved if the basic tool and the specialized attachment is used correctly.

Power saws, both as attachments to power drills and as integrated units, are among the most widely used of power tools. Saws are made in a variety of motor powers, and with various sizes of blade. The blade is circular and revolves on a spindle.

Variations on power saws are rebating attachments, which fit on to power drills and have a similar but much smaller blade and the jig saw, which has a thin serrated blade, which moves up and down to cut shapes.

The power saw is a versatile tool and can be used in conjunction with saw tables and benches to provide a permanent cutting jig, enabling a wide range of power woodworking jobs to be carried out.

Many of the jobs tackled with hand tools—such as cutting, rebating, mitreing, dowel-combed jointing—can be carried out with a power saw.

Obviously, if you intend to make a lot of use of a power saw, either use a larger drill with attachments, since small drills may not be up to the work, or buy an integrated saw. Again, choose a better one if you are going to use it very much.

Take care when using a saw that you do not strain the motor, this will be detectable by 'hunting' sounds and slowing down. Some makes of attachment have a clutch device which allows the blade to slip at a certain level of strain, to relieve motor stress.

Circular saws can be set for correct depths—just slightly more than the depth of timber—and should always work at a fast speed. Saws are fitted with a rip-saw fence to guide you accurately and can be operated at various angles for bevelling—there is a gauge on the unit to allow angles to be correctly set.

Before using the saw, remove any surface nails and screws as these will at once blunt and damage the teeth of the saw blade.

Used properly, a circular saw is perfectly safe. However, never switch it on with the hands near the blade; never make adjustments near the blade with the power plugged in; and always make sure that the retractable blade guard is in working order.

This is spring loaded and pushes back as the saw advances. Make it an automatic practice to unplug when making any adjustments at all.

The two basic attachments with the saw blade are a saw stand, on which the drill with a saw attachment is mounted, and a saw table, under which the saw drill attachment fits.

The attachment is only really suitable for light use; other than for occasional such work, it is far better to buy an integrated saw, capable of heavy duty.

When operating a power saw, start the motor before the blade touches the wood. The saw must always run at a high speed. Saws have a rip fence which keeps the blade running accurately to the line; this is set to the depth measurement of the cut.

If the blade wanders from the cutting line, never attempt an adjustment by twisting the saw, as this may jam the blade. Go back a short distance and resume cutting. If the blade binds persistently, it needs resharpening.

Blades
There are two main sizes of blade—125mm and 150mm. The smaller blade gives a depth of cut of 40mm and the larger 50mm. Circular-saw blades are available in several types and patterns.

Combination type Suitable for most purposes such as cutting thick or thin hardwoods and softwoods with or across the grain, as well as plywood, blockboard and hardboard.

Cross-cut blades possess fine teeth which cut smoothly across the grain of hardwood and softwood, and are also suitable for cutting plywood, hardboard and blockboard.

Rip blades These are used for coarse cutting with the grain.

Planer blade Has no sideways 'set' to its teeth, and relies on deep, widely spaced gullies for clearing away waste. Gives a neat cut; will saw a variety of thick or thin materials. Planer blades must be kept

If plate holes are cut in disc, correct
grinding angle can be checked from back

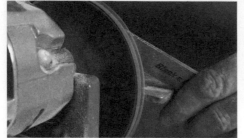

When standing over work, angle can
easily be checked from rear position

Bevels can also be produced by using
a replaceable disc on sanding unit

Disc is next located on adhesive. When
running, slots provide view through plate

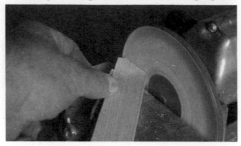

Rough edges and corners, can be taken
off; angles can also be made on wood

Bench lathe and attachments permit ambitious woodturning work to be carried out

sharp and must run at maximum revolutions, to avoid clogging, and an over-
heated motor.

A circular saw allows bends, mitres
and grooves to be cut.

The sole plate of the saw is hinged to
tilt and allows cuts to be made at any
angle between 45° and 90°. Minimum
depth is represented at 45° and maximum
at 90°. Three basic adjustments for depth,
angle and width of cut should always be
made and checked before any cutting.

Bench saw

A bench saw consists of a flat table top
with the saw blade projecting through it.
The blade is adjustable for depth and angle
of cut and protected by the sliding guard.

There are two guide fences which
allow timber to be cut correctly. The rip
fence parallel with the saw blade can be
slid sideways up the edge of the table.
Timber is guided along it into the blade
for parallel straight cutting, usually along
the grain.

The cross-cut guide is for cutting across
the width and grain of wood at any angle
and slides from front to back of the table
in a slot parallel with the blade.

A protractor on the front of the guide
enables angled cuts to be made.

Both fences can be removed so that
large sheets of material can be cut. It is
important to check the angle of the rip
fence periodically, as the blade may jam if
it is not exactly parallel with the blade.
Some bench saws have slip clutches to
disengage the motor.

Never direct short pieces of wood or

the ends of pieces into the blade with your
hands. Always use a push stick to direct
it. This is a simple piece of wood with a
v-cut at the front end.

Wood is also likely to slip on a saw
bench because the torque of the blade
tends to push it aside if it is not held firmly.
This may be a problem when using the
cross-cut guide set at an angle.

Usually, when cross-cutting, you should
hold with both hands on one side of the
blade, and let the offcut fall away. Pushing
from both sides closes up the cut around
the blade and may cause jamming.

To cut a mitre, set the protractor on
the cross-cut guide to an angle of 45° and
place the wood against the guide and slide
both wood and guide into the blade.

To cut a bevel along the edge of a piece
of wood, again set the blade at an angle of
45°. Some saws have built-in protractors
though on others the table tilts and not
the blade.

Firring

Firring consists of cutting a taper on a
long piece of wood so that it is narrower
at one end. Firring pieces are used for
rafters on flat roofs to create a slight
drainage slope.

An adjustable jig is the best way of
cutting these. It can be made from two
battens of medium length. These are set
face to face and fastened together by a
hinge at one end and a slotted metal strip,
secured with wingnuts, at the other.

By opening the jig to the extent desired
and tightening the nuts, an accurate
profile for repetition work is provided.

Kerfing

This allows a piece of timber to be bent to
produce an outside curve. This is achieved
by making a row of parallel cuts across
the wood on the inside of the curve through
half to three-quarters of the wood's thickness, all along the part to be curved. The
wood can then be bent, though it is best to
dampen or steam it first.

Use a cross-cut or planer blade to make
the cuts as a combination blade is too
coarse. Kerfing reduces the strength of
wood and should not be used for load-
bearing frames.

Housing joints

Housing and other grooves can be cut by
setting the blade to the depth required and
cutting the sides of the groove first; use
the fence to keep them straight.

Next, remove the fence and cut out the
wood in between by passing the wood over
the blade. Mark the limit of the groove on
top of the wood, to avoid cutting past the
edges.

For a stopped housing, you need to cut
the last distance by hand, using a chisel.
This method provides for an even depth of
cut all over the groove. Wood can be
removed in the same way when cutting
tenons.

Rebates

Rebates may be cut in two ways on a bench
saw. One is to cut along one side of the
rebate, using the fence, and turning the
wood through 90° to cut the other side.

It is quicker to mount the blade on
'wobble washers'. These are a pair of
angled washers which make the blade
wobble from side to side as it spins, so that
it cuts a wide groove.

The width of a rebate can be increased
by making several passes. Once you have
set the blade on its washers, place a section
of battening against the fence to protect
it.

For narrow cuts, adjust the blade to
cut into the battening. The depth of cut
can be adjusted in the normal way. You
can adjust the width of the wobble cut by
means of washers.

Jig-saws

The jig-saw and the jig-saw attachment
enable curves and shapes to be cut. While
safety rules should still be observed, these
are far safer to use than circular saws.

The moving blade can be touched
without hazard, though this is not recommended.

This attachment is limited to soft
materials, up to about 50mm thick, or
harder materials, such as hardwood, 25mm
thick. The jig-saw can be used either as a
hand-held or bench-mounted tool.

Rabbeter

The rebate attachment, or rabbeter
(rabeter), can be used either free in the
hand or as a bench unit with a lathe kit.
The rabbeter can, with different blades, or
cutters, be used to produce tongues, rebates, slots, decorative edges and grooves.

INDEX

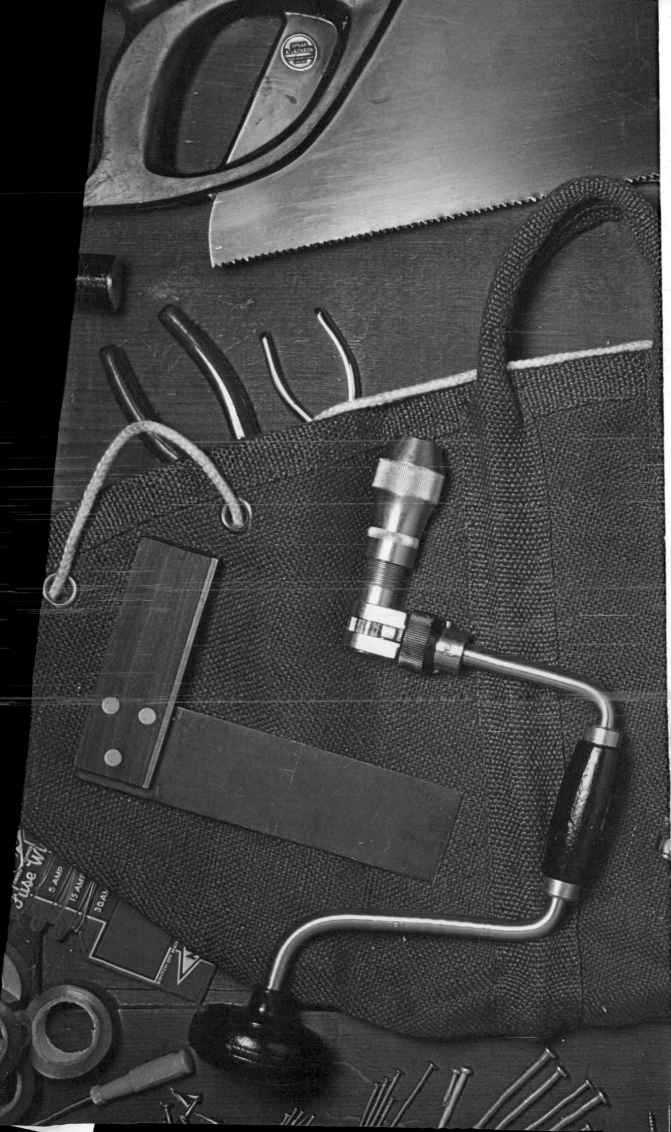